MILITARY ERRORS OF WORLD WAR TWO

MILITARY ERRORS OF WORLD WAR TWO

KENNETH MACKSEY

CASTLE BOOKS

This edition published in 2003 by Castle Books ®,
A division of Book Sales Inc.
114 Northfield Avenue
Edison, NJ 08837

This book is reprinted by arrangement with
Orion Publishing Group Ltd.
Orion House, 5 Upper St Martin's Lane, London WC2H 9EA

First published by Arms and Armour 1987
Paperback edition 1993, Reprinted 1994
Cassell Military Paperbacks edition 1998
Reprinted 1998, 1999 (three times), 2000, 2001

British Library Cataloguing-in-Publication Data : a
catalogue entry for this book is available from the British
Library

ISBN: 0-7858-1598-8

Printed in the United States of America

Produced by DAG Publications Ltd.
Designed by David Gibbons; edited by Michael Boxall

CONTENTS

LIST OF MAPS

INTRODUCTION

Wars and combat without mistakes are unknown if only because one side's faultlessness inevitably imposes errors upon its opponent. As an art compounded of improvisations, war creates a breeding ground for mistakes no matter how skilful or resourceful commanders and their followers may be. The sheer unpredictability of battle, which usually takes place on unknown ground and is accompanied by a fear that makes for uncertainty in the minds of the contenders, is a guarantee of unrehearsed chaos. In imperfect conditions, error is not necessarily shameful – just so long as every potential contingency has been foreseen and covered, and provided that the commanders are the best available for the task. When men of good conscience do their best and fail, forgiveness is permissible. But when incompetence and sloth lead to avoidable errors, criticism and censure there must be.

Residing in the cynical realms of the public mind is the myth that military leaders, as a tribe, are, by nature and upbringing, callous, untrained, irresponsible bunglers. This myth lies deeply seated in folklore and history, the retailing of which has frequently been accompanied by a pursuit of scapegoats. It commonly acquires plausibility due to downright ignorance of military art, let alone unawareness of the events and personal pressures bearing down upon leaders and led. Very few people know, and fewer still understand, the intricacies and stress of combat – a pursuit which has increased in complexity and obscurity as the technology of the past two centuries has proliferated. Of economic necessity, only a handful of sailors, soldiers and airmen can receive the benefits of staff college training, and from their ranks only an élite of higher commanders can be selected and promoted. Yet the myth of the gifted amateur's inborn superiority over the trained professional dies hard, partly, no doubt, because the critics themselves know nothing of the frequently adverse conditions with which commanders must contend, but largely, one suspects, because military commanders trade in death and so are vulnerable to public castigation for wastage of life. Yet those who hold these views seem habitually to overlook the fact that admirals, generals and air marshals are, like themselves, flesh and blood, subject (despite a rigorous training) to the same fallibilities and inadequacies, but who often must carry out their tasks in unimaginably horrendous conditions.

It is, nevertheless, my purpose to highlight a selection of command 'cock-ups' (to use the vernacular) which occurred during the Second World War and try to show how they came about. My basis of choice decrees that each episode illustrates fundamental or trend-setting aspects of the conduct of war by sea, land and air, and that it relates to events which significantly extended the length and scope of the war with consequent increase in loss of life, in destruction of property and in political change. I pass over or avoid, inasmuch as I can, those battles which seem to me to have been dissected excessively or whose inclusion would detract from the aim of the book – which is to investigate errors and not to do duty as a critical examination of the war. So, I look at the blunders and mistakes by entire command systems, not just the performance of individual commanders, although naturally it must be borne in mind that they are responsible for everything done in their name. Naturally I investigate evidence of personal incompetence and how it came about, but it is every bit as important to take into consideration a host of other factors which make it extremely difficult, if not impossible, for the individual to function efficiently or sensibly. Clashes of personality enter the lists, as do conflicting notions of allies, statemen and nations who very properly have an interest in what the military are proposing or doing. Misconceived doctrines arrived at through the sheer inability to foresee the future through a cloud of unimaginable innovations or changing circumstances have their impact, leading not only to the acquisition of inadequate equipment but also to the adoption of organizations and methods which hamper, if not cripple, the true function of command. All of these have to be looked at to see what effect they had on readiness for battle; on command and control systems; the gathering of information and the protection of security; the preparation of appreciations, plans and orders; logistical systems and so on – all of which were conducive to the standard of training and morale of ordinary fighting men who always are utterly dependent upon those in authority to prepare and launch them into combat with a reasonable chance of success and survival.

The examples chosen are designed to demonstrate how the inter-action of opponents led to a compounding of errors by all those involved, and the reactions – political and military – they generated. Setting aside the heinous and futile mistake by Japan and Germany, later compounded by Italy, to take up arms in the first place, it was the quite astonishing success of the Germans in conquering most (but not quite all) of Western Europe in 1940 which must be regarded as the fatal moment for the entire world. What followed – the involvement of Russia and the USA in 1941 – might never have occurred if only the Germans (who clearly were unaware of their astonishing supremacy in techniques) had not gambled and got away with it due to an incompetence on the French and British part which is hard to believe. If only the Germans had been held in Western Europe in the summer of 1940, neither the Russians nor the Americans might have been called upon to commit the errors they did when they themselves were struck – which is a parable for today without much doubt. And yet, if Adolf Hitler had not flinched from invading Britain in 1940 (as he could easily have done it he had integrated that culminating concept with the initial assault upon France), the Americans might have been spared the traumas of 1941 and later. And, too, the world might have been rid of a Russian-promoted Communism that was every bit as odious as Fascism.

Astonishing as the events of 1940 were, they are hardly more amazing than those which automatically followed. The inability of the Russians to reorganize quickly enough to take advantage in 1941 of the lessons learnt by study of 1940 German methods and, with numerically superior forces, check them in battle without relinquish-ing vast tracts of land space. The failure of the Americans and their Allies in the Pacific and Far East to cope with the initial Japanese onrush, even though the Americans had been preparing for the event for at least 20 years and had had ample warning of what was impend-ing. These two major catastrophies represent perhaps the greatest enigmas of all. Nevertheless it was these phenomena which made unavoidable the rest of the saga related here – the fierce and pro-longed U-boat war in the Atlantic (which might have been of shorter duration if Admiral King had not misdirected the American defence); the air battles over Germany (in which politics and personalities vied among one another to a detrimental extent); the costly battles to retake Western Europe, leading to the unnecessary failure at Arnhem and the inability to end the war in 1944, which would have preserved the greater part of Germany for Western rule; and the concluding battles in the Pacific in which both sides committed some remarkable mistakes for extraordinarily bizarre reasons.

Before scientific operational analysis of battlefield performance and new technology began to exert a precautionary as well as evolutionary influence, military commanders were compelled to base their judgements upon history, intuition and inspired guesswork. To some extent that is still the case, although it is less prevalent than it was. The educational and selection processes have made their impact and to an even greater extent than in pre-twentieth-century days when the rate of technical change was much slower, thus offering more time and opportunity to understand new weapons prior to their use. It is for the reader to consider and judge the extent to which a more scientific approach to decision making in war conditioned the responses of commanders between 1939 and 1945 and, if he wishes, to compare the effects of the experiences and lessons of the First World War with those of the Second. Then to extrapolate his thoughts towards the present day with its far greater availability of knowledge and data (albeit numbingly complicated) when applied to the deadly matter of waging war. If the results of that study give confidence in future analysis, he may conclude that it is not inconceivable that the sheer dimensions of the warnings made evident to the mass of the people, as well as those who decide, will act as the persuasive deterrent to any major escalation of conflict.

In the preparation of this book I have been helped immensely by many old friends and colleagues of whom David Brown (head of the Naval History Branch of the British Ministry of Defence), the staff of the Military Library of the Ministry of Defence and the Public Record Office are pre-eminent in their resourcefulness and courtesy. I am also, as on many other occasions, deeply in the debt of Lieutenant-Colonel Bill Woodhouse, RTR, for reading and criticizing the first draft and to Felicity Northover for endless patience in decyphering and typing my rough drafts.

1

THE SINS OF COMPLACENCY
Events before 1940

From reports sent in the summer of 1940 by Joseph Kennedy, the United States Ambassador in London, it appeared to President Franklin Roosevelt that at any moment Germany would invade England and that the British Empire, until a few weeks ago the greatest force for stability in the world, would collapse. But at so desperate a moment, when vital decision had to be taken as to whether or not to lend support to the ailing Empire or come to terms with the awesome prospect of compromising with the soaring ambitions of Adolf Hitler, there was no time for the US Government to investigate the causes of the disaster in what might prove a useless search for the mistakes and errors which had brought it about. When Roosevelt decided to ignore Kennedy's assessment that Britain had less than a fifty-fifty chance of survival – which was not too far wide of the mark – it was left to commentators, journalists and academics to indulge in a wild mixture of guess-work and prescient speculation as they tried to understand what had gone wrong.

How was it, they might ask in September, when rough weather and longer nights made invasion less likely, that the Germans had not, against all the odds, invaded Britain? On the face of it the reason lay in the defeat of the Luftwaffe by the Royal Air Force in the Battle of Britain. But, tracking backwards through the events of a summer resplendant in brilliant weather with mostly smooth seas, why had not the Germans come much earlier when, as many correctly surmised, the Royal Navy, the Army and the RAF were at their weakest after successive débâcles in Norway, at Dunkirk and in France? After all, the Germans could surely count! They must have realized that losses and damage to ships (many publicly admitted) were high; seen the thousands of guns, tanks, weapons and vehicles lying destroyed and abandoned on the battlefield; and noted the wreckage of hundreds of aircraft caught on the ground or shot down, and from this calculated the destruction of a majority of their enemy's strength. What matter, it could be reasoned, that 330,000 British, French and Belgian soldiers had been evacuated from Dunkirk in May if they were disarmed. And yet there was another question – how on earth did all those men manage to escape when the German Army and the Luftwaffe (setting aside what slight impact might be made by a weak German Navy) had been poised to capture Dunkirk, could dominate the sea escape routes with coastal guns and bomb the surrounded and defenceless armies into submission?

Precise answers to these questions were difficult – impossible at the time – to come by. Nevertheless, pursuing the line of investigation then, and in the decades to come, proved a fascinating study, frequently baffled by false trails and mistaken assumptions among publicists and historians who were absorbed by the urge to discover how it was that Germany, apparently unready for war, managed, within three months, to bring about the rout of Anglo-French forces, deemed the strongest in the world, and wreck the fabric of nations which, but 22 years before, had brought Germany herself to defeat in the greatest war in history. How was it that some ten to a dozen mechanized divisions and only a few hundred bombers had outmanoeuvred, outfought and outshot armies many times their size and numbers; armies, moreover, which deployed quite as many modern tanks and guns as the German enemy and almost as many aeroplanes whose performance was as good, if not better, than that of their opponents. People talked learnedly of the demise of French morale brought about by the political system and the undermining of their will to fight after the appalling losses of the First World War. But the Germans, it could be pointed out, had also suffered grievous losses, had been torn by civil strife and economic problems and, if reports coming out of Berlin were true, were by no means united in allegiance to their Führer. So what combination of errors and omissions had made the once mighty French Army give way, as it had last given way before Germany in 1870? And why had not the entirely mechanized British Army, which had pioneered armoured warfare and had been a leader in tank development, not done more to help their allies?

Memories, stretching back, recall the maps in the newspapers showing German arrowheads extending across France to the sea near Abbeville and northwards to the environs of Dunkirk where, for some unknown reason, they stopped just short of the port. Staunch resistance by the British at Boulogne and Calais was claimed as the reason for this halt. But soldiers who escaped from those briefly beleaguered ports would discount that. The defence had been too short-lived for significance except in gallantry. Eyes would move eastwards to where it all seemed to begin with the sinister announcement, less than a week after the Germans struck on 10 May, that a bulge had been forced in the much vaunted Maginot Line (which had been confidently described as impregnable) in the vicinity of Sedan, and that heavy fighting continued in attempts to eliminate this salient. Cynics and realists who recalled defeat in Norway in April and the surrender of the Dutch Army on 14 May after only four days' fighting, drew the worst and correct conclusions from this bulletin. Something was going wrong. The Germans had a built-in superiority, maybe a secret weapon, unmatched by the French and the British. A *poilu* of the French 55th Division, crouching in his trench on the slopes overlooking the River Meuse at Sedan on the evening of 13 May, might well have provided a key to the solution of one aspect of the puzzle. For he would have been witness to the unbridled panic which swept among his officers and comrades in the aftermath of prolonged bombing, the rending sound and effect of which they none of them had expected, seen or heard before: above all by reports of tanks already across the river and moving irresistibly up to envelop their positions as their own guns fell silent.

But simply to ask why the French infantry and gunners took flight when only a handful among them had seen anything of the enemy and when, in fact, the tanks they had heard (and not seen) were their own machines preparing to counter-attack, is almost to beg the question. For there was another more fundamental question yet to be answered. How was it that no less than three German panzer divisions and a mechanized infantry regiment, with their thousands of vehicles and hundreds of guns, could be there at all in so short a time after traversing the densely wooded Ardennes terrain, in the face of a strong screen of French troops? For previously there had been almost universal agreement among the General Staff and pundits of both the French *and* German Armies that such a penetration by a mechanized army was impossible. So, taking our reversed journey of inquiry a stage farther back, how was it that the best military brains of the upper hierarchy's generation had come, with obvious and notable exceptions, to make this crucial miscalculation and all at once find themselves confronted by a situation of surprise with unimagined and shattering consequences?

Sailors, soldiers and airmen are, or should be, the servants of the statesmen and politicians governing their nations. They are not, therefore, to be held responsible entirely for the state and equipment of their forces, unless, as is by no means unusual, they happen to have assumed the mantle of government as well. In this book, which aims to examine what are strictly 'command' errors, 'political' errors will receive only passing attention. Clear distinctions will appear, of course, as to the category into which an error falls – whether, for example, it is an error of personal incompetence, technical inadequacy or plain misfortune – with due consideration given to whether, in tennis parlance, the error is forced or unforced.

At this point it is worth mentioning, perhaps, that great military commanders of the past often tended to study victorious campaigns and battles of old in order to decide the measures needed to equip, train and direct into action the forces at their disposal. For example, von Schlieffen, the German Chief of Staff who designed the strategic plans governing what was to be his nation's plan of campaign against France and Russia in 1914, had a yearning to emulate Hannibal's victory at Cannae in 216 BC and studied the victorious campaigns of von Moltke in the 1860s and 1870s. And the Commanders who went to war in 1939 were, not surprisingly, preoccupied with the lessons of earlier struggles in which they had been involved as junior officers between 1914 and 1918. It is natural enough that a profession which functions well only upon ground of optimism has need to concentrate upon successes. The danger inherent in the process lies in the glory of ultimate victory obscuring both sides' mistakes in arriving at that happy moment of conclusion when all omissions, miscalculations and set-backs are forgiven, when the platitude that 'he who makes the least mistakes' wins the war conceals delusions enshrouded in a cloud of excuses.

The extent to which post-1918 military thought conditioned the plans and reactions of May 1940 was to be found in the shaping of armies and air forces throughout the rearmament phase of the 1930s. What else could they do, it might be asked, in an epoch when the use of operational analysis by armed forces was virtually non-existent, except in the playing of rudimentary war games? There did exist, however, a concern among politicians and the military that the previous conflict had demonstrated that surface warships remained supreme; that the underwater threat from submarines and mines had largely been controlled; that the unreliable tank and the increase in mechanized warfare had not altered the existing superiority of the defence on land, when conducted from fortified positions, over attackers in the open; and that air power would have only a limited, if growing, effect upon sea and land operations. At the same time a quite remarkably large proportion of the prophets agreed that air power directed against centres of population, industry and communications would have a quite catastrophic effect upon the means to wage war and upon civilian morale. Therefore, when circumstances demanded and money was made available by begrudging treasuries and politicians who reflected universal rejection of armaments in the aftermath of 'the war to end all wars', the weapons purchased, with few exceptions, were those designed to satisfy superficially studied notions with but little set aside for scientific research and the development of advanced ideas.

Navies continued to build improved battleships, cruisers and destroyers, and paid little more attention to unproven anti-submarine weapons than to improving submarines. They did concentrate significantly upon aircraft carriers but without, at the same time, recognizing that the bombers and torpedo aircraft they would carry could seriously threaten surface vessels whose anti-aircraft protection they tended to neglect. Armies and, as a respected authority on the subject, the victorious French Army in particular, continued to insist that infantry and artillery would reign supreme on the battlefield. They laid down that existing, unreliable tanks were only ancillary to infantry, and that fixed fortifications were a better guarantee of security than mobile forces, including the horsed cavalry to which so many officers professed such a sentimental attachment. Only air forces, through vigorous propaganda, managed to convince the world at large that they possessed the potential to win a war by action independent of the traditional role of navies and armies. It would be done, they claimed, not only by attacking industrial targets and centres of population, thus undermining the will of civilians to resist, but also by the sinking of so many ships and the destruction of such quantities of guns, tanks, lorries and horses as to dominate those surface forces that had forfeited air superiority.

So France, as an act of faith in the defensive policy her leading soldiers espoused, began the construction in the 1930s of the Maginot Line, a barrier of massive concrete and steel fortresses along her frontier with Germany – and neglected the remainder of her forces in order to pay for it. While Britain, supporter of the theory of omnipotent, independent air power so convincingly described by the Italian General Giulio Douhet, accepted the conclusion of Lord Trenchard, the Chief of Air Staff, that since the bomber would usually get through to its target, despite the efforts of fighter aircraft and anti-aircraft guns, the best antidote to the bomber was a strong bomber force as a deterrent to any likely aggressor. It followed that, with the traditional slice of funds continuing to be allocated to the Royal Navy and an increasing proportion going to the Royal Air Force when rearmament commenced in earnest in the mid 1930s, the British Army suffered severely from deprivation at the bottom of the list of priorities – a deliberate decision because a caucus of influential political opinion held the view that future British involvement on the continent of Europe should be avoided. Thus the Army was relegated to the task of policing the Empire with equipment and methods which would put it at a disadvantage should it actually find itself engaged in a sophisticated European war.

In days when centralized defence ministries did not exist and when each Service struggled for its share of funds through its representatives at ministerial level, the balancing of resources through bargaining could be extremely haphazard, and frequently at the whim of politicians who were uneducated in the military art. At a time when controversy of unprecedented complexity raged over the conflicting claims of land and air forces and in which an objective precise view was almost unobtainable, emotional attitudes were as likely to win the day as scientific ones – particularly having regard to the fact that virtually no politicians and only a few senior soldiers and airmen were scientifically or technically educated. More even than aircraft, mechanized and armoured vehicles staked claims for support which only an élite had come to terms with – all the more so because, ever since air and mechanized forces had come into being as the most revolutionary element of the fighting arms at the beginning of the First World War, they had been in contention not only for resources and in conflict in battle, but also engaged as complementary forces when made to work in conjunction with each other. That this remained self-evident stemmed from the claims of the armour enthusiasts that they, with air power's assistance, could overcome fortifications, restore mobility and, by long-range raids penetrating deep into the enemy rear, produce total victory by paralysis of the enemy's will.

The British, as leaders in armoured warfare from the start in 1914, and by their first use of tanks in 1916, continued as front runners. Their experiments with independent mechanized and armoured forces in the 1920s and early 1930s demonstrated, in conjunction with the introduction of vehicles of speeds of 20mph, radius of action up to 100 miles, flexible firepower and much improved reliability, that an armoured force was feasible provided that the anti-tank weapons, then being developed in parallel, never grew overwhelming. The issue of *relative* vulnerability was crucial in any comparison of aircraft or armoured fighting vehicle (AFV) power. When, in the early 1930s, bombers with speeds in excess of 200 miles an hour (and thus faster than existing fighter aircraft) appeared, it could be claimed that the bomber was almost invulnerable. Whereas the apostles of land vehicles had to admit that no matter how fast they moved, it could never be fast enough to avoid the fire of the latest high-velocity anti-tank guns, and that attempts to make tanks invulnerable with thick armour against all kinds of gun would fail and also be prohibitively expensive.

No better example of nations facing up to the problems of rearmament from a state of almost universal obsolescence in equipment and conflicting doctrines can be provided than that of the contenders of 1940 – the British, the French and the Germans – the rearmament of whose air forces and armies got into full swing after Adolf Hitler came to power in 1933. Each had to start practically from scratch since the weapons left over from 1918 were palpably outmoded. Each felt deprived of finance at a time of severe economic recession when fears of inducing runaway inflation by over-expenditure were prevalent. Naturally the stronger personalities who held sway managed, in varying degree against cloying bureaucracies and political wavering, to obtain the lion's share and sometimes put through radical measures. By the middle of the decade the doctrines, the organizations and the weapons to be built had, to all intents and purposes, been decided upon. France and Germany would concentrate upon the construction of air forces whose role was the support of their large armies, which would contain armoured forces of radically differing design. Britain gave priority to a strategic force of four-engined bombers, a sophisticated defence of the United Kingdom by fighters controlled by radio with information provided by a brand-new electronic scanning device called radar. In consequence, the resources allocated to support of any army to be sent into Europe were restricted, as were the number and type of AFVs to accompany that force – less than 50 'heavy' tanks (of over 20 tons) for infantry support, about a 100 'mediums' (between 10 and 20 tons) for deep penetration, and several hundred light tanks of about 6 tons which were useful for reconnaissance but death-traps in any other role.

Advanced technology (or lack of it) settled the controversy over the employment and equipment of air power. When Hermann Goering, a fighter ace of the First World War, Hitler's most trusted and senior subordinate, and Commander-in-Chief designate of the still clandestine German air force, set about the creation of the air arm which had been banned by the Treaty of Versailles in 1919, he acquired from the Navy and Army, in addition to a few 'Old Eagles' of the original Imperial air forces, a cadre of the most brilliant military thinkers and organizers, headed by two ex-members of the General Staff, Walther Wever and Albert Kesselring. As an advocate of both armoured warfare and of strategic bombing, Wever became Chief of Staff designate to the German air force and initiated a programme calling for a balanced force like the RAF, which could defend the homeland, co-operate with the Navy and the Army and, using four-engined bombers, deliver strategic attacks. But Wever was killed in a flying accident, as the result of his own pilot error, in the summer of 1936, on the eve of Germany's involvement in the Spanish Ci‧ il War. And Kesselring, who succeeded him, almost at once felt compelled to cancel the strategic force. First because he sensed that Hitler's driving ambition might pitch Germany into all-out war before the armed forces had reached their planned state of war-worthiness by 1943, making it imperative for priority of limited resources to be given to the Army. Second because the big bombers would be far too vulnerable by day against the latest 300mph plus monoplane fighters armed with cannon and soon coming into service to replace the old 200mph biplanes. And third because the technology to enable those bombers to navigate, find and hit their targets with sufficient accuracy by night was, as yet, unattainable. There would be those who, in hindsight, would castigate Kesselring's decision as a mistake. Time was to prove he and them both wrong and right. Wrong as the British were to discover when, far too late, it came to light that even the most heavily armed unescorted bomber could not survive against fighters by day, and that by night astral navigation and the existing bomb-sights were virtually instruments of scatter bombing. Right, in due course, when solutions to these problems, most expensively in lives, material and money, had been found.

Similarly a state of flux plagued the armies. Vehement debates in public and behind closed doors hampered the adoption of a new generation of AFVs to replace the infantry-support machines of France and Britain, and equip the secret, projected armoured (panzer) forces of Germany. Field Marshal Petain, the hero of defensive fighting at Verdun and elsewhere, who had deplored the loss of so many Frenchmen in abortive headlong infantry attacks throughout the First World War, had stuck doggedly to defensive concepts which were stolidly supported by the writings of General Narcisse Chauvineau, who prophesied a wholesale killing of tanks (and thus a blunting of the offensive) at the hands of the latest anti-tank guns when deployed in mass. But by 1936 the French had embarked upon the construction of a fleet of tanks with armour thick enough to defeat projectiles from the high-velocity 20mm to 50mm guns then in service, and had concluded not only that offensive operations were possible but, indeed, essential if the morale of the Army was not to be sapped by a passive state of mind. With this philosophy the British would concur, as also would they lean more heavily towards the French concept of infantry support and cavalry-type scouting by AFVs, despite being the prisoners of the doctrine of strategic deep penetration raids. The Germans, however, had ideas of their own.

As a symbol of its willingness to innovate, the German Army had encouraged Heinz Guderian, one of its most talented, if hot-headed, General Staff Officers, to study the technology and techniques of mechanization. A communications specialist, Guderian was among the handful of German soldiers who brilliantly combined the attributes of the fighting man and trained strategist with twentieth-century technical insight. Unlike many of his detractors, rivals and future enemies, he had imagination. It was due to his dynamic advocacy that the Germans, against precisely the kind of conservative opposition prevalent in France, Britain, the USA and elsewhere, created unique panzer divisions – formations of all arms, dominated by the AFV, with an ubiquitous role in every phase of war. Above all, fast-moving formations capable of advancing great distances against or encircling enemy opposition, controlled by commanders who rode with the spearhead and who spoke with subordinates by encoded radio or secure land-lines which could be laid as quickly as the vehicles advanced. For ubiquitous methods, such as these, AFVs of universal application were needed – and were largely denied to the German panzer army because of lack of funds. Guderian would have liked slow, heavy tanks to support the infantry, but could have them only by sacrificing the larger numbers of machines required by the fast panzer divisions. He chose, therefore, to deny AFVs to the infantry and cavalry formations in order adequately to equip the panzer divisions with a light and medium tank, as originally specified by the British in the 1920s, armed either with machine-guns and high-velocity anti-tank guns or machine-guns and a low-velocity howitzer; none of these machines to be sufficiently armoured to defeat the current type of anti-tank shot at normal battle ranges of about 500 yards.

The Spanish Civil war is invariably quoted as providing an opportunity for testing the technology and techniques of the Second World War, and certainly it confirmed obvious shortcomings in, for example, obsolescent biplane fighters when pitted against monoplane fighters and fast bombers; and the vulnerability of light tanks to the smallest anti-tank gun, particularly when those machines were employed slowly in dribs and drabs, instead of quickly in mass. But quite as many false as correct lessons were learned such as the exaggerated effects of air bombardment; certainly it unsettled inexperienced troops, but it lost the power to terrorize once its bark was recognized as worse than its bite, and troops noticed that accuracy, even by the latest German dive-bombers, was often questionable against pin-point targets. Likewise, the assertion by Colonel von Thoma, commander of the German tanks in Spain, that radio was unnecessary in AFVs, though it met with approbation from those in the Army seeking to slip resources from Guderian, was received with anger by that officer who was having difficulty enough in obtaining the funds for what he regarded as the most vital element of combat within the panzer divisions. In this Guderian would be proved right, but in his denial of some kind of AFV to the ordinary infantry divisions, wrong.

Germany's invasion of Poland in September 1939 – one of the most fatal of Hitler's political errors in that it brought on the world war he could have avoided – was the first real test of the wisdom of

> ## CRITICAL FLAWS
> ► Inadequate operational analysis of the design and development of new weapons and their relationship to techniques and tactics.
>
> ► An over-exaggerated respect for the effectiveness of air power and an underrating of mechanised land forces controlled by radio.
>
> ► Resistance among many Service chiefs to technical education.

Germany's pre-1939 command decisions and, like the Spanish venture, demonstrated as much that was wrong as was right. Outnumbered by a ratio of 3 to 1 and technically outclassed as the Polish Air Force was, it managed to survive against the Luftwaffe for two weeks until its early warning system and several airfields had been overrun. Even by day the Luftwaffe (its 1st Air Fleet under Kesselring) had found it difficult to find and hit Polish aircraft on the ground. Nor had it by any means managed to cow the Polish Army or population by intensive bombing or to play a decisive role in the forward edge of the land battle where it scored few hits on the enemy and far too frequently attacked friendly troops by accident. When Guderian told Hitler, in answer to the Führer's query as to whether some enemy guns had been knocked out by the dive-bombers, 'No, our panzers', it was rather more than a remark of pride. It was a justifiable claim that land forces still produced more positive results in terms of destruction as well as occupation of ground, than could air forces.

Yet if Hitler had complained, as senior Army officers would complain at the end of the month-long campaign, that the infantry had failed to advance with the élan of their forefathers, and demand that AFVs be placed in close support of infantry, he would have been justified. If it had taught nothing else, the First World War had proved that infantry supported only by small arms and artillery fire had the greatest difficulty surviving in trenches, let alone advancing in the open, but that, supported by AFVs, they rarely failed. And conversely, infantry under attack from AFVs had a habit of losing their nerve and bolting. In the aftermath of Poland, therefore, it was insisted that infantry be allocated an armoured component, the Germans opting for a cheap version of the infantry tank by up-armouring obsolete light tanks and fitting a forward-pointing gun with only limited traverse – machines which became known as self-propelled assault guns.

Both the Germans and the French drew useful lessons from the Polish campaign despite the continued resistance of conservative die-hards on both sides to whole-hearted revision. The Germans took drastic measures to improve co-operation between aircraft and ground forces and managed to resist an attempt by horsed cavalry leaders to raise a second cavalry division, despite irrefutable indications that the horse, as an assault vehicle, was doomed. And by the same measure, as will be seen, not all the senior German officers had yet grasped the full potential of the panzer division. That General Gamelin, the French C-in-C, had is, however, plain. Since 1936 he had failed in his endeavours to create a formation to match the panzer division. He was rejected by his Minister of War (a soldier by training) who said it would be 'foolish enough to sally out in front . . . in search of heaven knows what adventure', and frustrated by a bureaucratic system which was adept at neutralizing original ideas by a process of self-cancelling, inter-departmental arguments. When at last, after Poland, he did have his way, and formed four so-called armoured divisions (DCR), the heavy infantry-support tanks allocated were too slow for the task and the time to train their officers and men in the techniques required far too short even had it been possible to convince them of what was required.

2

THE INCONCEIVABLE CAMPAIGN
The German Conquest of Western Europe

From the German point of view it was to resolve into a matter of considerable good fortune when, on 10 January 1940, two Luftwaffe officers, Majors Reinberger and Hoenmanns, made the mistake of forced-landing in bad weather in Belgium and thereby presented the Belgians with plans for the forthcoming invasionof France via The Netherlands and Belgium. As it happened, the Allies, through three other excellent sources of information, including the spy known as A-54 within German Military Intelligence (Abwehr), were already apprised of what was in train. But the failure of the two officers to destroy the papers (which they should never have taken with them by air) provided essential corroboration of German intentions and set in train the mobilization of Dutch and Belgian troops. The invasion had to be called off, the troops, already on the move, returned to barracks and a total recasting of some fundamentally compromised plans put into motion. It was as if the error were determined by a Fate working on Germany's side, for the lost scheme had little to recommend it since it amounted only to an unoriginal, enlarged, modernized version of the famous wheel through the Low Countries, as executed by the Germans in 1914 and defeated at the Battle of the Marne, and which was already fully anticipated by the Allies. Butting head-on against an opponent entrenched behind a series of water obstacles, occupied by troops trained for exactly this kind of positional warfare, it was hardly likely that an approach on the line of greatest enemy expectation and strength could prevail.

Germany's fundamental weakness, quite apart from the relatively weak state of her forces when she prematurely entered the war (a mere 4,000 first line aircraft and about 300 modern tanks was not much upon which, in 1939, to base a struggle of potentially European if not world-wide dimensions), was the lack of a coherent strategy. Under Hitler's overall guidance as Head of State *and* Supreme Commander of the Armed Forces, working through the Oberkommando der Wehrmacht (OKW) which, to begin with, was little more than a secretariat, the Germans hopped from one conquest to the next under the opportunist whim of a born politician. There was no plan to annex Czechoslovakia in 1938/39 before the occupation of Austria in March 1938; and no scheme for the conquest of Poland until Czechoslovakia had been finally swallowed in March 1939. And since it was assumed France and Britain would decide against war on behalf of Poland, no plans to tackle Germany's western neighbours were prepared until October 1939. Even then, plans for attacking France were overtaken in April 1940 by another 'snap' operation, the invasion of Denmark and Norway which, successful as it would be, was a serious distraction of thought and of resources, particularly naval and air assets. It followed that fully considered long-sightedness, which is the essence of strategic planning and had always been a hallmark of the German General Staff's excellence, was at a premium, creating some quite unnecessary internal stresses in haste which were conducive of error. The proposition to make the main thrust into France through the Ardennes which was first suggested to the Army Command (OKH) in October 1939 by Lieutenant-General Erich von Manstein (Chief of Staff to General Gerd von Rundstedt's Army Group A) had not been well received, very likely because it added to the tension but, perhaps too, because it was interpreted as unwelcome criticism of the C-in-C and his Chief of Staff. Also because it tended to undercut Army Group B (which had the lion's share of resources for the main blow on the right wing and whose commander, General Fedor von Bock, was as ambitious as any self-respecting general); and quite probably because General Guderian's hand was recognized in the inception. For Guderian had also been consulted by OKW when Hitler had had a similar 'hunch' and was known to be very favourable. Moreover Guderian had persuaded von Manstein to more than double the size of the mechanized force over the original three mechanized divisions proposed for the thrust. Nevertheless, the Manstein plan would have been pigeon-holed had not the Luftwaffe officers committed their 'crime' and if von Manstein had not been given an opportunity to speak directly to Hitler.

It is among the most ironic of paradoxes of the period that, after von Manstein was posted to command an infantry corps (in order to silence his advocacy of the Ardennes plan) and the plan came up in February for adoption, it was von Rundstedt, who had previously, as von Manstein's commander, supported the plan, who found himself on the verge of being instructed to implement the greatly expanded scheme – and was none too happy about the prospect. Indeed, although by this time the Army Chief of Staff, Major-General Franz Halder, had come to appreciate the genius of the idea, there existed a majority of senior commanders who, while agreeing that the Ardennes could be penetrated, had no confidence in the three panzer corps earmarked being able to cross the heavily defended line of the River Meuse without a prolonged pause to bring up sufficient artillery and complete the extensive dumping of ammunition required for a traditional barrage to neutralize strong defences. Their error, of course, lay in their assessment of the effects of bombing, based on its relative innocuity in Poland against patriots who fought with sacrificial fervour; in dismissing Hitler's contention that the French were 'lacking in combat determination'; and in underrating the value of German Intelligence reports about French defences and the effect of surprise if a non-stop assault were made under the inspiration and drive of General Guderian, whose XIXth Corps would make the crucial lunge on the southern flank against Sedan.

From beginning to end, von Rundstedt was unhappy about the Ardennes scheme, part of Plan Yellow as it now became. At a supposedly social *Herrenabend* on 21 January as an interlude in exploratory war-gaming under von Rundstedt's direction, Guderian had been provoked by the army group commander into a typically outspoken defence of his belief of deep penetration by mechanized forces and had gone to bed with a bad cold and a vile temper, writing to his wife: 'It was a debate which I thought impossible in its lack of understanding and, in part, even hatefulness after the Polish campaign . . . It is completely fruitless ever to expect anything from this well-known group of "comrades".' And at a later date, when involved in the final presentation for Hitler's approval and again twitted by 'comrades' who doubted if he would even cross the river, let alone drive for the English Channel or Paris, he was reduced to fury. It helped, of course, that von Rundstedt now should make his peace. But the seeds of disaster existed in the inability of the 64-year-old Army Group Commander, and some of his subordinates, to come to terms with the plan. They dwelt in trepidation of 'Heinz Hot Head', as Guderian was sometimes known in addition to the more popular 'Quick Heinz'. And von Rundstedt was nothing like as flexible in his thinking as his admirers claimed.

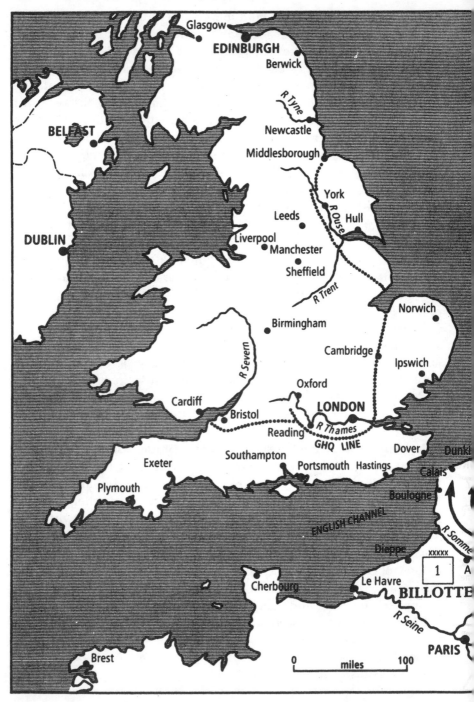

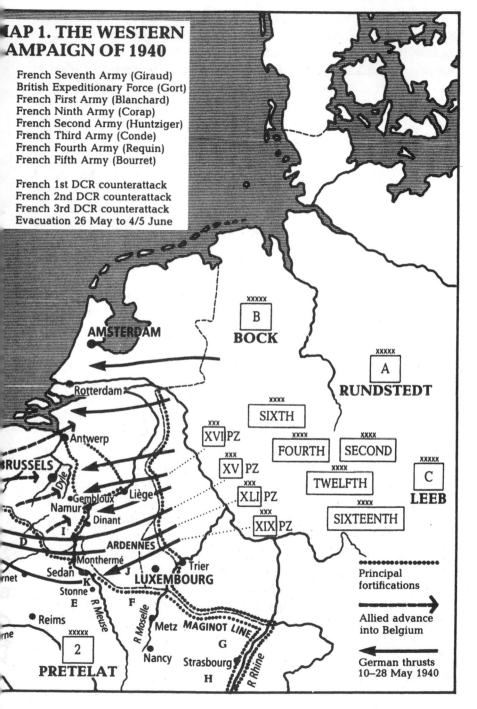

MAP 1. THE WESTERN CAMPAIGN OF 1940

French Seventh Army (Giraud)
British Expeditionary Force (Gort)
French First Army (Blanchard)
French Ninth Army (Corap)
French Second Army (Huntziger)
French Third Army (Conde)
French Fourth Army (Requin)
French Fifth Army (Bourret)

French 1st DCR counterattack
French 2nd DCR counterattack
French 3rd DCR counterattack
Evacuation 26 May to 4/5 June

AMSTERDAM

B
BOCK

A
RUNDSTEDT

Rotterdam

SIXTH

Antwerp

XVI PZ

FOURTH   SECOND

BRUSSELS

XV PZ

TWELFTH

C
LEEB

Dyle

XLI PZ

Gembloux   Liège

Namur

SIXTEENTH

Dinant

XIX PZ

I

ARDENNES

D

Monthermé

Trier

Principal
fortifications

Sedan

J   LUXEMBOURG

K

Stonne   E   F

Reims

R. Meuse

R. Moselle

Metz   MAGINOT LINE

Allied advance
into Belgium

2

G

Nancy   Strasbourg

R. Rhine

German thrusts
10–28 May 1940

PRETELAT   H

The *poilus* of the 55th French Division were the first to be aware that von Rundstedt was wrong and Guderian right when German bombers began high-level bombing attacks which would mount in violence throughout the morning of 13 May until reaching a climax at midday when, plunging from on high like gannets, the dive-bombers began plastering and terrorizing their sector with screams and roars of unimaginable volume. Already they were appalled by the apparent ease with which the enemy had appeared along the river front the previous evening, and shaken by stories from troops withdrawing across the river who were filled with apprehension about tanks of which they had, in fact, seen only a few. Already, indeed, the viruses of sloth, which ate deeply into the French system, were at work, exposing the errors of pre-war years which had permitted them to thrive unchecked. The 55th, 71st and 3rd North African Divisions within General Gransards's X Corps, which had the task of defending the Sedan sector, were under-equipped in weapons and composed of second-rate officers and men among whom, Gransard himself said, 'the ardour for work, for training and the desire to fight' were rare. '... the men are flabby and heavy ... In the artillery the men are older, the training is mediocre . . .' So why had the intellectually brilliant General Charles Huntziger, the Commander, Second Army, placed them in this under-fortified sector and put his better troops on their right behind a much stronger part of the Maginot Line proper? And why, as the threat became apparent, did he not hasten the reinforcement of Sedan and impress his subordinates with a sense of urgency? Simply because, it has to be said, he was as ignorant of the pace and power at which panzer divisions could deploy and attack as was von Rundstedt, despite his having taken an interest in their triumphs in Poland. Or perhaps because of that. For the reports he read were those of General Keller, the French Army's Inspector General of Tanks, who had written that he did not think the Germans would be capable of a *Blitzkrieg* against France as in Poland and that 'In future operations the primary role of the tank will be the same as in the past: to assist the infantry in reaching successive objectives.'

The falsity of this notion would have struck the poilus of 55th Division very forcibly, had they been aware of them, as their artillery began to fall silent under the air attack (the gunners driven to cover, their guns rarely directly hit); as, without warning, the pillboxes guarding the river line were knocked out by high-velocity shot from anti-aircraft guns, firing over open sights from the far bank, whose gunners aimed precisely through the weapon slits; and as enemy infantry in rubber boats, totally without field artillery or tank support, began to cross the river. In broad daylight, without a tank in sight (because they had not yet been brought forward) the German infantry won a foothold and began to infiltrate the heights. And as night approached to the accompaniment of encroaching sounds of battle, a dismal silence from their own artillery which, upon unconfirmed reports of enemy tanks across the river and advancing, had been permitted to withdraw, the X Corps fell apart. How did this happen? Again quite simply a demonstration of poor training, lack of combat determination and inept command and control by officers, some of whom pretended they had received the order to withdraw and led the spreading rout. For although there were tanks present they were, in fact, French tanks on their way to mount a counter-attack which might well have thrown back the superbly trained, battle experienced German infantry, but which, instead, had to be halted for fear of spreading the panic wider among the infantry, gunners and commanders of neighbouring units and formations.

Present in the débâcle resided the pyschosis of 'Tank Terror' which the Germans had suffered in 1917 and 1918, but which the French were experiencing for the first time. Unaware of its existence, they had obviously done nothing during training to innoculate themselves against it. Shaken by another unknown terror, the relatively innocuous dive-bombing, their morale was very liable to crack. So when, next day, German tanks really did appear, after crossing the river by rafts and bridges built during the night, there was nothing to hold them. From what he saw for himself in the forefront of the battle, Guderian judged that a wide hole had been torn in the enemy front and that, regardless of lack of orders, this was the moment to make full speed for the English Channel. Moreover, downstream at Monthermé and at Dinant where, respectively, Lieutenant-General Reinhardt's XLI Corps and Lieutenant-General Hoth's XV Corps were also across, the westward drive was also in progress against a shattered enemy.

Of almost equal significance was the situation on the front of the French First Army after it had moved forward into Belgium with the Ninth Army pivoting on its right. Here, on 14 May, the first big clash of armour took place when, in the vicinity of Hannut, General Prioux's

Cavalry Corps, carrying out its screening role, came into collision with leading elements of Lieutenant-General Hoeppner's XVI Corps. Both corps comprised two armoured divisions, the French DLMs (divisions légères mécaniques) possessing 174 tanks each, including the good SOMUA; the Germans with about 300 light and medium tanks each, none of them the equal of the SOMUA in armament or armour. This was the confrontation which at once demonstrated the superiority of the modern German doctrine of concentration of all arms against the old-fashioned French way of treating tanks like horses. Spread out across the First Army front and not once endeavouring to concentrate or to work with its artillery and mechanized infantry units, the French exposed themselves to piecemeal destruction by an opponent who manoeuvred in groups to destroy individual knots of resistance before advancing to vital ground in the French rear. There it disrupted the DLMs' command and control system and destroyed their logistic support. Moreover the French lost also in tank versus tank combat because of the fundamental design error of fitting their tanks, including the SOMUA and, in the Divisions Cuirassées de Réserve (DCRs), the Char B with a one-man turret. This made it almost impossible for the man who had to command the tank, load and aim the gun to do so efficiently and at a fast rate. Whereas, in the three-man turret of the German Mark III and IV tanks, the sub-division of tasks between commander, gunner and loader made for rapid and, within the ballistic and optical limitations of the equipment, fairly accurate shooting. But of even greater effect in giving the German AFVs the edge was their comprehensive radio network, with reliable sets in every tank, as against the French, only 25 per cent of whose tanks carried a (somewhat unreliable) set. The piecemeal defeat of the French Cavalry Corps at Hannut was then made absolute by the commander of Ninth Army's insistence upon sharing out the DLMs' tanks among the infantry. From this day's maltreatment by both foe and friend, neither of these two DLMs, nor the third of their number with Seventh Army, ever recovered even after they were released later to concentrate near Arras.

Next befell the dissolution of the French DCRs, the so-called armoured divisions which, under the command of leaders who lacked the vision of a Guderian, never were grouped two or three to a corps and, as a matter of habit, frequently were themselves dispersed. 1st DCR, sent forward on the 14th by Ninth Army to check the advance of

Hoth's XV Corps, was overrun on the 15th by the concentrated battle groups of 5th and 7th Panzer Divisions when it lay immobilized by shortage of fuel just as the fuel trucks were arriving. By the end of the day its strength had been reduced from 150 to 50 tanks and then to virtual extinction as it fled westwards. On the 15th, 2nd DCR's fighting echelon lost touch with its administrative echelon when the latter bumped quite unexpectedly into Guderian's XIX Corps which was miles ahead of where the French estimated it to be. Deprived of organized supply, the fighting echelon, including the tanks, was split up among the infantry and thus eliminated as a formation and condemned to destruction from a thousand cuts by the exultant Germans. 3rd DCR, ordered on the 14th to counter-attack XIX Corps' bridgehead at Sedan, exhibited all the signs of unpreparedness, sloth and inefficiency which typified the French offensive arm. Omitting the issue of a warning order to its units, divisional headquarters dallied in formulating a plan and giving formal orders, and delayed refuelling, after a leisurely approach march to the starting-line. So the attack was postponed, then cancelled and the usual process of dispersal began. Urged next day to try again, the same sluggishness pervaded with similar results. Here and there, notably at Stonne, the tough Char B tanks did get into action and, with their thick armour, made a profound impression upon German anti-tank gunners. But upon the minds of Guderian or his superior officer, General von Kleist, who commanded the Panzer Group consisting of XIX and XLI Corps, the impression was meagre. Only von Rundstedt was genuinely worried by the struggle at Stonne.

Apart from the incomplete 4th DCR under General Charles de Gaulle and the emasculated remains of the Cavalry Corps, the French Army's striking force had been wiped out in less than 48 hours. Thus the campaign, from the French point of view, was already lost and the Army's command and control mechanism was in disarray. Captain André Beaufre captures the atmosphere at the headquarters of General Georges, commander of the North East Front, as news of the collapse came through. Georges, terribly pale, said: 'Our front has been broken at Sedan. There has been a collapse . . . He flung himself into a chair and burst into tears.' It was a blow from which neither he nor the rest of the Army recovered as the German advance accelerated to such a pace that the old-fashioned communications system of telephone and somewhat unreliable radio network (whose codes had already been broken by the German cryptologists) was unable to cope.

Self-satisfaction, as a by-product of past victories with outmoded techniques; sloth, leading to incomprehension and generating incompetence among commanders, many of whom were too old to cope with the speed, stress and strain of modern war, had brought the French Army and the nation to ruin. Error would now pile uncontrollably upon error and need not be further examined here as we trace the unrelenting thrust of the panzer corps spearheads, record the fall of Holland on 14 May to a combined airborne and land attack, and mark the surge of von Bock's predominantly infantry and artillery Army Group B into Belgium. This, in fact, is the moment to examine German progress only and discover why all was not well in parts of their camp.

No sooner had the three panzer corps broken out from their bridgeheads on the 14th, than two very influential officers began to fret about the danger of a strong French counter-stroke against the lengthening southern flank. Concern had been expressed about this during the war-gaming but not, as it happened, by Hitler. Yet it was he who raised cries of alarm on the 16th in chorus with von Rundstedt over 3rd DCR's fragmentary attacks at Stonne. Each took council of the other's fears and transmitted their concern, on the 17th, to the Army Chief of Staff, Halder, who was serene in his contentment with developments. That day von Kleist, acting on orders from von Rundstedt (but not from Army Supreme Headquarters (OKH)) ordered Guderian to halt where he was at Montcornet and berated him for having exceeded instructions by advancing too far. There was an almighty row, 'Heinz Hot Head' resigned his command and von Kleist accepted the resignation. Information by radio of the event reached von Rundstedt who sent General Siegmund von List to reinstate Guderian – and the advance continued under the pretext of 'a reconnaissance in force' – with Guderian linked only by cable teleprinter and liaison officer to his own HQ and those of flanking formations so that his orders could not be monitored over the radio. Nevertheless, from this comedy of errors, time and momentum had been lost; the result, as Halder expressed it, of Hitler's fear of his own success.

Well supplied with Intelligence from decrypted enemy codes, from air and from ground reconnaissance, the Germans could move with almost faultless assurance towards their objectives. XV Corps reached the outskirts of Arras on the 20th, XLI and XIX Corps the Channel coast a few hours later. Also, they did it with logistic ease, never short of fuel or ammunition and still with at least 50 per cent of their tanks in running order and a high percentage of the remainder requiring but first or second line repairs since the numbers actually destroyed in combat were relatively few. All around lay an enemy in confusion who could not tell if the panzers would now turn south to capture Paris or move north to round up the French, British and Belgian troops who had their backs to the sea and a few undefended ports.

If there is any one date which Germany's enemies should celebrate as the day upon which Germany lost the war, it should be 21 May. On this day vital time was wasted while OKW and OKH, haunted by Hitler's and von Rundstedt's dread of the exposed (but never seriously threatened) south flank, paused to debate. At last they determined to strike northwards against Dunkirk, while the infantry divisions consolidated the south flank, the XVI Corps was brought round to strengthen Group von Kleist, and Army Group B pushed the withdrawing Allies to the north of Arras. It was also the day when a small force of British infantry with 70 heavily armoured tanks and the residue of the French Cavalry Corps produced panic by a move south-wards from Arras, to bite into the exposed flank of 7th Panzer Division in XV Corps as it resumed its advance in the afternoon. It was the day, too, when a decision to garrison the ports of Boulogne, Calais, Dunkirk and Ostend was taken, initially for the import of supplies now that communications with the main bases in the south had been cut; latterly, to extract the defeated armies if, in the meantime, they were not already enveloped and compelled to surrender.

And the chances that they might well be surrounded was at once made clear to the British, not simply from monitoring battlefield Intelligence but also from a new and crucial source – the general key (known as Red) to the Luftwaffe's top-level encyphered radio messages. The existence of the German electro-mechanical wired encyphering machine called Enigma had been known to the British for several years, and its keys were being cracked rather slowly by a Polish machine called the Bombe. During the Norwegian invasion, however, a British-improved, high-speed Bombe regularly broke the key (Yellow) used by the German army and air force in that campaign. But on 20 May (as a result of slips in German usage) the

Bombe quickly cracked the Luftwaffe Red, and did so for the duration of the war, delivering from 22 May onwards as many as 1,000 invaluable decoded messages per day.

Despite the unwanted pause on the 21st and despite the temporary, and as it turned out, unnecessary diversion of the forces directed against Dunkirk on the 22nd (because of the need to take precautions against any renewal of the so-called Allied counterstroke at Arras), the advance by Group von Kleist shot forward. No amount of Intelligence from the Bombe in the British Ultra organization could change the catastrophic Allied situation. All their forces were embroiled in the front line in Belgium and could not be brought back to bar the way to von Kleist against whom only light forces, some shipped across from England, were in place. At this desperate moment just about the only bit of luck which came the British way was the result of another lapse in security. On the 25th, a German Army liaison officer was captured near the front in possession of papers indicating a planned attack by the Germans into the gap left open by the withdrawal of the Belgian Army near Ypres. This gave just enough time to fill the hole by redeployment, which saved the British Army. But of incalculable importance for future usage, the capture presented the complete German Order of Battle to provide the basis of all Intelligence data upon the vital subject of German deployment in every theatre of war.

Perhaps the greatest error made by the Germans on the 21st was that perpetrated jointly by Hitler and his Chief of Naval Staff, Admiral Erich Raeder. Realizing that within a few weeks' time the entire sea coast from North Cape to Biarritz would be likely to have fallen into German hands and that Hitler's next invasion might be of England, the Admiral reminded his Führer that, quite recently, the impracticability of such an attempt had been agreed. 'But what of now?' he asked, hoping devoutly for rejection of that risky enterprise which he feared – and mightily gratified when Hitler, giving the matter short consideration, said 'No', on the grounds that Britain's hopeless situation must now compel her to sue for peace. We will revert to his momentous decision later, merely mentioning here that, once more, the Supreme Commander had allowed logical military contingency planning to lapse by default.

Nevertheless, there were good grounds for concluding that if the British Expeditionary Force, along with the remnants of the French

First Army was, as the British War Office conceded, wiped out when Dunkirk inevitably fell, the national will to resist might be destroyed. Boulogne was found indefensible and was captured on the morning of the 24 May by 2nd Panzer Division. 1st Panzer Division by-passed Calais, leaving that port to be assaulted by 10th Panzer Division and captured, after a stiff fight against a British brigade, on the 26th. On the morning of the 24th Group von Kleist, with three panzer divisions and the equivalent of two motorized infantry divisions, was within 15 miles of Dunkirk, advancing on a wide front with only a single low-grade French infantry division and a weak British infantry force standing in the way of the envelopment of the port within 24 hours. The fact that innundations might make movement off the roads difficult was irrelevant since the roads could not be adequately defended. And the first manifestations of air attacks by aircraft from England was a mere nuisance. Dunkirk was to be had for the asking when, out of the blue, the celebrated order to halt was received.

All sorts of reasons have been suggested for the aberration on the German part, the commonest target for blame being Hitler himself. Here the simple chronological sequence in the issue of orders will be related to demonstrate what is now generally accepted by historians, that the order originated with von Rundstedt whose fears were fed by Hitler and never checked by OKH. On the afternoon of the 24th von Rundstedt called the halt, anxious as ever to 'close up units to the front', regardless of a steady flow of mechanized forces within reach of the coast – and did so without permission from OKH whose instructions were for Army Group A to be the hammer and Army Group B the anvil to the east of Dunkirk. Not until the evening of the 24th, after von Brauchitsch, the C-in-C, had endured a very unpleasant interview with the Führer, was the halt confirmed on Hitler's authority, along with orders that the destruction of the enemy in Dunkirk was to be completed by the Luftwaffe. The reasons given for holding back the Army reflect to perfection von Rundstedt's misgivings and ignorance of mechanization – fear of the threat from the south, concern over the 50 per cent decline in tank strength (still leaving about 1,500 tanks in running order with many on the verge of repair) and a desire to conserve strength against the day when the Army must strike southward to complete the conquest of France. The reason for handing the torch to the Luftwaffe was quite simply that of opportunism on the part of its C-in-C, Field Marshal Hermann

Goering, who seized upon the Army's discomforture as a golden opportunity to win laurels for his own force, despite the Luftwaffe's unreadiness and patent inability to do so. For its bomber force, attenuated by losses and unserviceability, was incapable of operating accurately in darkness (when most of the evacuation by sea from Dunkirk would take place), and its short-range fighter force was restricted because forward airfields had yet to be properly established. But after all, as one German authority has remarked, Goering's military abilities never really rose above those of a battalion commander and, in any case, the frailty of the much vaunted prowess of the Luftwaffe, and its inherent limitations as a decisive arm in its own independent right, had yet to be fully revealed.

Too late, on the 26th, von Rundstedt who, according to Halder, 'could not stand it any longer', went up front 'to get the lay of the land' for the next moves of his armour. Shortly afterwards Hitler, who was frequently in touch with von Rundstedt, relented to allow the Army to advance again on Dunkirk, 'in order to prevent further evacuations'. But by then the port's perimeter had been occupied by strong Allied forces brought back from the east, and the Luftwaffe was finding it most difficult to sink shipping – a task for which it had not yet seriously trained and which was made still more difficult when bad weather and, to a lesser extent, the activities of RAF fighters put it beyond reach.

Before the disgusted gaze of the German Army, those elements of the Allied armies which got back to Dunkirk sailed away, hampered, but never stopped, by artillery fire and bombing. Meanwhile the mobile forces were called off in order to prepare for the conquest of France – a mere formality, as it must inevitably be, in the certain knowledge that the best of the opposing forces already had been eliminated. This was the moment, in the opinion of General Kesselring, and with support from his chief, the ever-ambitious Goering, when immediate steps should have been taken to pursue the British across the sea to England and overrun the island before a state of adequate defence could be established. But the fatal decision of 21 May against an invasion of Britain and Hitler's reinforced confidence that the British were now certain to give way, precluded this. Everything would be hurled against France. Only gradually, after France had fallen in June and the early days of July, brightly illuminated by celebrations of victory, but marred by pronouncements of

CRITICAL FLAWS

▶ **Absence on the German part of a long-term strategic plan.**

▶ **Inferior training of French troops contributing to vulnerable morale and operational ineptitude – above all when faced by aircraft and tanks.**

▶ **Dispersal of French mechanized formations and their Army's reliance upon static defences.**

▶ **Inability of several key German commanders to envisage the feasibility and effects of mechanized deep penetration operations on land.**

▶ **Profligate use by the Germans, in particular the Luftwaffe, of insecure radio communications.**

▶ **The fallibility of Goering's claim that a decision at Dunkirk could be achieved by air power alone.**

dogged resistance from the British Prime Minister, Winston Churchill, did reality intrude. And by then, just like the days prior to Dunkirk, a pause in momentum and lack of a fully developed strategy had sown the seeds of ultimate failure.

3

THE FATAL POSTPONEMENT
The Battle for Britain

The basic reason for Germany's failure to invade Britain in 1940 is very likely to be found in the lack of any preconceived will or intention to do so, with the result that not until after the outbreak of war was the problem contemplated. Another reason for holding back, even when France stood on the verge of collapse and the BEF seemed doomed to annihilation, lay in paucity of Intelligence. Because of lack of intention, only a rudimentary information gathering operation had been mounted against Britain. Of British strength and dispositions, let alone morale and plans, the Germans in the summer of 1940 had only cursory knowledge, a vacuum in Intelligence which they never managed to fill.

Far from want of trying, Britain was also extremely ignorant of Germany's condition although, in June, firmly convinced that an invasion must be imminent. The capture, due to carelessness, of important British Secret Intelligence Service (SIS) agents by the Germans in November 1939 and a series of related disasters, compounded by the overrunning of Europe by German forces, had deprived Britain of her best sources of information. From the British Official History of Intelligence, one is led to the conclusion that prior to and, to some extent, during the Battle of Britain, British estimates of the German economy and industrial production erred, sometimes wildly, on the side of suggesting imminent collapse; while in regard to available military strength, notably the strength of the Luftwaffe, they significantly over estimated. Of course, once the conquest of the West had been completed it was realized that Germany's economic strength had been immeasurably enhanced, but an estimate of a Luftwaffe strength of 5,000 available aircraft against the actual strength of about 2,800 available on 1 August 1940, inevitably placed an inhibiting influence on the defensive measures of Air Marshal Sir Hugh Dowding, C-in-C, Fighter Command.

From the outset both sides appreciated that a successful invasion depended upon air power. In June the British were in terror that the

41

Germans might try, as Kesselring desired, to execute a raid with airborne troops. The magnitude of the German error in not at once, or at the latest in early July, attempting to do so can be measured by pointing out that the Home Fleet, in the aftermath of Dunkirk, was at its weakest for many a day, stretched to the fullest extent by the need to protect the coastline, neutralize the French fleet before it could fall into German hands and maintain the flow of convoys bringing food, raw materials and weapons from overseas: and that the Army could muster a bare 200 heavy and medium tanks, plus some 300 light types, only 786 field guns and a mere 167 anti-tank guns to be used by formations and units which were still in a state of confusion in the aftermath of evacuation from France. As for the Royal Air Force, its radar early warning system was still incomplete; its single-engine fighter strength, seriously depleted by combat over France (which had reduced the number of fighters in reserve depots on 4 June to a mere 36), stood at about 1,000, with fewer than 1,200 trained pilots to fly them when the rate of fighter production was about 15 a day and of trained pilots only 6 a day.

Of course, the Germans could not under any circumstances have known the extent of the British weakness, but they were already aware of the slight technical superiority of their single-engine fighters over those of the British, and boasted of their pilots' greater experience and sounder tactics. Nor was it too difficult to calculate from all the material which had fallen into their hands in France the amount of damage done. Just as that information, alone, should have generated a more realistic German appreciation than it did, so too should a study of the results obtained by bombing have indicated that, in the existing state of the art, air power lacked the potency claimed of it. Yet, in the aftermath of his Luftwaffe's shortcomings in Poland, and in the West, to win absolute air superiority until enemy early warning systems and airfields were physically occupied, Goering was still to the fore in boasting that his organization could, on its own, subjugate Britain, enabling the Navy and the Army, almost as a formality, to cross the Channel. To which the Navy and the Army responded by making it a condition that he do so before they moved; the naval high command rather hoping he would fail and save them from a desperate business, the Army adopting a sanguine view by visualizing the whole business as a sort of up-scaled river-crossing operation of the sort they were perfectly competent to execute.

Because the Germans declined to invade early in July, as they could well have done had they started preparations after making an affirmative decision on 21 May when Raeder asked the question of Hitler, they never discovered the misguided state of British dispositions at that time. For British Intelligence, largely ignorant of German deployment and totally ignorant of their enemy's plans, continued until October to postulate that the principal invading force would assemble in the Baltic, as well as the North Sea ports, and effect the main landing in East Anglia. Nobody can say how this guess was arrived at, as guess it had to be due to the impossibility of obtaining air photographs of the Baltic ports until the latest Spitfire high-altitude long-range reconnaissance machine would be operational in October. It was probably manufactured to satisfy the deployment that existed prior to Dunkirk; others hint that the guess drew inspiration from the plot of Erskine Childer's *The Riddle of the Sands*, a novel which described just such a plan before the First World War. Be that as it may, the Germans opted to come by the shortest, most easily supported and obvious route across the Straits of Dover where the British defences, dictated by the naïve Intelligence forecast, were, with the fortunate and notable exception of fighter aircraft defence, extremely weak.

How misconceived those defences were can be judged by the measures planned by the Navy and the Army in the event of invasion. Admiral Sir Charles Forbes, the C-in-C, Home Fleet, intended, with Admiralty approval, to retain the Battle Fleet at Scapa Flow unless major units of the German Fleet put to sea. For the defence of the North Sea he relied upon cruisers and destroyers spread between four ports from Tyne to Sheerness, with a mere 5 destroyers at Dover and another 5 at Portsmouth. At all costs, and with good reason, Forbes was determined to avoid committing his big ships to the shallower, wreck and mine infested English Channel, and no sooner did intensive air attacks fall upon Dover and a destroyer was lost and several damaged, than he withdrew the destroyers from there to Portsmouth, opening the door to Kent and Sussex. As for the defences of Kent (where the Germans intended to land four divisions by air and sea on the first day), but one meagrely equipped, inexperienced division guarded the coast with orders to withdraw inland to the so-called GHQ Line covering London once the enemy gained a foothold – as they could not help but do. This was the state of mind of south-east England's defenders in July, an outlook which had changed but little by September when, day by day, aerial photographs began to show shipping assembling in the ports from Antwerp to Cherbourg, and watchers on the cliffs of Dover could count the invasion craft moving down Channel. Sticking to their preconceived notions, the naval staffs dismissed these convoys as part of normal trade, 'perhaps to alleviate the problems caused by the blockage of canals and rivers'; or by the suggestion on 12 September, that 'some of the traffic might have destinations as far off as Spain or Portugal'.

In September, the opposition to the Germans would have been much greater than in July. By then, too, a stronger suspicion existed in British commanders' minds that they might cross the Channel, leading to a pronounced reallocation of troops to the south coast. The nights were growing longer and the weather less benign, making the task of the German Navy increasingly hazardous. Above all, the Luftwaffe had demonstrated its inability to overcome a British air defence system, which had been given just sufficient time in June and July to extend its radar coverage, build nearly 1,000 more fighters and produce a few more anti-aircraft guns to protect vital points. Moreover, the Luftwaffe's commanders had, once more, committed a basic military sin, that of turning aside from the prime object of defeating the RAF and thus failing to 'maintain the selected aim' as all the Staff Colleges and the Manuals demanded.

Nevertheless, the air Battle of Britain was a much closer run thing than the British Official History and many other accounts admit. Having reached a point on 6 September when the invasion fleet was already assembling, almost unopposed, Goering, fed with misleading Intelligence which was formulated by his staffs on the exaggerated and unauthenticated claims by his own pilots of enemy aircraft shot down, drew the false conclusion that the RAF was beaten. He was nearly right – but not quite. Some airfields had been made untenable, others were in a bad way, pockmarked by craters. Communications networks were stretched and the early warning system threatened. Indeed, had the Germans not erroneously concluded from earlier attempts, that it was impossible to wreck radar installations by bombing, that vital element in the chain of fighter control would have been put out of action for good. Even so, the fighter squadrons were losing more aircraft than their German fighter opponents and beginning to feel the pinch of inadequate maintenance facilities on

---

CRITICAL FLAWS

▶ Poor German Intelligence contributing to their misreading of British determination and weakness, deterring them from invading Britain soon after Dunkirk.

▶ Fundamentally incorrect British Intelligence appreciations leading to a misappreciation of German strength and intentions.

▶ German failure to concentrate upon the neutralization of British early warning radar and the destruction of RAF Fighter Command.

---

bombed airfields. Still more worrying was the serious shortage of well-trained pilots, of whom only an experienced minority had the skill to shoot down the enemy, while the majority of fledglings made up the numbers, and provided easier targets for their more numerous and better trained opponents. Arguably, if the Germans had continued to batter the fighter airfields and compel the failing RAF fighters to accept battle within the range of German fighters operating from France, Air Marshal Dowding's Fighter Command might well have been driven from the invasion area in southern England. In which case a foothold could have been made.

Everything changed when Goering suddenly switched the attacks from the airfields to the port of London and the capital itself. Not only did these raids fail to cow the population, as they were intended to do, and not only did the airfields benefit from a respite sufficient to restore their efficiency, but the whole balance of advantage in the aerial combat was reversed. Operating at the extremities of their range while escorting bombers to London, the German fighters could be engaged in air space not of their own choosing but that of their opponents who could dive from altitude after being granted enough time to climb and position themselves. Within a week of the crisis point of the first attack on London on 7 September, the RAF had recuperated its fighter strength. A week later the Luftwaffe conceded defeat and reverted to hit-and-run attacks and scattered night bombing. Inevitably the invasion had to be postponed and finally cancelled.

It is no exaggeration to say that the failure to invade England and knock her out of the war was ultimately fatal to Germany. If she had achieved that aim in 1940 Hitler's hands would have been freed to pursue his policy of picking off nations, one by one, in his own time. Very likely the Royal Navy would have been neutralized. Probably key points of the British Empire would have fallen into German hands as he created a United States of Europe under German hegemony. In which case the President of the USA would have agreed with Ambassador Kennedy and might have withdrawn all help from Britain, preferring to reach a settlement with a major continental power which, if it chose to tackle Soviet Russia (as Hitler had already decided to do) might be irresistible.

4

SIDE STEPS TOWARDS RUSSIA
Preliminaries to the Invasion

Of the innumerable recorded pronouncements of reaction to the news that Hitler intended to or actually had launched an invasion of Russia, one theme predominated. Incredulity! Astonishment, even within his own circle and certainly among his commanders, that he should risk newly won gains by invading so vast a nation with which a pact of friendship had been signed less than a year ago. Amazement that he should even contemplate so enormous a project while the British remained undefeated, thus creating the very situation so frequently forsworn – a war on two fronts. Amazement, too, among his enemies when gradually, during the months following the Battle of Britain, evidence began to accumulate that Russia might be Germany's next victim. Yet it was only necessary for those who scratched their heads in wonderment, to read what the Führer had said and written about the Russian Communist menace ever since he took up arms against their agents in the post-1918 struggles. To Germans of centre and right wing political views, Communism was an abomination which had plunged the nation into a bloody civil war, wrecked an ordered society and destroyed the economy. To Hitler and his Nazi party, as well as the great majority of the military officers, it was a menace which had to be destroyed, although the wisdom of doing so by force at this particular juncture was open to question.

Setting aside the politics and psychology of Hitler's announcement in mid July 1940 to his closest colleagues, it is necessary to ask how it was that Hitler and his commanders came to believe that they could defeat the arguably strongest and largest military power in the world. At root, of course, they by now believed absolutely in the invincibility of their military machine, justifiably putting unwavering trust in the prowess and fidelity of the officers and men and in the organization which had proved completely superior in Poland, Norway, Holland, Belgium and France – and which had been prevented from crushing Britain merely by the existence of the English Channel. Vast as Russia looked on the map and on paper, and considerable as had been her investment in armaments over the past decade, nothing the Germans had seen of them when together they had met in the closing stage of the Polish campaign, or what they had learned about the Russian attack on Finland at the beginning of 1940, was impressive. The officers had seemed a poor lot (which was hardly surprising in the aftermath of Premier Josef Stalin's purges in the 1930s), the men none too well trained and the equipment obsolescent. From the Japanese they had also gleaned news of a patchy performance during various frontier incidents in Manchuria, but carelessly they overlooked the fact that Japan's forces were extremely well trained and equipped, and that in the latter stages of the Finnish war the Russians had performed quite creditably.

Of hard Intelligence on the Russian Order of Battle, deployment, new equipment, communications and economic situation the Germans were notably lacking. In the same way as they had paid little attention to Britain, they had not invested much in the gathering of information about a nation whose inherently secretive nature and extremely tight security made such activities incredibly difficult. It was far from clever, moreover, that the infantry-trained General Staff Officer responsible in OKH for Intelligence about the Soviet forces had many other duties, was not an expert on the Soviet Union or the Red Army and could not speak Russian. Therefore it was hardly surprising that the only detailed information acquired concerned the frontier regions across which ground patrols and aircraft often penetrated in furtive and thoroughly illegal reconnaissance. In consequence interpretation of Intelligence was generally mediocre. Few people, as time went on, retained faith in the reports circulated, quite apart from the fact that remedial action to cope with what was, rightly or wrongly, predicted, frequently was lax. Such are the products of over-confidence. The fact remains that the Wehrmacht plunged into Russia under the impression that there were 200 Russian divisions in being; only to discover, two months later, that the count had risen to 360, a figure which had been revised to over 400 by the beginning of December 1941. And while it was known that the Russian railway gauge was different from Germany's, and the roads inferior, by no means sufficient trouble was taken to compensate these critical factors in administrative and logistic planning which fell short of the desirable in nearly every department.

Britain and, ironically, to a lesser extent Russia, were far better informed about German intentions and strength from myriad sources and yet inhibited by the incredulity theme, unwilling to admit the evidence repeatedly set before them. Aside from speculation about a German attack on Russia, which began even before the fall of France, the first firm indications of a build-up of strength along Germany's eastern frontier and a reduction of exports from Germany to Russia, appeared in September. Henceforward they steadily multiplied – and as steadily were cancelled out by contradictory reports, many of which were planted by the Germans to suggest that an invasion of Britain still had top priority. The British policy of persistently sowing seeds of discontent in an endeavour to detach Russia from alliance with Germany resulted in much Intelligence passed from London to Moscow being discounted by the inveterately devious Stalin as merely one aspect of British deviousness. Of course, the British dared not tell Stalin all they knew (and had sometimes to mislead him) since significant tracts of information had been obtained via Ultra decoding of Enigma, and the very existence of this source was a priceless national asset which could not be disclosed to a nation which paraded its alliance with Germany.

To cut a very complex story short, the Russians had in their possession by April 1941 a mass of corroborative evidence to show that Germany was planning an invasion. Yet Stalin, who held all the reins of Government and acted as Supreme Commander, declined to believe it and took minimal countermeasures. It is suggested generally that this reluctance was due probably to his assumption that German deviousness tallied with his own and that, while posturing, they would not do anything so stupid as to invade. Viktor Suvorov, on the other hand, makes the interesting suggestion, backed by evidence,* that Stalin was himself planning an invasion of Germany, timed for 10 July, and that one reason why the forces on Russia's western frontier in June were caught unprepared was because they were poised for attack, not defence. If Suvorov is right, Stalin's error was a double one in steadfastly rejecting all professional pleas to call the armed forces to immediate readiness until the closing hours of 21 June; and all the more remarkable that he was finally persuaded at the last moment on the testimony of a German sergeant who deserted

---

*Articles in the Journal of the RUSI, since June 1985.

and crossed the frontier with a convincing story of what was to happen next day.

In the early hours of Sunday 22 June, as German aircraft warmed up their engines and the Army's columns closed up to the frontier, the Red Army staff in Moscow was feverishly attempting to dispatch a warning to their threatened airfields and frontier formations. But the Russian communications system, largely dependent upon telephone and cable and served only by rather inferior radio sets, had a notoriously poor traffic capacity. In any case it was the morning after the night before and a great many people, including some very responsible officers, were sleeping off a convivial Saturday night's happy hour or more. When bombs began to fall upon serried lines of undispersed aircraft, shells to buffet the frontier posts and German tanks and soldiers swept down upon bleary-eyed Russian infantry-men, roused from their slumbers by the opening shots, none but a few warning signals had been relayed to their intended destinations.

If the German attack upon Russia could have been launched without additional dispersal of resources other than those needed to keep Britain in check, what was known initially as Operation 'Otto' (and finally as 'Barbarossa') might well have succeeded – although leave may be taken for thinking that if Hitler had managed to launch it in September 1940 (as once was seriously discussed!) instead of pressing on with the Battle of Britain, it must have failed if only because of the nearness of winter. As it was, many diversions stole time and resources from the forces available, and not a few were as a direct result of having omitted to conquer the British Isles.

Inexorably the British threat dragged Germany into diversionary operations she could ill afford when the exacting and massive Barbarossa commitment loomed ahead. Before the plans were anything like complete, Germany's southern flank needed more attention than Hitler had bargained for. He had hoped to seal off from Britain the Mediterranean at its western end by seizing Gibraltar with Spain's connivance. But Spain's Dictator, General Franco, had had enough of war, which had devastated his country, and declined to collaborate. At the same time Hitler had to cope with the weighty millstone cast around the Axis neck by fellow Dictator Benito Mussolini. It had seemed innocuous enough as Italy joined in on Germany's side when the war looked won in sunny June. But come autumn's chill, it was already plain that simply to keep Italy in the war would divert weapons and raw materials from Germany's by no means lavish stocks – let alone propping Italy up when an unannounced (as well as unapproved) invasion of Greece ran into stiff resistance followed by ignominious retreat into Albania. This reverse, followed in December by a crushing defeat by the British of the Italian Army in North Africa (to which we will return later), and a headlong retreat from the frontier of Egypt towards Benghazi and, who could tell? Extinction of Italy's enthusiasm for war by the loss of her entire North African empire, could not be ignored.

Unwillingly Hitler had to take extra measures to safeguard Barbarossa's southern flank. By means of power diplomacy, Hungary, Roumania and Bulgaria had been brought initially into the Axis fold as bases for the invasion of Russia and for the defence of the vital Roumanian oilfields. Now they became springboards for a diplomatic takeover of Yugoslavia and an invasion of Greece. At the same time two mechanized divisions, known as the Africa Corps (Lieutenant-General Erwin Rommel) were sent to Tripoli to guarantee the survival of the panicking Italian Army in North Africa which, on 5 February, was annihilated by the British at the Battle of Beda Fomm. Each expansion in the south was a subtraction from Barbarossa as well as the cause of delay in its execution, a subtraction enlarged to alarming proportions when the British, by diplomatic intrigue, managed to instigate a *coup d'état* in Yugoslavia which overthrew the Government and brought to naught the arrangement whereby the country would fall unresistingly under Axis domination. With every indication that British bombers as well as troops would soon be within range of Roumania and the Barbarossa supply lines, a major invasion of Yugoslavia as well as Greece had to be undertaken at short notice.

These were heady days for the headstrong Führer, whose conceit at the prowess of his armed forces received another boost when the ruthless invasion of Yugoslavia and Greece conquered both countries in a matter of weeks. And did so at the very moment when, quite unexpectedly because it was clean contrary to instructions, General Rommel, instead of standing as ordered on the defensive in North Africa, attacked and threw the British back to the Egyptian frontier with heavy losses. Momentum gathered momentum. Carried away by his men's apparent irrestible battlecraft, and throwing to the winds the Army's strategic plan, Hitler permitted the invasion of Crete, and committed two airborne divisions to its capture.

Crete was another of Goering's prestigious ventures, conceived in the name of glory by the ambitious commander of XI Airborne Corps, Lieutenant-General Kurt Student. Student proposed it to Goering, who, in mid April, despite an earlier decision to leave Crete alone since it posed no great threat, obtained Hitler's permission to launch the attack in May provided that it was completed quickly. The remarkable speed with which the Luftwaffe prepared the launching airfields in Greece and assembled nearly 1,200 aircraft and gliders was offset by insufficient time to obtain Intelligence. Virtually the only information which could be gathered in less than a month was what reconnaissance aircraft could discover, and they found out virtually nothing about the strength and deployment of the not inconsiderable island garrison which they underestimated by a factor of 3–5, a disadvantage compounded by the fact that the British were extremely well aware of what was in train.

Ultra, as had been the norm since its first use in Norway and, with continuous and increasing fluency, since Dunkirk, was enhanced by a significant growth in the Y radio intercept service which enjoyed particular success in the Mediterranean, listening to Luftwaffe tactical traffic – some in code, some in plain language. Ever-enthusiastic radio communicators, and horribly mistaken in thinking that Enigma was unbreakable, the Luftwaffe, to a far greater extent than the German Army (which also made its contribution, however), was a profuse supplier of priceless Intelligence which, beyond much doubt, ensured the escape of the bulk of the British Army from Greece and gave precise warning of the impending attack on Crete – which was exclusively a Luftwaffe-controlled operation.

Provided by Ultra with precise details of the enemy landing zones, but overestimating the number of troops available, the British were also conversant with the landing techniques of the airborne troops, having captured their training manual in 1940. Moreover the British garrison could not only concentrate with confidence against the known enemy objectives, they had a further advantage in the possession of a few tanks – but possibly not enough – to be able to mount counter-attacks immediately the enemy landed and before they had time to consolidate. Outnumbering the forces committed by the Germans, the British were, however, almost devoid of aircraft, woefully short of artillery and provided with so few radio sets that links below brigade level were limited usually to a single set of

---

CRITICAL FLAWS

▶ **Germany's invasion of Russia before she had eliminated Britain linked to:**

▶ **The attempt to conquer Russia with inadequate knowledge of that country and its resources, and inadequate resources for the task**

▶ **Further diversion of German forces to the Balkans and the Mediterranean theatre of operations**

▶ **British failure at Crete to make full use of available Intelligence**

---

dubious reliability. Despite these deficiencies, it remains the opinion of competent authorities that the attack should have been defeated, particularly with the quality of information provided which made possible an assured concentration of forces against the three identified inland landing zones.

So why did Major-General Bernard Freyburg, the island's commander, decide that the principal threat would be against the coast from a naval invasion and that the German aircraft would land on the beaches? Freyberg, as Ronald Lewin has remarked, was 'a fighting general'. The command problems of Crete, thrust upon him unexpectedly by General Wavell, C-in-C, Middle East, were 'too big for him' – which is a way of saying that Wavell made a crucial error in this selection of a commander. Freyberg simply did not comprehend the characteristics and limitations of airborne forces and could not bring himself to believe the entire German operation depended upon them. In underestimating the vital importance of the airfields, particularly Maleme airfield which was the main Luftwaffe objective, he did not impress upon his subordinates the importance of their defence. The defence of Maleme by 22nd New Zealand Battalion (Colonel Andrew), as part of 5th NZ Brigade, with two heavy Matilda tanks in support, was not made 'vital', leaving the garrison unsupported as it was assailed by parachutists and glider-borne troops in large numbers. Without any form of communication with his companies and only a single and fading radio link with Brigade HQ, Andrew (a First World War VC) was to experience the disappointment of losing both tanks in their vain counter-attack and, in the absence of reports from his companies dominating the airfield itself, came to the conclusion that the position was untenable when, arguably, the enemy pressure was contained and the position defensible. Denied reinforcements by 5th Brigade, under no instruction to 'hold at all costs', Andrew ordered the company dominating the airfield to abandon its position. The New Zealand official historian, who fought at Maleme with 23rd NZ Bn, remarks that 'By withdrawing from Point 107 and the airfield he [Andrew] gave the enemy the only chance of exploiting the lodgement they had gained.' It was an excusable choice in the appalling circumstances, but an error – and one seized upon by the Germans who were facing failure elsewhere and whose seaborne force would be intercepted and almost destroyed that night.

The airhead at Maleme would become the base which Student would reinforce and from which the victorious advance to conquer Crete would spring. But the victory was a pyrrhic one, costing 170 Ju 52 transports and some 4,000 élite troops, killed or missing; machines and men whose presence in Russia a month later might well, as will be seen, have been decisive. And an event which was to have even longer-term effects on German strategy because the heavy losses convinced Hitler of the impracticability of large-scale airborne operations, deterring him from ever again sanctioning a major assault by an airborne formation.

5

THE PRODUCT OF OVER-CONFIDENCE
Battles in Russia, 1941

In the books of many military pedants, prime among the Principles of War is the identification and maintenance of the aim of an operation, along with a corollary that there must be one aim and one aim only. Prior to their invasion of Russia, the Germans adopted three military aims each enjoying its turn of higher precedence over the others, conjointly adding up to the lack of a main aim, to confusion and to severe contention in the conduct of Barbarossa. As much Russian soil as possible was to be occupied to protect Berlin and eastern Germany from air attack. The Russian Army was to be destroyed. Vital political and economic centres such as Leningrad, Moscow, the Ukraine and the Donets Basin were to be occupied. It could be said that simply by advancing on a wide front to seize those objectives all three aims ought to be satisfied. But German shortage of numbers precluded that. Across a 1,000-mile frontage with a mere 2,700 aircraft available (fewer than against the West in 1940) and 2,000 of the good Mark III and IV tanks, plus many lighter machines and assault guns (a stronger force than that of 1940), the discrete axes of advance had to be directed parsimoniously against selected objectives which would yield the most profitable results. There was little room for error in choosing the best from among several promising thrust lines.

To begin with, in Russia, as had been the case in France, the majority of mistakes were made by the defenders. Not only were the Russians at an overall technical and tactical disadvantage to the Germans in the air and on the ground in virtually every department of fire power, mobility, communications, training, tactics and combat experience, but they permitted themselves, for the reasons already described, to be taken completely by surprise at dawn on 22 June. Their technical weaknesses, of course, were in part the result of having commenced large-scale production of aircraft and AFVs some three or four years before the Germans. In quantity they might be superior by a factor of from three to five, but inferiority in the quality of outdated machines repeatedly mitigated against combat survival, quite apart from depleting the striking power by superior weapons.

In the air the Russians were outflown. Even the optimistic Goering was staggered by the losses of the Red Air Force at the start of the campaign – nearly 1,500 wrecks to be counted on the ground, and more than 300 claimed in the air in the first 24 hours for the loss of but two German aircraft; nearly 5,000 claimed within the first week for the loss of 179 German aircraft. It was not just a disaster to the Russians which permitted the Luftwaffe to do as it pleased throughout the summer campaign, above all to provide invaluable reconnaissance facilities to cover the gaps between armies which ground reconnaissance simply could not hope to fill. It was an appalling long-term setback inflicted upon the entire structure of the airforce, its crews and ground support, which did most harm. Never did the Red Air Force fully recover from this blow. Almost until the end of 1944 the Luftwaffe was able to operate obsolete aircraft, which could not have prevailed in the West, over the Russian front – which was very fortunate indeed when it is borne in mind that, in the exhilarating summer of 1941, earlier omissions and mistakes by Hitler, Goering and General Ernst Udet, his Director of the Technical Department, were already beginning to let the Luftwaffe fall behind its opponents in combat worthiness.

Russian AFV losses during the first five months of the war were every bit as enormous as those of their aircraft – some 17,000 is one score quoted against 2,700 German – which are interesting figures since they represent about 65 per cent of the total strength of each side's AFVs on 22 June. But it is the tactical handling of those AFVs which provides the most striking contrasts in proficiency, the well-practised, radio-controlled German units completely outmanoeuvring and outfighting their deprived opponents. Technical edge on the ground was important, of course, although not so important as in aerial combat where it was vital. In any case, the new heavy KV1 and medium T34/76 tanks coming into service were, to German chagrin, considerably superior to their own machines and very difficult to knock out. As in France, what counted was command, control and technique. True, it was revealed that the Russian crews were poorly trained and shot badly. AFVs tended to follow crest lines, nicely silhouetted for the picking off. Tank commanders who failed to take up covered firing positions, exposed their vehicles in the open and were seemingly innocent of properly practised battle drills which led to failure in mutual co-operation as well as co-ordination with artillery, infantry and engineers. But it was the higher command which was at a loss against professional experts, and the Soviet system, as run by Stalin, which had to take the blame for allowing the officers and men's state of training to lapse.

The ruthless purging of the best-trained and most intelligent officers carried out by Stalin in the 1930s, to prevent the Red Army threatening his authority, tended to harm the armoured branch more severely than the other arms because they had the best leaders. Terror lead to imposed caution among the survivors along with vacillation by policy makers. When lessons from the Spanish Civil War and the 'incidents' against Japan suggested that operations by independent armoured forces were impracticable, Stalin in November 1939 ordered the disbandment of the independent tank corps and the dedication of tanks to pure infantry support on the French model. After the German triumph in spring 1940 he hastily ordained a reversal to an earlier organization of mechanized corps of all arms – and on an enormous scale. But when it came to filling vast establishments with machines and, above all, providing proficient commanders at all levels, particularly senior ones, a dire shortage of officers who understood, let alone were capable of handling, such large and specialized formations, revealed itself. Many of those who took up senior appointments already were proven failures in battle, but had outlived their rivals by toeing the party line and making a habit of referring contentious problems upwards. Only a few of high quality, such as General K. K. Rokossovski, survived the purge and were reinstated to command as the talent shortage developed. In an environment where initiative was at a premium, and frequently stifled by threats of the firing-squad from political commissars, what hope there was of inexperienced commanders training their men imaginatively and taking bold measures in the field withered in a desert of ignorance and repression. And always it was the junior officers and men who suffered from the fundamental errors of Stalin and his frightened entourage.

Against highly imaginative and aggressive German commanders – von Bock and Guderian were the most prominent among a host of outstanding armoured leaders – the Red Army was lost. With a flurry of deep penetrations and double envelopments, the Panzer Corps leapt miles ahead of the marching and horse-drawn German infantry

MAP 2. THE EASTERN FRONT: THE GERMAN AXES OF ADVANCE, 1941 AND 1942

A   Finnish Front
B   'Stalin Line'
C   Front line at the end of September 1941
D   Front line in early December 1941
E   Stabilized front line, spring 1942
F   Limit of German penetration, September 1942

G   Italian Twelfth Army (Ambrozio)
H   German Second Army (Weichs)
I   Hungarian Third Army
J   German Twelfth Army (List)
K   German First Panzer Group (Kleist)
L   German XI Airborne Corps (Student)
M   German Africa Corps (Rommel)
N   British Western Desert Force

The Conquest of the Balkans, Summer 1941

LENINGRAD

Novgorod

Yaroslavl

Gorki

Kazan

Kalinin

MOSCOW

R Oka

E

B

Smolensk

Tula

D

Vitebsk

Lipetsk

Saratov

R Volga

R Berezina

C

Bryansk

Kursk

Voronezh

Pripet

Gomel

R Don

Stalingrad

Marshes

Chernigov

Kharkov

R Donets

F

Kiev

UKRAINE

R Dnieper

Kirov

Donetsk

Rostov

Azov

R S Bug

Dniester

Jassy

Odessa

Novorossisk

CAUCASUS MOUNTAINS

HAREST

Sevastopol

Black Sea

ube

Varna

miles   200

divisions, carving great inroads into the rear areas, encircling vast hordes of stupified men, destroying machines and virtually annihilating the Red Army formations which barred the way to Leningrad, Moscow and Kiev. Once more the panzer leaders found their mobility unchallenged by an enemy whose mass was destroyed *in situ*, condemning driblets of surviving AFVs and guns to disperse into uncoordinated groups of refugees fleeing pell-mell to the shelter of forest and marsh.

Taking the force aimed at Moscow as a prime example of German strategy, the operations of von Bock's Army Group Centre demonstrate from the outset how strength of execution took full advantage of Russian errors and misconceptions, and how vacillation of direction produced fatal errors. From the beginning the Army Group's two panzer armies (Second, under Guderian, and Third, under Hoth) far outran the marching infantry, as in France, but this time on a longer leash than in 1940 and were permitted to complete the encirclements of dense enemy mass. Within a week these two armies, striking deeply from Poland and East Prussia, had closed their pincers at Minsk, netting some 27 Russian divisions for later digestion by the infantry, even as the advanced mobile elements were already probing farther east, already a week's march ahead of the infantry, in the direction of Smolensk and Moscow. Seventeen days later and 250 miles onward, Second Panzer Army had reached Smolensk, regarded as one of the psychological as well as communication and industrial vital objectives, its occupation creating a blocking position across the retreat of an estimated 300,000 Russians from 12 to 14 divisions. On the face of it a triumph for von Bock and for Guderian. But only if the pocket could be completely sealed, the entire enemy force wiped out and the advance continued almost without pause before the enemy was able to restore his position by counter-attack (as he was already endeavouring to do) or re-establishment of viable defences between Yelnya and Yartsevo on the road to Moscow.

At this stage, signs of strain began to appear in reports by the German commanders broadcast by Enigma coded radio messages which the British intercepted and decrypted. The scale of Russian counter-attacks from the south against Guderian and from the north against Hoth were far stronger than anticipated and demanded the diversion of panzer corps to defeat them instead of concentrating upon sealing the gap and preventing a breakout from the Smolensk pocket. Moreover, an error on the part of Hoth's leading panzer corps left open a gap at the intended junction with Guderian to the north of Smolensk, with the result that the enemy began to flood through. The movement in this gap was actually visible to Field Marshal Kesselring, commanding the Second Air Fleet, as he personally flew over it and urgently called on the two panzer army commanders for joint action. But Hoth had detached a corps to deal with an enemy threat at Velikiye Luki and as yet was unaware of the gap, while Guderian said he could not spare any more troops, although he tried to stop the movement with artillery fire while calling upon Kesselring for intensive air attacks – which the airman could only partially comply with, knowing full well that the effect would be only marginal by day and ineffectual at night. Overall hung a suspicion that Guderian was deliberately ignoring the gap since his private intention was to seize Yelnya as the next step in the drive to Moscow – which had yet to be authorized. Von Bock's calls to close the gap were at first ineffectual and Kesselring's personal appeal to Goering, to bring pressure upon Hitler to insist upon it, got nowhere. It was shortage of supplies as much as troops which was at the root of the trouble, a situation brought about by heavy rain on frail roads and the clogging of the main arteries by too many vehicles, none of which could have gone cross country. Unfortunately, XI Airborne Corps which, as Kesselring sadly pointed out, might have closed the gap, was out of action, licking its wounds after Crete. This indicated in the most eloquent way possible, how unwise had been the launching of that unnecessary operation in the interests of the greater glory of Goering, Student and the Luftwaffe.

By Kesselring's estimate, some 100,000 Russian troops escaped from the Smolensk trap, one set-back among a mounting list of debits to the German account, though not the fundamental cause of lost German momentum on the Central Front or anywhere else. In searching for the basic reason behind the faltering German progress after July, it is necessary to delve deeply into past miscalculations and current misdemeanours at ministerial and high command level. Now the German armed forces were on the verge of paying a very high price for having entered into a major war before completing the preparations. Overwhelmingly effectively as the Wehrmacht had performed against anachronistic opposition in 1939 and 1940, it lacked depth and substance at its industrial and logistic base, presenting a facade for which Hitler, Goering and all the other members of his party had to bear responsibility, including Wehrmacht officers who had fallen too readily into line with a bluff carried too far.

The cracks in the Wehrmacht's structure began to appear towards the end of August, about eleven weeks after the start of the campaign and, of immense significance, a little longer than the longest campaign yet waged by the German Army since 1918. Poland had lasted four weeks, Norway nine, Holland, Belgium and France seven, the Balkans three. At the end of each of these outings the Army's equipment had been returned to the home base for major refurbishment, just in time to avoid extensive calls being made on field workshops which, in any case, were not geared to tackle more than running repairs. To make matters worse, the factories were not keeping pace with the total losses incurred. This was hardly surprising when it is recalled that, throughout the rearmament programme, supply and production had been limited in order to avoid monetary inflation. Now stocks of reserve equipment and supplies were falling to a low level. Furthermore, crucial items of equipment were proving inadequate in Russian conditions – which was hardly the fault of designers who had not been instructed to prepare for a war of aggression in an immense country of such primitive communications and extremes of climate. Engines wore out prematurely because air filters could not cope with the dust of the steppe. Two-wheeled drive trucks bellied in mud when torrential rain converted low grade roads into rutted quagmires. Tank tracks would fail in soft ground or when frozen solid in winter's tight grip. Lubricants also gave trouble in extreme cold. Fuel reserves were falling low. For a force which depended on machines for its offensive capability and its survival as none had depended to the same extent before, these were crippling defects. Many of the deficiencies had been foreseen and, as often as not, sidestepped or ignored on grounds of economy or because Hitler and many of his commanders had deluded themselves into believing the war would be won long before winter took its toll.

An advance by General von Leeb's Army Group North to the gates of Leningrad, the encirclement of the hordes at Minsk and Smolensk and a brilliant lunge into the Ukraine by von Rundstedt's Army Group South had created havoc in the Red Army, but failed to make the Greater Russian people give up the struggle or make Stalin sue for peace. It was arguable that a concentrated stroke aimed at the capture of Moscow might have brought about this collapse, but progress in that direction, as will be seen, was halted early in August. It is much more likely that the people of the already conquered territories would have joined in a crusade in collaboration with the Germans in order to win their independence from the oppressive Russians. Estonians, Latvians, Lithuanians, White Russians, Ukrainians, and many thousands of Poles, who welcomed the Germans as liberators, would have helped if only Hitler and the Nazi party not been wedded to racial doctrines which placed the Jewish and Slavic peoples into the category of vermin, to be antagonized by brutal treatment, and later by extermination policies, which threw them back into the arms of Stalin. Even the Greater Russians might have cracked if Hitler, supported by OKW and OKM, had not issued his infamous Commissar Order laying down that commisars and Communist intelligentsia were to be liquidated upon capture – an instruction which simply stiffened the Soviet leadership who had nothing to lose by continuing to resist and maintain their positions by measures as pitiless as those of the Germans. It is a supreme folly of war to drive an enemy into a corner and simultaneously deny him the slightest hope of survival. Yet these were the policies persistently adopted at one time or another by all the contenders throughout the war; the Russians, Germans and Japanese merely being guilty of most of the worst excesses, to the short-term stiffening of their own resistance, no doubt, but in the long term, to the corruption of their peoples.

Under the shadow of continuing Russian resistance, and aware of logistic shortcomings and the need to call a pause while stocks were brought forward and equipment repaired, the German high command vacillated over the best way to complete their promised victory. The OKH aim was by now settled upon seizing Moscow, a threat which would compel the Red Army to stand and fight (instead of avoiding confrontations as it was increasingly prone to do); the loss of which would disrupt the Soviet Government, deny important industrial facilities and communications centres, effectively cut the country in two and dramatically undermine morale. But Hitler's aim now perversely switched to destroying enemy forces by means of local actions which, incidentally, would win valuable ground in due course – schemes which went into abeyance when the Russians obligingly launched their heavy and abortive counter-offensives in the vicinity of Smolensk at the end of July.

The crunch came on 15 August when Hitler came down hard against a further stroke against Moscow. Instead, and to the dismay of OKH and Army Group Centre, he insisted in a directive dated 21 August that Guderian's Second Panzer Army should strike southwards in collaboration with Army Group South to encompass the complete encirclement of the four Russian armies deployed in the defence of the Ukraine. In the face of a concurrent denial by the Führer of adequate AFV reinforcements to the Eastern Front, and his contention that the earlier encirclements had proved disappointing when up to 25 per cent of the enemy had escaped, one is tempted to ask if the Führer's perversity in bullying and overruling his generals at times took precedence over trying to defeat the Russians. It is not by any means impossible that a failed Austrian artist who, as a wartime soldier, had never risen above the rank of corporal, should take pleasure in lording it over an aristrocratic Prussian field marshal, bearing in mind always the traditional antipathy existing between the Prussians and the south Germans. So deep by now was the rift that von Brauchitsch and Halder (a Bavarian) seriously contemplated resignation, but instead decided to persevere in the hope of changing Hitler's mind. Staunch in their arguably self-interested resolve to seize Moscow, the Commander of Army Group Centre, von Bock, and his most charismatic panzer army commander, Guderian, strove to support OKH in its endeavours to change the Führer's mind.

A meeting at Rastenburg on 23 August marks a turning-point of the war, let alone of the campaign. Clearly Halder felt that if anybody could persuade the Führer to go for Moscow it would be Guderian who, for many years, had had Hitler's ear and who, at that very moment, was being suggested clandestinely as a good replacement as C-in-C for von Brauchitsch, a careerist of little moral courage, who was quite unable to withstand the Führer's vehemence. On this occasion, von Brauchitsch forbade Guderian to discuss Moscow with Hitler. But in a discussion between the Führer and the senior officers of OKW only, Guderian raised it and was turned down by Hitler with a stream of irrelevant economic, political and military arguments and the patronising remark, 'My generals know nothing about the economic aspects of war . . .' And Guderian had bowed to the tirade in the old-established Prussian tradition that he could not 'debate a resolved issue with the Head of State in the presence of his company'. No doubt Guderian was restrained for fear a row might nullify his chances of becoming C-in-C, with its opportunities to save Germany from ruin. But in appearing to condone the diversion into the Ukraine, Guderian earned Halder's undying enmity for failing in one meeting to pull off a coup which he and the C-in-C had failed to accomplish over a period of weeks. Moreover, he also omitted to tell Guderian that already the order directing Army Group Centre to advance south had been issued, along with the injunction to use a strong force, '. . . preferably commanded by Generaloberst Guderian'. But whatever the reasons for this black comedy of misunderstanding and jealousies, the outcome was impending disaster.

The drive towards Moscow remained in suspense as the conquest of the Ukraine and the preparation to besiege Leningrad received priority. Yet another enormous haul of prisoners and equipment was scooped up in the German net. Once more sizeable Russian forces escaped as the defences along the road to Moscow were again stiffened from an inexhaustible reserve of manpower, albeit meagrely equipped. But the closing of the Ukraine pocket on 16 September acted as the catalyst for Hitler at last to give the go-ahead to advance on Moscow – just over 200 miles from Smolensk and, therefore, by the standards of normal panzer army progress, well within reach before the worst of winter's scourging. But Russian winters are abnormal by west European standards and the German Army which turned eastwards again on 30 September was on the eve of paying the full penalty for the accumulated errors perpetrated by its leaders since the campaign began.

Nevertheless the offensive began well, catching the Russians completely by surprise, presumably because they could not bring themselves to believe anything so incredible would happen – despite ample warning since 10 September from London, based on decrypts about Hitler's 'great plan' to destroy the Russian armies of the centre. The Russian defeat which ensued must also, however, be put down to the continued inept handling of their forces, compounded by their losses of so much equipment. When the order went out to the defending armies to cease all local attacks and fight where they stood, it was tantamount to a prescription for suicide in the face of such masters of mobility as were the leaders of the three panzer armies. With 14 panzer divisions and 8 motorized infantry divisions, the Germans ran rings round the Russians; a process facilitated by the Red Army's reversion to the grouping of tanks in infantry supporting brigades, to the virtual elimination of armoured corps or the panzer division. Yet little more could have been done given the impoverished state of the Red Army. The overrunning of factories and the threat to those remaining, which were in process of resiting to the eastward, had seriously curtailed production of all kinds of equipment, making it impossible to sustain more than a handful of mechanized units. These were the bitter consequences of Stalin's original, fundamental errors in castrating the officer corps and of proving incapable of understanding that, even if Hitler were as ruthless as he, he followed different lines of reasoning. All of which pointed to the inherent dangers of over-centralization when one man seizes all the reins in his hands because he is afraid or incapable of sharing power with others. Over-centralization is the enemy of initiative, terror the scourge of creativity.

Winter and paucity of administative foresight defeated the last German offensive against Moscow. Setting aside the original mistake of assuming (what was an impossible calculation) that the Russians would be totally defeated prior to winter's onset, that was no excuse for omitting to make provision for men's winter clothing and vehicles' protection against extreme cold. That was sheer incompetence. Win or lose, the Army and the Luftwaffe were bound to be standing guard in Russia throughout the winter of 1941/42 and would need something warmer than summer uniforms in 30° of frost, even if engaged only in garrison duties. The full significance of winter's impact was rubbed in between 5 and 7 October as the first snows fell, as the roads were reduced to chaos, as men and machines' efficiency fell into serious decline – and the Germans at Vyazma completed the encirclement of no less than six Russian armies, comprising about 600,000 men, plus a further two armies at Bryansk. At that moment, with the West Front in ruins, its commander, General Zhukov, recalling later that '. . . all roads to Moscow are, in essence, open', and a mass exodus in panic from the capital taking place, the Germans were incapable of exploiting the opportunity their fighting men had created.

The very familiar problem of mopping up the encircled masses which had hampered the summer offensives, now, in conjunction with the snowfalls, stalled the autumn attack and gave the Red Army command just sufficient time to re-establish lines of resistance nearer the capital. In a way the Russians were trading space and human beings for time, the sweat of people building defences by manual labour and the sacrifice of the massed dead and prisoners at the front set against the exhaustion of the German war machine. It was an evocative equation which scarred the conscience even of hard-driving commanders on both sides as they freely traded lives for victory. A pattern was formed, held in place by the fluctuating weather. When hard frost solidified mired tracks and fields, the Germans would shoot forward again only occasionally shaken by sudden eruptions of the latest Russian KV–1 and T–34 tanks which were beyond the firepower of German tanks to defeat with their short 50mm guns; and which would lead to recriminations from Guderian that his earlier recommendations to fit a more powerful piece had been ignored on the short-sighted grounds of insufficient necessity and overruling economy. But when the thaw came and everything came to a halt, firepower was neutralized and the defence held fast.

In fits and starts, the leading elements of Army Group Centre came in sight of Moscow on 5 December as the war entered one of its most fateful weeks, comparable in metamorphosis of course and power to the initial decision to invade Poland, the calling off of the invasion of Britain and the inter-related resolution to attack Russia. Already the Germans were aware that they had shot their bolt. Men and machines were functioning at 20 per cent efficiency, and Guderian was lying sleepless at night, torturing his brain '. . . as to what I can do to help my poor men who are unprotected in this crazy weather. It is terrible, unimaginable.' The offensive had to be stopped. On 6 December, with Hitler's approval, Army Group Centre ordered a tactical retreat from exposed salients, on each side of Moscow, to defensible positions. At once a Russian counter-offensive began. Next day Japan struck at the American Fleet in port at Pearl Harbor and began general hostilities against the USA, Britain and the Dutch in the Pacific and Far East. On 11 December, as he had indicated to Japan the previous August, Hitler, taking Mussolini's Italy with him, in turn declared war upon America.

August 1941 had been a mad month in the German calendar when vacillation and recrimination had let slip what chance remained of winning a conclusive victory in the East; when Hitler, drenched in the blood-letting he had started, remarked to Guderian that if he had believed the panzer generals' 1937 estimate of 17,000 Russian tanks in service he would not have invaded; and when, by assuring the Japanese of his support to the hilt if they came into collision with the

USA, he encouraged them to spread the war to world-wide dimensions and thus unleash the fury and boundless resources of the
greatest industrial nation on earth. There is little doubt that if a
concentrated drive upon Moscow had commenced in August, it would
have reached its objective. Whether that would have ended the war is
another, contentious matter, but the outcome could have been very
different from the failure which ensued as the result of the diffused
efforts actually attempted. Similarly, the continuance of von
Brauchitsch as Army C-in-C instead of his being replaced by
Guderian or somebody more likely to stand up to the Führer, could
only have made for an improvement in the quality of command
decisions – although by no means a guarantee that the megalomaniac
Hitler would have abandoned his headstrong methods. But at least
Guderian was incapable of externally holding his peace. Always the
chances of an explosion were present, as he had demonstrated quite
often prior to 5 December 1941 and as he would deliberately repeat
on 24 December in a fearless contravention of faulty orders which
earned him the sack. Better that and the example it set, many people
might argue, than forever lying prostrated as a doormat for Hitler.

If the war years preceding 1942 lent credence to the theory that, in
adversity, a combatant's military errors are publicly castigated and
magnified, while in victory they tend to be overlooked or forgiven,
then 1942, often regarded as the turning-point in the fortunes of the
main contestants of the Second World War, demonstrated how, at a
moment of balance, each other's mistakes could often be self-
cancelling. To preserve his own prestige in the eyes of his followers,
Hitler denigrated and sacked a number of senior officers, including
the C-in-C, all three Army Group commanders and several more
whose age and the exertions of the past two years, and particularly
the past two months, told against them. Taking over as Army C-in-C
himself, in addition to being Head of State and Supreme Commander,
he defied theoretical military logic by issuing an inflexible Stand Fast
order which prohibited even local retreats without permission. By so
doing he stopped what might have been a rot amounting to headlong
flight by the entire Army under the guise of a tactical withdrawal. It
was a shrewd, psychologically correct decision which stiffened morale
at the precise moment when well-educated officers, who had studied
Napoleon's winter retreat in 1812, were forecasting a similar disaster
and were losing their grip. Now the waverers would be disciplined by

harder commanders whose ambitions had yet fully to be satisfied by the acclaim of the populace, who were eager to try their hand and win the favour of a Führer who let it be known that retreats were unforgiveable – thus inducing officers to base their defences upon settlements which controlled strategic points, where a modicum of shelter against the elements, as well as enemy fire, could be obtained, and as bases whence armoured counter-attacks could be mounted against enemy penetrations by the handful of AFVs remaining. In effect, the basis of many defence systems of the past and in the decades to come.

At a point when both sides had reached the bottom of the barrel in respect of their material resources and when the Russians were in desperate need of a pause to rebuild the hierarchy and organization of their shattered, and yet triumphant forces, Stalin opted for an all-out offensive on all fronts in January. It was against the advice of Zhukov, who represented the new guard of commanders, but supported by the old guard commanders and political commissars whose incompetence, and to some extent sycophancy to Stalin, had exacerbated the defeats of 1941. Stalin's concept of at once hitting the shaken Germans and thus undermining their recuperation sufficiently to prevent a renewal of the offensive in the spring, was disputed (at his peril) by Zhukov on the grounds that there were too few guns and tanks to overcome any enemy who, despite his setbacks, continued to fight well. And fighting well, it might be added, out of a sense of sheer desperation inspired by horror at the prospect of falling into Soviet hands – exactly the same reasons for which Russians persevered out of fear of liquidation by the Germans.

Stalin had his way, supported in Council by the sycophants. He plunged inadequately trained, armed and supported infantry masses into headlong advances against opponents who fought back doggedly and inflicted immense losses. Cannon-fodder, thrown into the open in sub-zero temperatures which sapped the stamina and morale of all but the most hardy and dedicated, was eaten up. Before the offensive petered out in exhaustion early in March, having admittedly recovered considerable tracts of ground, the exact reverse of what Stalin had intended had been achieved. Profligacy with manpower, as a substitute for weapons and machinery, had imposed unavoidable tactical errors upon junior commanders and men. Incompetence at all levels thrived upon mistakes in abundance. Apart from the violence of the German resistance, the Russians suffered from the handicaps of their own well-known inadequacies of fire power and logistic support which denied them the strength to overcome enemy defences and the stamina to exploit whatever successes they won. In effect, the failure to capture nodal points, which controlled the arteries of supply, condemned troops infiltrating the German defences to a lashing from the icy blast and enemy fire power as the prelude to being struck on unsheltered terrain by deft German counter-attacks delivered economically with consummate timing and direction. By the minimum of effort, the Germans managed to take advantage of the Russian's prodigality while conserving their own forces, actually weakening the Red Army to the state at which it would be in no condition to withstand the cut and thrust of rested and refurbished panzer armies when the weather improved.

Thus Hitler's controversial, but correct, stand fast had benefited from Stalin's miscalculated and injudiciously ambitious counter-offensive. Not for the first time in history, an insufficiency of material resources had lain at the roof of failure. Once more, as so frequently in the past, one contender's demoralization had been transposed into a sense of confidence by an opponent's over-confidence. As the Russians faded the Germans felt strong enough to swing back on the offensive with another, still deeper plunge into the wastes of Russia, striking out for the Caucasian oilfields and the fatally attractively named city of Stalingrad on the banks of the River Volga.

There is no intention here of studiously debating the errors of 1942 on the Russian front. Faultily as the Red Army would employ its units in the early stages of the German offensive, and erratically as they fought until penned into Stalingrad, the major error was the Germans' quite unnecessary attempt to seize a place of but marginal strategic importance. The very fact that the Germans did engage in a positional struggle for prestige purposes – and lose it – when their forte was the prosecution of mobility, was of the very essence of stupidity born out of the political intuition and racial arrogance of one man.

Looked at in the context of the whole war's development in 1942, however, the German drive into the Caucasus and towards the Middle East and the gateway to India introduces another dimension – or would have if the Axis powers had planned their strategies in unison. For at the moment the Germans launched forth eastwards, on 28 June, there was no well-considered and agreed scheme between Germany, Italy and Japan to co-ordinate their efforts and, perhaps,

CRITICAL FLAWS

▶ German vacillation over the choice of strategic objectives, leading to a failure to achieve the main aim; all made worse by Hitler's progressive over-centralization of command in OKW and himself.

▶ Stalin's failure to alert his forces in time to take defensive precautions.

▶ Immature tactics of the Russian mobile forces.

▶ German antagonism, by barbarous behaviour, of a potentially friendly population in Russia's eastern zone.

▶ German failure to prepare for a winter campaign.

▶ Further weakening of Russian forces due to Stalin's perseverance with a prolonged winter offensive in 1942.

▶ Failure of the Axis partners to act in concert.

effect a juncture on the Indian subcontinent. All that existed in a few people's minds and on some draft papers, was Plan Orient, drawn up in June 1941 on Hitler's instructions, to cater for the eventual co-ordination of an attack southwards through the Caucasus linking up with an advance northwards from Egypt. But with no mention of collaboration with Japan at that stage, or even a year later, when that nation had expanded her empire to within striking distance of Australia and to the frontier of Burma with India. As an alliance, the Berlin Tokyo relationship had little to pride itself in the matter of genuine mutual assistance in the military sphere. When Hitler leapt to Japan's side in declaring war upon America four days after Pearl Harbor, there was nothing like a reciprocal act on Japan's part in declaring war on Russia. Prudently the Japanese opted to apply pressure on Stalin by force of threat alone. Practical mutual support, it seems to have been assumed, would have to wait until events declared themselves and the two sides drew measurably closer to each other on land. The only real assistance the shadowy Plan Orient gave the Axis was a fearful assumption by the Allies that it really existed and demanded strenuous diversionary countermeasures in Syria, Iraq and Persia to guard against invasion via the Caucasus. Yet on 28 June 1942, when the expected drive through the Caucasus revealed itself, there was, indeed, good reason to expect the evolution of a gigantic, strategic pincer movement. For at the moment, the southern arm, to the surprise of both the Axis and the Allies was, by a plethora of accidents, errors and indiscretions, within a tactical bound of Cairo and the British Empire's jugular vein, the Suez Canal.

6

THE TROUBLES OF INEPTITUDE
Western Desert Campaigns
December 1940 to February 1942

Referring to the benefit of Italians as allies, a German general, to the author's knowledge, once remarked, 'Well, its your turn to have them next time.' He was being derogatory, of course, and not by any means entirely fair. Given a cause they can believe in, the Italians fight as well as and better than many. The mistake Mussolini made in June 1940 was leading them into a war, for which Italy was unready, in a cause for which the people had no enthusiasm. Entering the war at Germany's side looked a safe bet, however. France was beaten and Britain was assumed to be on the point of surrender. It scarcely mattered, therefore, that Italy had insufficient steel, oil and coal to wage a major war (and was dependent on Germany for extra supplies); that her navy's good ships were deprived of bunker fuel and her air force's and army's equipment almost wholly obsolete. Her aircraft had far lower performance than those of the RAF, her tanks were no better than machine-gun carriers, and her artillery dated, in some types, from the nineteenth century and were more suitable as museum pieces.

It was scarcely surprising that when Britain continued to fight and began steadily to provide her forces in the Mediterranean, in North and East Africa with modern equipment that the Italians began to wilt. And that as Italy suffered a series of blows after her initial offensives into Egypt, the Sudan and Greece had been blunted, her leaders should be consumed by dread of what the British might do to them and of what the Germans might do to Italy as a result. These fears came to ahead when a mere 30,000 well-trained British troops, equipped with only a few score modern AFVs and aircraft, routed the Italian Army in Egypt and drove it headlong into Cyrenaica in December 1940. Employing tactics which had sufficed against tribesmen in East and North Africa, the Italians had been completely outmanoeuvred and made virtually defenceless against an extension of the British advance towards Benghazi and Tripoli. The prospect of the total loss of the Italian North-African empire together with every likelihood of control of the central Mediterranean falling into British hands and of the war being brought to the Italian mainland, loomed very large indeed.

Yet in London, as 1940 drew to a close, ambitious plans aimed at knocking Italy out of the war by seizing the island of Pantellaria, off Sicily, or making a raid with 5,000 commandos against Rome, to capture Mussolini and his Government, were, for excellent practical reasons, regarded as extremely long shots. While in Cairo, C-in-C, Middle East, General Sir Archibald Wavell, had his mind fixed upon the elimination of the Italian East-African empire, in his rear, as a preliminary to making some sort of sortie into the European mainland if the opportunity occurred. So far as the Italian invasion of Egypt was concerned, his order to Lieutenant-General Sir Richard O'Connor, commander of the Western Desert Force, demanded containment of the enemy advance before the port of Mersa Matruh; and having done that most artfully, along with conservation of force, to execute a five-day raid upon the halted enemy in an endeavour to cripple Italian offensive zeal on what he, Wavell, regarded as a purely defensive flank.

If Wavell appreciated the importance of seizing the entire North-African shore, re-opening the Mediterranean to British shipping and thus contriving a vast saving of vital carrying capacity by obviating the need to send everything to and from the Middle East round the Cape of Good Hope, he gave no pronounced sign of it. Indeed, he did not even bother to visit the Western Desert Force to see for himself. And even after O'Connor had won a smashing victory at the start of the raid on 9 December, he was to discover not only that no worth-while administrative arrangements had been made to enable his main force of one armoured and one infantry division to exploit victory, but that, in any case, the infantry division was to be removed to East Africa, its replacement not due at the front for nearly two weeks.

Although Wavell, under pressure from Winston Churchill in London, at last provided O'Connor with the facilities to pursue the Italians and eventually annihilate their army at Beda Fomm at the beginning of February, he never tried to go the whole hog and plan for an extension of the advance to Tripoli. Instead, he clung to a conviction that Greece should be assisted in her struggle against Italy when the threat of German invasion became clear. Until recently it was thought that the responsibility for sending ill-afforded British troops and aircraft to Greece in March 1941 lay with Churchill. But, as Ronald Lewin has shown in his biography of Wavell, *The Chief*, it was the C-in-C's own choice. He was granted permission to abstain in order to concentrate his main effort in Cyrenaica where, already in January, clear evidence of an increasing Luftwaffe presence, to be followed in February by army units, had been provided by SIGINT (Signals Intelligence) and Ultra. It cannot, of course, be stated with certainty that an immediate and carefully planned exploitation from Beda Fomm to Tripoli, reinforced by the resources diverted to Greece, would have been fully successful. But the chances were good, bearing in mind the abysmally low state of Italian morale and military strength, the extent of German commitment to the forthcoming Balkan and Russian campaigns and, therefore, the few German troops immediately available for Africa – one light mechanized division followed more than a month later by a single panzer division. And taking into consideration, too, the blockade of North Africa which the Royal Navy and RAF, based upon Benghazi and Malta, could have imposed to hamper the shipment of troops and supplies.

Wavell's decision to relegate North Africa to a subsidiary role in favour of an entry into the Balkans may be adjudged a strategic error of the first magnitude which had a profound effect upon the future course of the war, one whose political sense was also dubious. For it won few friends in the Balkans and it presented the Germans with a firm, almost unopposed, foothold in North Africa whence they could mount a dangerous threat to the Suez Canal. Of lesser importance, it brought to world attention the name of a commander whose impact was out of proportion to his intellectual capacity. Lieutenant-General Erwin Rommel was an extremely brave infantry officer who had been rated unsuitable for entry into the élite German General Staff, despite being the holder of the Order Pour le Mérite. Although never a member of the Nazi Party, he owed his subsequent advancement to command of a panzer division to his sponsorship as a hero by Josef Goebbels, the Reich Propaganda Minister, and the patronage of Hitler. His tactical flair and rampant opportunism (which made him a kindred spirit with the Führer) had won him well-publicized fame for his exploits in France in 1940. Now his appointment to command the Africa Corps represented a reward which not only provided a tempting opportunity but gave him a star role on a minor stage, instead of a subsidiary part in the Russian theatre.

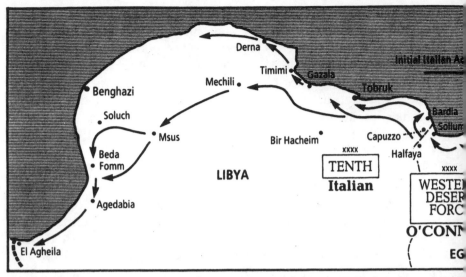

A. Wavell's Offensive, 9 December 1940 to 7 February 1941

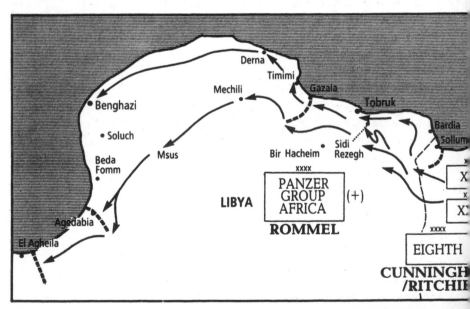

C. Auchinleck's Offensives, 18 November to 31 December 19
Operation 'Crusader'

MAP 3. CAMPAIGNS IN THE WESTERN DESERT, 1940–1941

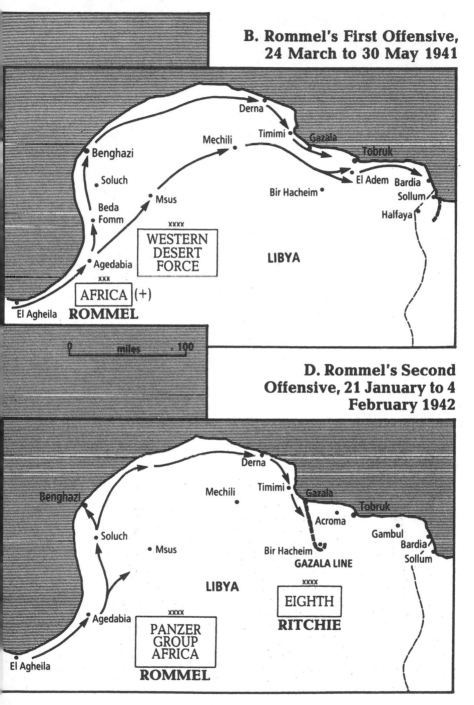

B. Rommel's First Offensive, 24 March to 30 May 1941

D. Rommel's Second Offensive, 21 January to 4 February 1942

Rommel's instructions from OKH were to secure Libya, but to abstain from offensive operations until his corps and its logistic support was complete in May – sensible orders when applied to a force with no experience of desert warfare, in a subsidiary theatre of war. A strategy, too, which GHQ in Cairo realistically anticipated when it deployed an immobile infantry force guarding Benghazi and a recently arrived and inexperienced armoured division covering the Cyrenaica frontier at El Agheila. British Intelligence's miscalculation of relative strengths took only slight account of the superior training of the small but growing German contingent, as it nestled like a cuckoo in the Italian nest, and none at all of Rommel of whom little was known. Intent upon Greece and perhaps out of wishful thinking, Wavell grossly underrated the German threat as 'probably much exaggerated'.

When Rommel broke the rules and, phase by phase against orders and military logic while continuously on the threshold of logistic bankruptcy and his men's physical exhaustion, drove the British back, the advantage of acute tactical insight over uninspired British orthodoxy paid off hand over fist. When, for example, his attack upon the strongly held defile at Mersa Brega was pinned down by infantry and ripe for an armoured counterstroke, the British divisional commander demurred on the grounds that insufficient daylight remained, and withdrew – a step backwards which removed the cork from the bottle to release a triumphant Rommel with unfettered access to the wide open desert where he practised mobility to the extremes of recklessness. For he was not to know that the British armour would fail as much from mechanical breakdown as tactical ineptitude, nor that the diversion of so many troops to Greece deprived his opponent of strong reserves. Simply sensing the enemy's collapse and listening to panic on what few radios the British possessed told him all he wanted to know. Nevertheless, as he lunged for the ports of Benghazi and Tobruk and for Egypt beyond, he revealed the hallmark of his performance in the campaigns to come, a propensity to gamble which repeatedly threw the British off balance into error.

To understand why so many errors were made by the British when opposing Rommel in the years to come, it must be borne in mind that the technique and practice of handling large mechanized forces in battle was only sketchily grasped by their commanders in the desert, particularly after General O'Connor and one or two other leaders, who had learnt so much when fighting the Italians, had been captured by Rommel in his advance to Tobruk. None of the radical pioneers who had developed armoured warfare prior to the war were in command in the Middle East. Few of those who would come out from Britain in command of fresh units and formations would have had the opportunity to practise the new art when equipment, due to delays in production and battle losses, was in such short supply. Moreover, it could hardly be claimed that more than a handful of the senior officers were of the calibre desired. Many of the older members – senior cavalry, tank regiment, artillery and infantry officers, who had been resistant or slow to adapt to mechanization, had yet to be found wanting and sacked as formation commanders in order to make room for the more adaptable youngsters who were learning to command units and sub-units. Building a brand-new military technique and tradition in the shadow of defeat is not an overnight task. The British were fairly easy meat for predatory German commanders with more than one victorious campaign behind them and with a wealth of talent as replacements.

Repeatedly even the best of the British commanders were thwarted by inferior staff work and communications systems which prevented their giving orders rapidly and reliably. They were also starved of immediate transmission of information and Intelligence about the enemy upon which effective operational moves depended. Moreover, as often as not through insecure transmission of those messages which were passed, the enemy gleaned invaluable information upon which to base his own moves. But even when communications worked reasonably well, defects in weapons condemned the British troops to fight at a technical disadvantage which was to no mean extent the product of pre-war mistakes, and which was exacerbated by tactical misconceptions.

As in France in 1940, mechanical failures robbed AFVs of their full potential. The latest Crusader cruiser tank swiftly gained a reputation for unreliability second to none – and mainly because of a simple error in draining the water-pump prior to shipment to the Middle East and failing to fill it again after arrival. 'For want of a buckle . . .?' Yet all too frequently it was some trivial defect which would incapacitate a machine and reduce combat worthiness significantly – let alone undermine the operator's confidence and morale. Among tank crews of both sides there abided justifiable dissatisfaction with their AFVs' propensity to catch fire, usually from unprotected ammunition, and disquiet at the difficulty of finding the range and hitting targets without vast expenditure of ammunition. In this respect the Germans did better than the British since they opted to shoot while stationary while the British persisted with an all too obviously innaccurate method of engaging while on the move. The British, however, expressed bitter complaints that their guns would not penetrate the German armour, which should have aroused suspicions since it was known that the Germans were only just beginning to doubt the efficacy of the 30mm armour of their Mark III and IV tanks which the 40mm gun could penetrate out to 500 yards. It was to nobody's credit in the technical world that they were slow to appreciate the double advantage enjoyed by the Germans with their superior, capped armour-piercing shot and their face-hardened armour which caused uncapped British shot to disintegrate on impact.

At the heart of the British Army's inertia in failing to tackle technical faults without delay was to be found the pernicious pre-war attitude of so many officers, including many Tank Corps officers, that technology was beneath their dignity. Few had received a technical education. Many were dismissive of technologists whom they tended to despise and whose doctrines they could not understand. So it is not surprising that those officers who were technically educated or technically aware had great difficulty introducing reform even in wartime. For example, the War Office had succeeded in resisting the formation of an AFV Directorate until June 1940, and did all in its power thereafter to sustain a system which demonstrably had permitted the design and development of inferior machines. Likewise, it was not until November 1941 that GHQ Middle East formed an AFV (Technical) Branch to tackle on the spot the all too obvious defects of tanks in battle and take action to put matters right. As one example of the desperate need for this branch one has only to quote the example of the German Mk IV tank which had been in British possession since April 1941 and waited until March 1942 before somebody took the trouble to investigate and discover that it had face-hardened armour.

Inevitably misleading technical information, which quite frequently was arrived at by guesswork instead of scientific investigation, impinged upon tactics. Although it had been known since May 1940 that the Germans had been using their very powerful 88mm anti-aircraft gun in a dual anti-tank role, for a long time there remained a delusion, due to inadequate testing, that it could not penetrate a heavy Matilda tank beyond 440 yards whereas, in fact, it could do so at 2,000! As a result, during the Battleaxe counterstroke launched by the British along the Egyptian frontier in June 1941, Matildas were confidently sent against 88s and were torn to pieces. Simultaneously faster, lighter armoured AFVs, endeavouring to close to within the 500 yards at which, they were told, their 40mm guns would penetrate the enemy tanks' armour, were sent to their doom since, (a) they were unlikely to score hits on the move and (b) they were unlikely to penetrate when they did hit. Yet it was tactics such as these which conditioned the methods adopted during the major British Crusader offensive of November 1941 in an endeavour to defeat enemy armour in battle, relieve besieged Tobruk and clear Cyrenaica of the Axis forces.

Not that Rommel did not seem to do all in his power, at times, to facilitate the British task. Always deprived of men, machines and supplies by the low priority accorded his force by OKH, and the depredations of the British who frequently sank his ships, it helped the British to be reading not only Enigma, but also the lower grade cypher used by the Italians with their Swedish-designed C38m machine; taken together they gave ample warning of the routeing of ships, the strength of what was now known as Panzer Group Africa, and Rommel's intentions. As a result the British were fully prepared to dodge a so-called reconnaissance in force by Rommel in mid-September, when two battle groups aimed at a presumed (but non-existent) British supply dump inside Egypt, and to harass the German columns without coming to harm themselves. But they can hardly have expected Rommel's subsequent move when, instead of prudently retiring, he rashly struck eastwards in an endeavour to swat the wasp-like enemy light forces, ran out of fuel, came under intensive air and artillery attack, suffered heavy casualties, and was lucky to evade capture in the course of an undignified run for safety leaving a trail of equipment in his wake. Congratulate himself as he would upon the capture of enemy documents purporting to show a British intent to retire further into Egypt, thus permitting him to concentrate exclusively upon a long-planned and essential assault upon Tobruk, he had, none the less, suffered a serious set-back which was all the more dire because of the loss or damage of 67 tanks out of

21st Panzer Division's strength of 110. As a result his force would be incapable of offensive operations until the latter half of November – as the British, through SIGINT, were perfectly aware.

It was partly as a result of self-delusion that Rommel was extremely slow to react to the British Crusader offensive when it was launched into Cyrenaica on the 18th; and also partly due to complete ignorance of the enemy strength and the aim or scope of his advance. For until the British broke radio silence after their advance, they managed to preserve their secrets while always remaining better informed about Rommel than he was about them. So why, when they also had many more tanks and guns than the German/Italian force, did the British not overwhelm it at once?

For a start the British plan was at fault, based as it was upon the concept that the massed armour, comprising some 730 tanks, backed by reserves, could seek out and destroy in tank versus tank combat a *known* enemy force of about 385 serviceable tanks with sparse reserves. It did not take into account that, as tank killers, the British tanks technically were not up to the job, nor that enemy tactics tended to avoid direct tank versus tank combat, preferring to leave the main tank-killing role to dug-in anti-tank guns of the latest, powerful long-barrelled 50mm type (along with the 88mm guns). Thus Rommel's gunners nearly always had the advantage by shooting at known ranges, by surprise as in ambush, from concealed positions on vital ground of their own choosing against an opponent who, by the very nature of his 'search and destroy' policy, was liable to wander, dispersed, into killing grounds of the enemy's design. And that even when British armour did meet its German counterparts, it was compelled to shoot inaccurately on the move while trying to get within the mandatory armour penetrating distance of 400 or 500 yards. The cause of these faulty tactics was to be found in the history of British belief, since the first tank versus tank fight in 1918, of the ultimate inevitability of tank versus tank jousting and the defects of their tank design philosophy previously described in Chapter 1. But mainly the blame lay in the inexperience of senior commanders who, for a variety of reasons and accidents, had not come to understand the fundamentals of all-arms mechanized warfare.

With only one exception, from the new C-in-C, Middle East (General Sir Claude Auchinleck) to divisional level, the senior commanders were innocent of practise in armoured warfare. Auchinleck was an Indian Army infantryman with little experience of the British Army and virtually none of AFVs. General Sir Alan Cunningham, the newly appointed commander of the Western Desert Force (now renamed Eighth Army), was better qualified, having recently arrived from East Africa where he had won an overwhelming victory over demoralized Italians and conducted a brilliant pursuit deep into Abbysinia. But as a gunner, his knowledge of infantry fighting was far more profound than of AFVs and his concepts of armoured warfare were conditioned accordingly. XIII Corps' commander was an infantryman, XXX Corps' (as nominated) a member of the Royal Tank Regiment, a most able officer of great promise who unfortunately, together with his battle experienced Chief of Staff, was killed in an air crash shortly before the battle. His successor as leader of XXX Corps, the armoured striking force, was Major-General C. W. Norrie, the commander of the newly arrived 1st Armoured Division, whose only experience of armoured warfare had been at regimental level in France in 1940. The rest were newcomers and infantrymen. Blameworthy as all these men might be for what eventually went wrong, their mere presence in high command was the product of the pre-war system and British way of thinking about war which had denied them an army adjusted for modern operations.

The conduct of the dispersed advance to contact by the British and the reluctance of Rommel to take it seriously, abandon his intended assault upon Tobruk and concentrate his forces for battle were abundant with error and largely responsible for the extraordinarily untidy and complicated clash which ensued. Fanning out from the desert flank in the direction of Tobruk, British XXX Corps was denied its anticipated collision with the Africa Corps because the latter's commander, General Ludwig Crüwell, was prevented by Rommel from concentrating his forces. Both sides therefore drifted into piecemeal engagements in the neighbourhood of the escarpment overlooking Sidi Rezegh airfield. Paying no particular interest to the vital ground as a pivot for manoeuvre, the British repeatedly bumped into emplaced German anti-tank guns, to be shot up; or charged stationary enemy armour to receive similar treatment. Yet this need never have happened if Norrie had stuck to the original plan and kept XXX Corps concentrated near Gabr Saleh. Instead he divided his armoured brigades in order to go hunting for the enemy, thus permitting Rommel and Crüwell to pick them off in turn. Rommel, indeed, might well have been lured to destruction if XXX Corps had been deployed upon vital ground instead of that selected by Cunningham as a compromise solution between the wishes of Norrie, to plunge deeper, and the desire of General Godwin-Austen, commanding the predominantly infantry XIII Corps advancing along the coast, to have the main armoured force nearby in case of attack.

Norrie was unwise to disperse his armour, but the initial error lay with Cunningham who had condoned a defective deployment by allowing XIII Corps' fears to hamper XXX Corps' freedom of action. By so doing, too, he had set the tone for this battle, and for a great many to come, by permitting the monotonous bleating of infantry commanders calling for the tanks to come to their aid at the slightest hint of an enemy armoured threat. A bleating with some justification, however, since the obsolete 40mm anti-tank guns with which they were equipped were no match for the latest, better armoured German tanks – though, let it be remembered, the tanks they were crying for had only the same 40mm gun as themselves. Where the infantry really went wrong was in not taking full advantage of the other guns already in their possession – the 25pdr (83.4mm) field artillery pieces which, admittedly, were not pin-point accurate, and the 3.7in anti-aircraft guns which were every bit as effective against armour as was the German 88mm. But British gunner purists insisted that the 3.7in was meant to concentrate against aircraft, and only shoot against tanks in emergency. So no one (including Cunningham, a gunner himself) took steps to overrule them.

Rommel and Crüwell also made unnecesary mistakes, the worst being the charge by the mass of Africa Corps on 23 November into the teeth of South African 40mm anti-tank guns and artillery of XXX Corps to the south of Sidi Rezegh, which caused heavy casualties to both sides – but showed that emplaced British infantry, unsupported by tanks, could, at a price, hold their own against the German armour. Yet at that moment, when British strength had, momentarily, been reduced to 44 fit tanks, Rommel, as was his way, decided to do something extravagant, even though his tank strength was down to 100 and his supply situation desperate. To the despair of Crüwell and the staff, he led a swing through the desert to the south, with the intention of cutting in behind the main British forces at the frontier and annihilating them at his leisure. He did so on instinct because previous moves of that sort had undermined the British resolve.

And he did so without valid evidence to indicate whether the British were ripe for disruption in this way, and without taking into account that, by departing from the vicinity of Sidi Rezegh, he was not only surrendering possession of vital ground to the British but denying himself the material fruits of victory. Among the scores of immobilized AFVs littering the battlefield were a large number of machines fit for quick repair. If Rommel had tarried in order to recuperate his own vehicle state, while securing or destroying the abandoned British vehicles, he would have achieved a decisive advantage. Instead he gave the British an opportunity to rebuild their strength on the vital ground and demolish irreplaceable German AFVs, while Africa Corps blundered about at the frontier, suffering further losses from breakdowns and from attacking British artillery head-on.

Yet Rommel almost achieved his psychological aim by what became known as 'the Dash for the Wire'. When German columns intermingled with fleeing elements of the British administrative echelons and even put HQ XXX Corps to flight, Cunningham faltered. Distressed reports of the extremely high tank losses at Sidi Rezegh made him react in the same technically uneducated manner as von Rundstedt before Dunkirk; being brought under fire at HQ 7th Armoured Division by German artillery and being forced to make a hair-raising escape by car and plane; he was compelled to witness the débâcle of XXX Corps, all of which contributed to his loss of composure. To his Chief of Staff and to Auchlineck, when the latter came forward to see for himself, it was apparent he had lost his nerve. Auchinleck's decision to relieve the exhausted Cunningham of command, and his insistence upon continuance of the offensive have usually been portrayed as the staunch if risky acts of a great commander, as it was; but with the proviso that SIGINT informed him to perfection of German logistic vulnerability, indicating that if Rommel persisted in retaining Africa Corps in the frontier zone, the annihilation of the Axis force was calculably assured. Auchinleck, indeed, might have been still more confident had he known that, at that crucial moment, Rommel, by his own impetuosity, was lost, broken down in the desert and out of touch with his command; and that the saving order which eventually withdrew the German armour to Sidi Rezegh to counter the looming menace of the British build-up there came from a courageous General Staff officer who risked court martial to override his commander's instructions. These things were of

secondary importance to Auchinleck's dilemma in finding a replacement for Cunningham and simultaneously winning a battle which
hung in the balance – and of those two dilemmas the selection of the
next commander was by far the most telling in its effects on the
present and the future.

In less exacting circumstances, Auchinleck might have promoted
one or other of the Corps commanders to take over Eighth Army, but
at the height of the battle that was impracticable. There was no one
else of the required combination of experience and seniority available
in the theatre, so Auchinleck appointed a stopgap – his own Deputy
Chief of the General Staff, Major General Neil Ritchie, through whom
he could channel his own will and intentions until the aftermath gave
time for the appointment of a more suitable officer. In the circumstances the arrangement was made to work. As Rommel unavailingly
strove to restore his incompetently forfeited position at Sidi Rezegh,
he was worn down by relentless British pressure applied by Ritchie in
response to a stream of long-winded letters and instructions from
Auchinleck who, effectively, retained personal if remote control of the
Eighth Army. But it was hardly a sound command system since, with
the best will in the world, Ritchie's subordinate formation commanders could never be sure who the real boss was. With the result
that the malady of querying ideas and orders which had festered
under Cunningham now became chronic – though partially concealed
by local victory when Rommel was at last compelled to face the reality
of his own parlous state and withdraw from Cyrenaica.

British tank losses under Ritchie's command in the closing stages
of the battle continued to be heavy and stemmed from the same
technical weaknesses and tactical ineptitudes as before. As one
British tank driver plaintively recorded in his diary: 'Quite frankly, I
was not so strong for this charging business' – as many a comrade
would have concurred when asked to close with emplaced enemy
tanks and guns as if their vehicles were horses at Balaclava. Nevertheless, charges were ordered to the last, and with disastrous effects.
Even as Rommel completed his final steps backwards and, making
good use of a shipment of tanks landed recently at Benghazi (unreported by British Intelligence), twice ambushed the pursuing British
armour and inflicted heavy casualties. The unreported presence of
these German tanks could not be placed at Ritchie's door. It was the
Intelligence staff at GHQ which had overlooked a SIGINT report

indicating that tanks were included in a shipment, and the necessarily complex system of securely transmitting ex-Ultra information to users which had led to confusion and omissions. Nevertheless, subsequent failures on the British part to cope with Rommel and his men had to be laid at the door of Auchinleck and Ritchie since they were the men in command. 'Upon the King – it is always upon the king.'

To begin with, Auchinleck could be criticized for confirming Ritchie in command instead of replacing him in the aftermath of 'Crusader' by somebody of higher calibre, even flown from the United Kingdom. There were such generals, as time would show. Furthermore, they both could have made better use of the Intelligence available and done something to improve training and counteract deficiencies in operational procedures – although Rommel allowed them only the shortest possible time to do so. In fairness it has to be said that security surrounding the launching of Rommel's riposte on 21 January 1942 was redoubled because he even withheld information as to his intentions from his Italian allies and Field Marshal Kesselring, the German C-in-C, South, for fear they would veto what was a hazardous but finely calculated risk. The glaring difference between this German plan and its British counterpoise lay in the relative handling of information by the two sides. Supplied by a mixture of lower grade SIGINT and, most fruitfully, by the ability to read the high-grade diplomatic code of the American liaison officer in Cairo when he reported the British strengths and weaknesses to Washington, Rommel's Intelligence staff was able to deduce that, for a fleeting period towards the end of January, the British strength at the front would be inferior to the reinforced German forces, an imbalance caused in part by British logistic problems and to some extent over-confidence as the result of faulty Intelligence synthesis.

At root of the British misappreciation was the fact that, as Hinsley points out in the official History of British Intelligence in the Second World War (vol 2), British commanders and staffs had yet to abandon the habit of consulting 'I' only when they felt the need for information about the enemy's situation instead of tackling the vital problem of decision-making. In fact, there was sufficient SIGINT concerning the improvement in the Axis logistic situation, through the latest shipments, to conclude that the enemy's situation was much improved. Instead, 'I' at GHQ and HQ Eighth Army enthusiastically preferred to believe only that evidence which suited their wishes, on the lines, as

Auchinleck put it, 'that the enemy is hard pressed more than we dared think' and, as his Deputy Director Military Intelligence (DDMI) wrote, 'we have Rommel in the can'. As a result the troops deployed forward of Benghazi were weak – the newly arrived 2nd Armoured Brigade, in 1st Armoured Division (its mechanical state spoilt by a 450-mile road run from railhead at Mersa Matruh, its desert training incomplete) and the equivalent of three infantry brigades unsupported by armour. Even so the British of XIII Corps (still commanded by Godwin-Austen) might have made a better fist of it than they did, and much of the blame must be laid on the shoulders of three of the four generals chiefly involved in the fiasco – on Ritchie, whose spirits waxed and waned with each piece of bad tidings from the front and each morsel of optimism from 'I'; on Messervy, who commanded 1st Armoured Division at the front; and on Auchinleck who carried out an almost ceaseless debate by signal and letter with Ritchie. Disagreements within the British camp were frequently overheard by the German radio intercept service and the impression correctly was acquired that the British were suffering severe losses and were in a state of disarray.

But Ritchie made the British situation a lot worse when he interpreted as signs of impending enemy withdrawal, Intelligence reports saying Rommel was short of fuel (which he usually was because of the manner in which he operated) and that he was about to fall back on the defensive (which falsely he had told the Italians in order to mollify their objections to his having attacked in the first place). Concluding that this was a 'God-sent opportunity to hit him [Rommel] really hard when he puts out his neck . . .', as appeared all too likely when the only RAF reconnaissance report to come to hand (because of bad weather) spoke solely of a (feint) German column making for Mechili, Ritchie laid XIII Corps wide open to envelopment by the main German thrust towards Benghazi. In mounting confusion came the inevitable headlong retreat to the next line of defence at Gazala, covering Tobruk, where Rommel really did run out of fuel. And the pay-off for General Godwin-Austen, who had read correctly the scale and portent of Rommel's riposte? Rustication! He, who had commanded XIII Corps with real ability throughout 'Crusader' and who, on the record and from seniority, was more entitled to be commander of Eighth Army than Ritchie, his junior, now found Auchinleck only too ready to accept his request to be relieved of command. It mattered not that Ritchie had been wrong in over-riding Godwin-Austen's sensible decision to evacuate Benghazi once the 1st Armoured Division had been defeated. It apparently did matter to Auchinleck that he should be loyal to his friends and staff. But it may have mattered still more to Auchinleck that, by retaining Ritchie as Eighth Army commander, he could continue also to command that Army by remote control – and in so doing laid up for himself a mine of trouble for the future.

In time of war the opportunities to win laurels and fame are often fleeting and rarely repeated. When a commander has a glittering prize snatched away because of his own incompetence or because of the enemy's undeniable superiority – or even through bad luck, which is common to all – he has, if he is fair, but little to complain about. Complain he may when, like some among Rommel's commanders, they are unjustly demoted or lost to captivity due to their leader's incompetence or his seeking of a scapegoat: or, in the case of Auchinleck's generals, by the naked favouritism shown for the by no means outstanding Ritchie. Denied just reward, commanders can begin to ferment poisons of resentment within a hierarchy, causing speculation as to who will fall next and producing fractious relationships which sacrifice a military community's most priceless asset – mutual confidence among peers. It has to be said that Auchinleck, who actually drew comfort from a state of underlying weakness among his enemies (reported conversations of malcontent German generals), might have done well to consider the disaffection simmering in his own camp.

Uncertainty among the British at the highest level of command and amid a prolonged debate between London, Cairo and Eighth Army in the desert as to the moment when the offensive could be resumed, or whether the Germans would manage to strike first – or whether the Germans, rebuffed in Russia, might yet strike southwards through the Caucasus or through Turkey, seethed in parallel with disenchantment among commanders at lower levels. Recriminations which increasingly surfaced among infantrymen, who complained of lack of support from the armour; tankmen who felt let down by the leadership, hampered by the infantry and sometimes unsupported by gunners, who felt they were fighting a war on their own, were brought about very largely due to lack of an enforced common doctrine with clearly laid down rules of inter-arm co-operation. Mistrust abounded as each arm tended to go its own way. Jealousies were commonplace and allowed to fester by a higher command which often failed to command, tending instead to debate matters as if in committee. Inferiority of equipment – above all that of AFVs and the need for a much more powerful anti-tank gun than the obsolete 40mm 2pdr had something to do with it. That was about to be rectified, but vital errors in battle would continue a while longer and on several occasions were the result of an unhealthy respect for the genius of the enemy commander as the German propaganda, which sedulously burnished Rommel's image at home, also raised his stock among the British.

Success in battle produced rich rewards for the commander of Panzer Army Africa; many gifts came from the delighted Adolf Hitler who, in January 1942, was only too anxious to receive tidings of victory when news of nothing but defeat and withdrawal came from Russia. As plans matured to resume the offensive in Russia and seize the Caucasian oilfield, the advantage of linking this drive with a threat to, if not the occupation of, Egypt became obvious. With that in mind, Kesselring had been sent to the Mediterranean in December 1941 to make the best he could of fresh forces being earmarked for that theatre of war. Superb strategist that he was, it was obvious to him that Rommel's main handicap was logistics and that until the island of Malta had been captured and its offensive operations against the lines of communications stopped once and for all, no invasion of Egypt should be undertaken. He would agree with Rommel that the capture of Tobruk was a vital prerequisite to the invasion, but Malta, he argued with Hitler, OKW, OKH, Mussolini, the Italian Comando Supremo and Rommel, had to be seized first.

No one was as enthusiastic as Kesselring about what came to be known as Operation 'Hercules'. Rommel put Tobruk first. The others were frightened – Hitler notoriously so when he cast his mind back to the price paid for Crete. The debate rambled on into April with no firm decision arrived at. In the meantime, Kesselring had stepped the air offensive against Malta until, at the cost of between 250–300 aircraft in April alone and the creation of a bomb shortage, he could boast to a sceptical Mussolini on 11 April that 'Malta as a naval base no longer demands consideration.' So Rommel could sigh with relief as supplies flowed into North Africa barely impeded because the British offensive capability against shipping had been neutralized. Kesselring's unwise boast to Mussolini was the undoing of 'Hercules'

CRITICAL FLAWS

▶ Italy's entry into a war for which she was basically unprepared.

▶ Wavell's uncalled for diversion of forces to Greece instead of using them to exploit his victory in North Africa.

▶ Rommel's chronic underrating of logistic factors.

▶ The inadequate indoctrination of most British commanders in the handling of mobile desert forces.

▶ Auchinleck's poor selection of commanders and his techniques of command.

▶ Hitler's unwillingness to invade Malta.

---

because it gave Mussolini and Hitler the excuse to postpone until July the invasion of Malta (leaving it to the Luftwaffe to continue the neutralization of the island with forces attenuated by the need to divert effort to Russia for the summer campaign), and for Rommel's favoured attack on Tobruk ('Theseus') to take place at the end of May. It was a fatal error which could never be redeemed because it set in motion an irreversible train of events.

7

THE CORRUPTION OF EGO
Gazala to El Alamein, 1942

The battle that broke out at Gazala on 26 May, when Rommel swung the mass of his armoured forces wide of the French-held fortress of Bir Hakeim on an approach march aimed at reaching vital ground to the southwest of Tobruk by nightfall, was to evolve in a totally different manner from that envisaged by the contenders. The Intelligence factor necessarily lay at the root of error, compounded by false assumptions and failures in human relationships to an extent more pronounced than in most battles taking place at what was, after all, only Army level and on a very small scale compared to battles past and future in Russia and Western Europe. To begin with, Rommel was unaware of the deployment of the mass of armour in British XXX Corps, but took it for granted he would bring it to battle outside Tobruk, in rear of the fortified infantry and artillery-held 'boxes' strung out from the coast among minefields to Bir Hakeim, 45 miles inland. Nor was he aware of a significant improvement in the British armoury, the arrival of several hundred of the new, 57mm (6pdr) anti-tank guns, and of more than 150 American-built Grant tanks fitted with a 75mm gun which, unlike previous British armament, could fire high-explosive as well as armour-piercing shot.

Characteristically, Rommel assumed that the enemy would perform as ineptly as in the past, and deemed it sufficient to adopt a sort of 'Crusader'-like plan, in reverse, by inserting his main armoured force in the British rear to defeat the British armour and trigger the familiar galloping rot. When Africa Corps's Chief of Staff, Colonel Bayerlein, suggested that the British armour might at first refuse battle and then strike at the exposed German right flank, Rommel replied 'You're crazy, they'll never do that!' And because he believed all would be over quickly, he rejected prior elimination of the Bir Hakeim box, thus dangerously extending his lines of communication.

Auchinleck and Ritchie were far better informed, mainly through SIGINT, of the enemy's strength and timing yet, and to some extent for that reason, committed quite unnecessary errors. They were well aware that the German attack would forestall their own offensive by some three weeks and they knew almost to perfection the greatly increased German AFV and aircraft state including the arrival of a number of the latest much more powerfully armed and armoured Mark III tanks together with a few of the even more menacing Mark IV. Uneasily they were aware, too, of amphibious and airborne forces in waiting, having rejected an earlier correct suspicion that they might be earmarked for Malta. Really only the thrust line of the main punch was denied them, although, at the last moment, information from a very, and suspiciously, talkative German prisoner and certain radio intercepts actually did disclose it. Instead, HQ Eighth Army, preferred Auchinleck's earlier conclusion that the main thrust would come in the north, directed straight at Tobruk in a manner totally uncharacteristic of the Rommel of old, but in a manner all too similar to their own way of operating. In fact, Auchinleck and his staff had been deluded by the enemy deception plan which sought to give this impression. Moreover few officers lower down the chain liked to contradict the C-in-C, particularly in the light of his previous 'extensive and usually very accurate sources of Intelligence'. Naturally, junior officers at the lower levels were kept in ignorance of Ultra and could not know when the C-in-C was working on hard facts or just surmising, as was presently the case.

Yet Auchinleck had got it right when he told Ritchie to concentrate XXX Corps's armour to the east, as Bayerlein thought he should, and disappointed when he learnt that it was dispersed, as Rommel assumed it might be. Indeed, 7th Armoured Division, with its high proportion of Grant tanks in 4th Armoured Brigade, was placed well forward to the south in the path of any flanking attack which might occur. It was made plain by Auchinleck to Ritchie that he disapproved, but he did nothing to correct the error or, perhaps, better still, relieve Eighth Army of its commander, appoint somebody else or take over himself. John Connell, Auchinleck's biographer, argues convincingly that, for several reasons, this was not opportune and also stresses that '. . . it simply was not in character. He trusted his subordinates . . . He did not abandon his trust when they disagreed with him.' Meanwhile Ritchie seemed to think that any misunderstanding between the C-in-C and himself was the result of a very senior staff officer 'being given the wrong information from the map board here' and that Auchinleck approved of his final dispositions. And, amid the verbosity of their all too frequent epistles to each other, Auchinleck eventually received the impression that his wishes had been complied with. Inevitably Auchinleck, following the subsequent battle from reports relayed to the map in his office, would be living in a fool's paradise partly of his own creation.

Such harm as initially was to be caused by this faulty deployment might have been mitigated if only General Messervy, now commanding 7th Armoured Division, had reacted at once to the reports which made it clear on the night of 26th/27th that the enemy was throwing his weight round Bir Hakeim. The reason he delayed the order telling 4th Armoured Brigade to leave its harbour area and occupy pre-planned battle positions, was founded upon that same sense of doubt introduced by Auchinleck's original appreciation that the main attack would fall in the north. Acting on his own initiative after a warning order from XXX Corps at 0230 hrs on 29 May, Messervy hesitated until dawn when he was ordered by XXX Corps to send 4th Armoured Brigade forward – straight into the teeth of an Africa Corps which desired nothing better than to catch a surprised enemy in the open and on the move. Heavy losses were inflicted on the new Grant tanks whose high silhouette made them easy to see, whose riveted armour was not entirely proof against the long 50mm gun and whose commanders, intent upon using the 75mm gun in its hull-mounted position, denied themselves the normal tactical advantage of shooting from hulldown posifions with the upper turret-mounted 37mm gun, even though that piece was a better armour penetrator than the 75mm. Soon, a similar fate overtook 22nd Armoured Brigade, which also had been prevented from taking up position before it was attacked, its majority of less reliable Crusader tanks falling easier victim than its Grants.

By the end of a day, when the points of Rommel's columns had reached their objectives and the carcasses of wrecked or broken-down vehicles littered the desert, he was claiming victory in the belief that he had destroyed the bulk of the British armour and that the intercepted radio messages were telling of yet another collapse in British command, control and morale. To the extent only that HQ 7th Armoured Division, together with its commander, had been overrun and captured due to unwisely hanging about in its exposed location, this was untrue. Command and control remained firm, as did unit, armoured vehicles and gun commanders who stuck to their task and began to close in upon the German spearheads from all sides. Now it was the Germans who began to feel the weight of the Grant's firepower, the 75mm high-explosive shells inflicting heavy losses at long range upon anti-tank guns which previously had endured nothing worse than scattered machine-gun fire from British tanks. Now, too, his tank losses became serious with some 30 per cent of their number out of action at nightfall. Worse still, supplies were held up. An attempt by the Italians to seize Bir Hakeim had failed. Not even the long way round was safe for the trucks and Bayerlein's worst fears were realized in every detail.

Try as hard as Rommel would, next day the 28th, to achieve his original object and criticize as he might the piecemeal manner in which the British armour was sent into battle, the fact remained that Rommel had rashly spread his own force across the desert in a wild gamble and, by midday, was out of touch with many of its elements and sensing defeat. On the 29th, with supplies desperately short and tank strength little better than 50 per cent, he had no option but to withdraw. But in choosing to occupy a position to the north of Bir Hakeim in the vicinity of Sidi Muftah (which soon was to become known as the Cauldron) he did so while totally oblivious to the fact that the ground to the west was strongly fortified by the 150th Brigade, thereby cutting him off from supplies.

As innumerable critics have declaimed, this was the moment for Ritchie to strike hard with unified forces against an opponent in sore plight – as convincingly portrayed by 'I' which had recovered from the nadir of its pre-battle performance. He had simply to support 150th Brigade box, prevent Rommel's attempt to open up a supply lane through the minefield and then bring down a crushing air and artillery bombardment upon the Cauldron prior to overwhelming it with a massed tank and infantry attack. But the Luftwaffe, reinforced by Kesselring and superbly handled, was making life difficult for the RAF and, in any case, the doctrine, technique and communications system required to co-ordinate air and ground operations in the forefront of the battlefield were still badly undeveloped by the British, a condition for which the RAF, with its independent philosophy, was not entirely blameless. But by breaking down its forces into brigade groups co-ordinated by divisions in a loose framework of control overseen by corps and army headquarters, Eighth Army had, with Auchinleck's encouragement, rescinded the traditional function of command, eliminating the chances of achieving rapid concentration of effort. And in no department was dispersal of effort more fatal than that of the artillery which was spread evenly around the battlefield, mostly employed by batteries of 8 guns, sometimes by regiments of 24 guns, rarely by divisions of 72, and never by the corps with several hundred guns controlled by telephone as in 1918, now even easier to arrange with the extensive radio networks available.

Fully aware of the dire straits in which the enemy stood at a moment when, from shortage of water and much else, Rommel was within 24 hours of suing for terms of surrender, Ritchie ponderously dallied. Undoubtedly the realization of Rommel's plight had something to do with the listless British attempts to capitalize on their advantageous position. Enjoying a known tank numerical superiority of about 500 to 250 and a still greater superiority in artillery power, there was injected into the backs of senior commanders' minds the idea that, come what may, the enemy must fall as the result of his own isolation. Maybe this is why they indulged themselves in protracted discussions as to the pros and cons of the best course of action to take, always feeling that time was on their side. But the fact that it took a whole week from the moment Rommel had backed into the Cauldron to the moment when a fully co-ordinated Corps attack was made is almost beyond belief unless one draws the conclusion that, at the upper levels, the Eighth Army's leadership was unworthy of the brave men under their command.

Take for example the attempt by Major-General Herbert Lumsden's 1st Armoured Division on 30 May to assail the Cauldron with two armoured brigades, with a third in reserve – a force of Corps dimensions amounting to well over half the British tank strength. If it had been launched by General Norrie, commanding XXX Corps, on the 29th, it would have caught Rommel's defences in weak condition. But Norrie had a habit of delegating responsibility, and the ponderous British battle procedures, which hampered swift reconnaissance, assembly and launching of co-ordinated all arms forces into battle, repeatedly delayed the attempt which, when at last it did start, fell apart. One brigade was distracted by German counter-action, another fell into disorder in a sandstorm; the third, in reserve, was held back until the afternoon and was unable to make an impression when it ran into entrenched enemy opposition. Tank losses were heavy against the screen of Rommel's defences, and the attack was called off. A

MAP 4. THE CAMPAIGNS IN NORTH AFRICA, 1942–1943

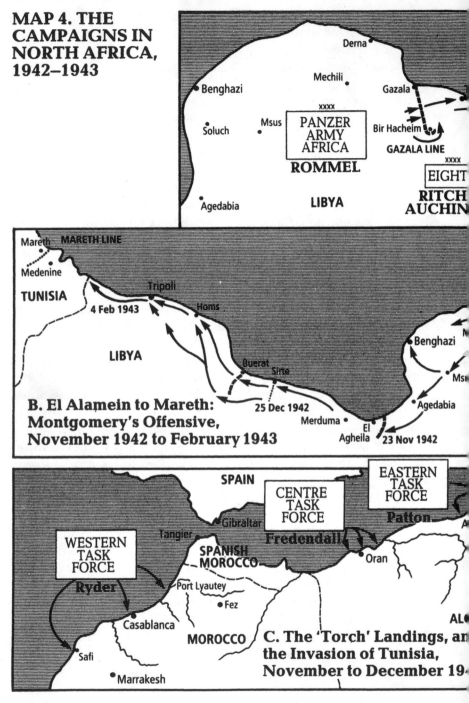

B. El Alamein to Mareth: Montgomery's Offensive, November 1942 to February 1943

C. The 'Torch' Landings, an the Invasion of Tunisia, November to December 19

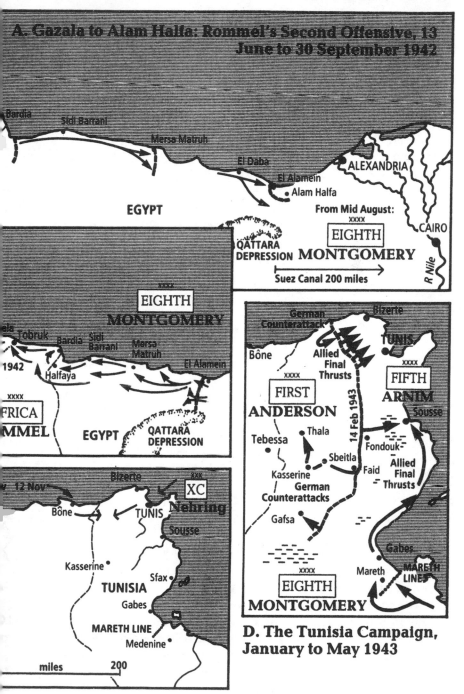

A. Gazala to Alam Halfa: Rommel's Second Offensive, 13 June to 30 September 1942

Bardia

Sidi Barrani

Mersa Matruh

El Daba

El Alamein

ALEXANDRIA

Alam Halfa

EGYPT

QATTARA DEPRESSION

From Mid August:

xxxx

EIGHTH

MONTGOMERY

CAIRO

R Nile

Suez Canal 200 miles

xxxx

EIGHTH

MONTGOMERY

els

Tobruk

Bardia

Sidi Barrani

Mersa Matruh

El Alamein

1942

Halfaya

xxxx

FRICA

MMEL

EGYPT

QATTARA DEPRESSION

German Counterattack

Bizerte

TUNIS

Bône

Allied Final Thrusts

xxxx

FIRST

ANDERSON

14 Feb 1943

xxxx

FIFTH

ARNIM

Sousse

Thala

Tebessa

Sbeitla

Fondouk

Faid

Allied Final Thrusts

Kasserine

German Counterattacks

Gafsa

Gabes

xxxx

EIGHTH

MONTGOMERY

Mareth

MARETH LINES

v 12 Nov

Bizerte

xxx

XC

Nehring

Bône

TUNIS

Sousse

Kasserine

Sfax

TUNISIA

Gabes

MARETH LINE

Medenine

miles   200

D. The Tunisia Campaign, January to May 1943

column trying to replenish 150th Brigade was ambushed and destroyed on 1 June, and a night relief operation under command of Messervy (who had escaped from captivity to resume command of 7th Armoured Division) was called off because the infantry brigade concerned could not be ready in time. Yet, in the immediate aftermath of the capture of 150th Brigade's box by a Rommel who now knew that the crisis was past, Ritchie was writing to Auchinleck that he still considered 'the situation favourable to us and getting better daily' – which inspired another exchange of long messages between the two leaders as they debated what next to do.

In the full knowledge from SIGINT of the state and deployment of the Cauldron's defences and that Rommel was relying upon the British to repeat a frontal attack against them, Ritchie proceeded to condone a plan on the basis of a suggestion by Messervy, designed to do just that. Lieutenant-General H. E. Gott, commander of XIII Corps, and the most experienced of the desert leaders, declined to assume responsibility for it. So Norrie tackled the job with XXX Corps – and told Messervy and Major-General Briggs, commanding 5th Indian Division, to execute it – without himself actually controlling the event. Ritchie presided at a conference, agreed to what was arranged and then sat down to write a six-page letter of explanation to Auchinleck asking for his approval.

It was all rather like a Staff College exercise in which the students submitted their written papers to the Directing Staff and waited for comments in red ink. Urgency was never of the essence. And the plan, a clumsy, three-stage operation by infantry and armoured formations, bore all the resemblance of a set-piece infantry assault of 1918 pattern – as was almost inevitable bearing in mind that all the senior commanders involved, with the exception of Norrie, were infantrymen and that infantrymen, by the very nature of their task and training, are conditioned, from start to finish, to think in terms of head-on assault as the culminating act of war. Conceived on 2 June, discussed on the 3rd, approved by Auchinleck on the 4th and executed on the 5th, it started short of adequate reconnaissance and by dropping the initial artillery concentrations on empty desert. In consequence the armour and infantry rolled forward against an unshaken enemy, sweeping away the Italians who barred their way and driving into the sights of the German anti-tank gunners with disastrous results. Here a total failure to combine infantry with armoured formations led to a shambles. 22nd Armoured Brigade and 9th Indian Infantry Brigade went into action subject to a complete misunderstanding of their respective, interlocking roles. They got nowhere. Elsewhere, 32nd Armoured Brigade, equipped with heavy Matilda tanks, attacked 21st Panzer Division in position with the support of a mere twelve pieces of artillery and lost 50 out of 70 tanks engaged. At the end of a day in which the British tank strength was more than halved; when 2nd Armoured Brigade, which had been issued with a new code, read 'west' for 'east' and moved in the opposite direction to that ordered by Messervy; when command and control (such as it ever was) broke down due to its inflexibility and the incompetence of those in charge; and when good troops were to a very large extent left to their own devices and unit by sub-unit found their own way out of the vortex or into destruction or captivity, Rommel (who had already begun the reduction of Bir Hakeim he should have undertaken on 26 May) struck out to bring ruin to the already shattered Eighth Army.

Kesselring, who was no great admirer of Rommel, paid tribute to his 'amazingly expert technique in directing a desert command post' – a technique which was foreign to the opponents whom he now over-ran. Within the next few days the British armour was reduced to rags and tatters and chased either back into Egypt or into Tobruk. Fully apprised through SIGINT of Rommel's intentions and plans, Auchinleck had originally set his mind against another siege of Tobruk because he wished to avoid locking up troops which, any day now, might be required to face a German drive through the Caucasus or Turkey. In any case, SIGINT seemed to indicate that the enemy was in no logistic condition to persist with a major offensive – a view with which, as it happened, the Axis High Command concurred. But from London, Churchill made it known that he expected Tobruk to be held. And from Ritchie on 14 June would come a factually incorrect signal giving the impression that the enemy in the desert was being contained. Auchinleck changed his mind and permitted the 'temporary' garrisoning of the port, without perhaps fully realizing that it had been stripped of a high proportion of its original defences to stiffen the Gazala line. But Auchinleck in Cairo, it has to be said, knew more in some ways about the enemy than he did about the true situation of Eighth Army up in the desert. There Rommel was preparing to eliminate the El Adem box, which stood in the way of Tobruk, his most prized objective.

By sheer brilliance Rommel would take Tobruk and inflict upon Eighth Army a stinging and, from the British fighting soldier's point of view, quite unnecessary defeat. In its aftermath would come a sacking of failed British generals. With Auchinleck's necessary approval, this brought about the removal of Messervy and, a few days later, of Major-General Pete Rees, whose only sin was correctly to point out to Gott that, with the forces at his disposal, he could not hold the frontier region for 72 hours. On the 25th, four days after the port had fallen, came Ritchie's turn, the removal of a commander who had never commanded in the proper sense of the word, who was too slow in his reactions to cope with the pace of Rommel (or most other German panzer generals for that matter) and to whom the texture and mode of the modern mechanized battlefield was, as it had been to so many of his subordinates, a closed book. Into his shoes stepped Auchinleck who, with Churchill's approval, now combined command of Middle East forces with those of Eighth Army as he felt compelled to strip the northern frontier of his command in Syria on the eve of the German offensive into the Caucasus. For already Rommel was making it plain that there was to be no respite for the shattered Eighth Army – which also came as a shock to Field Marshal Kesselring when, shortly after congratulating Rommel on capturing Tobruk and telling himself that Malta must now be the next objective, it came to his notice that Rommel was hell-bent on going to Cairo.

Promoted to field marshal and with the unstinted backing of Propaganda Minister, Josef Goebbels, Rommel had only to go to Hitler and Mussolini to receive full support for a change of plan – the further postponement of the invasion of Malta in favour of a drive to the Suez Canal. In rebuttal of Kesselring, who was very properly about to switch the Luftwaffe against Malta because the island's operations against the Axis supply lines were once more on the increase, and to whom the prospect of a logistics disaster was plain, Rommel claimed that the vast stores captured at Tobruk should see him through in what was, he admitted, a gamble. And to Italian generals who protested, he merely had to remark that Mussolini, tempted by the vision of riding through Cairo on a white horse, had given his approval. Yet he mollified them with the concession that, if things went awry, he could easily retreat to the safety of the frontier. It was not as if his Panzer Army represented a mighty, unwieldy host. It was light of foot and of everything else, with its divisional manpower reduced to an average of little more than a thousand men, and its tank strength to less than a hundred – though of this shortage the British were unaware at the moment SIGINT began to warn them of what was in train. Yet what Rommel lacked in numbers he made up for in sheer audacity and a self-confidence which he transmitted by personal example to his troops, who were engaged with an opponent whose competitive spirit was undermined by inferior command and leadership.

Auchinleck was much to be blamed for the British state of discontent. His involvement had been personal, his interference with his commanders pronounced. Even to accept that he had not been sent the best men, there is a distinct feeling that no matter who commanded in the desert he would have been at the receiving end of a stream of long-winded advice and well-meant encouragement, much of it of dubious quality due to communications problems and misunderstandings produced by the tyranny of distance. Nevertheless, Auchinleck was arguably right when he decided to abandon the frontier and the long-established bastion at Mersa Matruh in order to retreat into the as yet unprepared El Alamein position. Yet even though the front at El Alamein was a mere 35 miles long between the sea and the impassible Qattara Depression, its length was beyond the British capability to fill and make unflankable since their numerical strength was also seriously depleted. When Rommel received SIGINT of Auchinleck's decision to abandon Mersa Matruh it was mightily encouraging, particularly as Africa Corps and the Italian XX Corps began to penetrate its defences on the evening of 26 June and the British radio nets, as usual, emitted their chorus of woe. But, even in the uncertainty caused by vague orders from Gott to his XIII Corps holding the desert front, and in this underlying knowledge that a withdrawal was impending, the British so very nearly defeated Rommel at this point. By concentrated artillery fire in the approaches to Mersa Matruh itself, they hammered him to a standstill. If Gott, whose nerve was already cracking at the end of two years of almost constant battle, had not made the incorrect assumption that the New Zealand Division was in process of disintegration on the 27th and, instead of telling his corps to withdraw, had insisted that it stand firm, the German advance might have been stopped there and then. For already Rommel's logistic situation was overstrained by an excessive consumption of petrol in loose sand, and his casualties were heavy.

But Auchinleck had calculated that neither the strength nor the confusion within his entire force (not least in the state of its communications system) made it prudent to risk a battle against an enemy at the top of his form – and Gott's performance underlined the wisdom of that appreciation. He continued to prepare the Alamein defences for occupation by Eighth Army.

The fundamental flaw in Rommel's posture became clearer with every hour that passed as his own strength wilted and that of the British burgeoned under the firm command and leadership of Auchinleck who had only to keep his head – and those of his troops – to win. Pushing himself to the limits of endurance and persuading many of his followers to do the same, there never was much prospect of Rommel reaching Cairo and the Canal with so few troops at the end of such extended lines of communication against a reinforced enemy who chose to fight. The struggle known as the First Battle of Alamein, which raged throughout most of July, represented the fulcrum of the war in North Africa. It was inevitable at this point of balance, when the British began to counter-attack in what degener-ated into a battle of attrition, that both sides would make many tactical mistakes. It can be shown that Rommel persisted over-long in his endeavours to break through the crust of the newly formed British line, just as it can be demonstrated that the British attacks against a desperate opponent suffered from the all too familiar defects of nearly all their battles throughout the Auchinleck regime. Weary armies led by tired men who had run out of ideas were bound to make mistakes.

On the British side there was the lost opportunity of 4 July when, in conjunction with SIGINT showing enemy reversion to the defen-sive, the hasty counter-attack ordered by Auchinleck failed because neither Norrie's XXX Corps nor Gott's XIII Corps advanced with the vigour demanded of them by the C-in-C. So while it was plain that both corps commanders had shot their bolt and justifiable to sack Norrie on the 6th, it is astonishing that, a month later, the Prime Minister and Auchinleck were underwriting the appointment of Gott as commander of Eighth Army. To which one might add the opinion, held by many authorities, that if a roving German fighter pilot had not shot down and killed Gott within a few hours of this appointment, Rommel might yet have won the next battle.

Over the years a factional and tedious campaign has been waged by historians as to the merits of Auchinleck's generalship as measured by his victory at First Alamein, linked to the alleged injustice of his replacement as C-in-C by General Alexander, and as Eighth Army Commander by Montgomery in the aftermath of that victory and on the eve of perhaps winning the Second and finally the Third Battles of Alamein. The debaters too frequently overlook the fact that, had it not been for Auchinleck's numerous mistakes in selection of commanders and staff, irresolution by remote control, imposition or condonation of misconceived organizations, clumsy methods and poor communications, plus the misreading of Intelligence, First Alamein should never have taken place at all since the Axis could have been held and finally defeated in Cyrenaica as they so nearly were on several occasions.

On the other side of the hill, the Axis command is not lightly to be excused for so riskily exposing itself to destruction at the moment of triumph, well supplied with information about the British state as it was by SIGINT. In this latter aspect, however, it was dealt a serious blow when, in mid-July, the source of high-grade Intelligence from the US Military Attaché in Cairo dried up because the Allies, through their own SIGINT, had rumbled the leak; and when they lost the services of their outstandingly expert radio intercept unit under the direction of Alfred Seeböhm. He was captured at the front during a British local attack; unwisely, he was too far forward, probably because, at Mersa Matruh, he had been reproved for evacuating his threatened position too early. The British attack was expected. But the loss to Rommel of a priceless asset through carelessness was an immeasurable disaster. Never again would he be so well provided with Intelligence.

At the same time it did not need much intelligence to appreciate that the exposed Axis position was a neck stuck out for the chopping. Tactically, now was the time for Rommel to withdraw. Yet Rommel must either have been insincere or incredibly naïve when he discussed that possibility with his colleagues. With Hitler and Mussolini publicly committed to the capture of Cairo, and the German Army thrusting deeply into the Caucasus, psychologically, politically and strategically it was inconceivable to expect permission for a withdrawal. Similarly it was too much to expect that Rommel would stand about supinely, awaiting a renewed British attack later in the autumn, without himself making one further attempt to break through. The Battle of Alam Halfa which he lost in three days at the end of August was merely the inevitable last act of the folly committed by not invading Malta in the aftermath of the fall of Tobruk – and it was typical of Rommel that, as his troubles piled up, he blamed everyone except himself for what had gone wrong. But the main, underlying reason for the military situation's swinging in the Allied favour was to be found elsewhere, two years previously when Hitler had failed to understand, what Kesselring and a handful of enlightened individuals meant when they pointed out that, unless Britain were eliminated immediately from the contest, Germany's position relative to the opposition would progressively decline from its current peak of supremacy.

It was, therefore, a nice irony that it was Kesselring who now found himself embroiled with the first major dilemma when Axis strength fell short of the capability to exert the necessary strength to retain the initiative. It can be laid at Kesselring's door that when his inability sufficiently to supply Rommel became obvious, he should have pleaded to have the offensive called off instead of feeding Rommel with palliatives, stating, for example, that enough fuel would be provided. Yet all Kesselring actually did was try as hard as he could to improve the logistic situation, without ever giving guarantees. He was not to know that the reason so many supply ships and oil tankers were being sunk was due to British reading of both German and Italian codes to the extent, in due course, that they could economize in effort by striking mainly at the most valuable ships. But perhaps it should have been spotted that fuel supplies flown in by air would not have consumed their own weight in movement to the front if they had been landed close to the troops instead of well to the rear. In part this was due to Rommel's habitual disassociation from logistic affairs, his brusque dismissal of such matters as belonging to the realms of his Quartermaster. But it was a mistake his enemy rarely made and it cost him battles.

Perhaps Kesselring, an expert administrator, should have picked up these flaws, but at that crucial moment in August he was taxing his energies in pressing a renewed air offensive against Malta and struggling to stiffen Rommel's offensive spirit in the realization that the Army Commander was a sick man, whose cutting edge of combative spirit (like Gott's) had been blunted. Here, again, Kesselring was being realistic, not only in appreciating that it was politically impossible not to attack but that it was also politically impossible to remove Rommel from command (much as he wished to do so) because the

Africa Army Commander had been built up into such a public hero that his removal at that moment was inconceivable, even if Hitler and Goebbels could have been persuaded of its necessity.

So the Battle of Alam Halfa (Second Alamein) was fought and lost by Rommel, just as, in due course, Third Alamein would be lost because Hitler, pulling his puppet's strings, resolutely insisted upon applying the formula which had worked in Russia at the beginning of the year, by refusing to permit a step backwards without his permission. Henceforward the Axis commanders would suffer, as Ritchie had suffered, from increasingly close surveillance and interference in their functions at long range by higher authority. This was a handicap compounded by the ravages of Germany's inferiority in resources which would steadily worsen – and which, through an excellent if insecure communications organization, was by no means limited only to the Mediterranean theatre of war. It would plague Rommel when, in October, his time came to counter the Eighth Army's offensive and it was discovered that in General Montgomery there was a British commander who, by meticulous training and preparation, had largely eliminated the principal sources of error which had so far plagued the British and which, to some extent, had been caused by his predecessor. Now it was Rommel's turn to be pounded by an opponent who tended to be (and has been criticized for being) over-cautious. But Montgomery was of a different stamp from Rommel, ever zealous in his efforts to 'tidy up battlefields' to reduce the chances of tactical and logistic error; determined not to be stampeded by Rommel into repeating the mistakes of the past; above all, forcing Rommel into many errors by imposing upon him the need to retake vital ground with counter-attacks for which a hot welcome was always provided, leading to a ruthless wearing down process to annihilate the German armoured formations.

Let the comedy of errors attending the crisis on 2–4 November during Third Alamein illustrate how command could be upset by confused communications. By the evening of the 2nd the Axis armour was at its last gasp, its anti-tank gun screen stretched to the limit and the Italian infantry beginning to surrender in large numbers under intensive British attacks behind an awe-inspiring artillery barrage. Out of sheer necessity Rommel signalled to Berlin and Rome his intention to withdraw and began, with a complicated plan, to thin out infantry formations from the front. By midday on the 3rd, the process

---

CRITICAL FLAWS

▶ The tardy initial deployment of British armour at Gazala

▶ Rommel's failure to secure his lines of communication by capturing Bir Hakeim at the outset.

▶ Failure by the British to counter-attack Rommel swiftly while he was off balance.

▶ Inept British handling of dispersed artillery in support of armour.

▶ Auchinleck's mistake in agreeing to hold Tobruk instead of evacuating it as originally intended.

▶ Hitler's mistake in permitting Rommel to advance on Cairo and preventing Kesselring invading Malta.

---

was well advanced when exhortations were received from Hitler and Mussolini asking him to stand firm. To Rommel this looked like an order, a rejection of his signalled intention to withdraw. In fact, it was not. The signals, delayed by encoding and decoding, has crossed. But Rommel, while signalling the dangers of remaining, called off the withdrawal, and then breathed a sigh of relief when the expected British *coup de grâce* did not materialize, due to delay on Montgomery's part for time to assemble an irresistible blow that night, followed by the breakout on the 4th.

By the time Kesselring visited Rommel's HQ next morning, the result of the pulverizing British attack were all too plain. Dramatically Rommel accused the C-in-C as the man who 'has done us all an ill-turn', in the emotional and mistaken belief that Kesselring was the one behind Hitler's counter-order. In better possession of the facts, from his central position, Kesselring was able to placate the excited Rommel and, without hesitation, act as the rescuing angel by taking personal responsibility for rescinding Hitler's order (which Rommel did not dream of doing!) and saving rather more from the wreck than might have been the case if the misinterpreted signals had been unchallenged. Even so the Axis would have lost far more if radio intercept of a German signal had not indicated the presence of a strong German force near Fuka and caused the New Zealand Division to waste time concentrating. Or if 1st Armoured Division, as the spearhead of the pursuit, had not been delayed in starting on the 4th due to petrol shortage, and prevented on the 6th, for the same reason, from catching the enemy near Mersa Matruh, errors which could only be laid at the doors of logistics staffs that, after more than two years of desert war, should have anticipated the problem. Not fatal errors; simply the kind which made the difference between victory and a total victory, such as O'Connor had won at Beda Fomm in 1941. The sort which would let the war go on just that little bit longer than it should have done.

8

THE DELUSIONS OF INSPIRATION
The Battle of the Atlantic, First Phase

It is among the war's great paradoxes that, in the autumn of 1942, a period during which the German U-boats held a clear advantage in the Battle of the Atlantic, the Allies managed to sail without interception large troop convoys from the USA and Britain to land armies at three places between Casablanca and Algiers. Also that, in April and May 1943 the U-boat offensive collapsed with sinkings of merchant ships down and sinkings of U-boats rocketing to no less than 46 in May alone, and this after a winter in which the convoy battles seemed to move dramatic-ally the German way, and in March, the biggest single U-boat versus convoy battle in history. How was it that a situation described by the British Admiralty in March as one in which 'it appeared possible that we should not be able to continue (to regard) convoy as an effective form of defence' was transformed into one in which Grand Admiral Karl Doenitz, Commander-in-Chief of the German Navy, had to admit on 23 May in the aftermath of a catastrophic failure to score successes in a major convoy action: 'Losses, even heavy losses, must be borne when they are accompanied by corresponding sinkings. In May in the Atlantic the sinkings of about 10,000 tons had to be paid for by the loss of one boat while not long ago only one loss came with the sinking of 100,000 tons. Thus [German] losses in May have reached an intolerable level.' And with that he had admitted defeat by withdrawing his packs from the central battle while searching for a remedy to a problem the cause of which was unknown to his scientists, his staff and himself.

The failure of the U-boat offensive, just as much as the one-time promise of its victory, can be traced back to the state of the art at the end of the First World War, and the debate and technical and tactical developments which took place in the years of peace and at the immediate onset of war in 1939. The consensus on all sides for much of that period had recorded somewhat tepid support for the U-boat's chances of prevailing aginst modern defensive measures. It had been demonstrated, in the teeth of initial objections and an unwillingness to study the subject scientifically and statistically, that losses to ships in convoy were significantly reduced and that the institution of a convoy system was by no means as disruptive of trade or wasteful of escorts as its opponents guessed – and 'guessed' is the proper word, even when referring to the First Sea Lord at the Admiralty, Sir John Jellicoe. It had also generally been accepted that the combination of detection of submarines by sonar (known then as ASDIC) with attack by depth-charges would act as potent deterrents to underwater craft so that the submarine would not play a leading role in sea warfare.

In consequence, the emphasis on naval construction throughout the rearmanent period of the 1930s was upon battleships, aircraft carriers, cruisers and destroyers, with funds for cheap, small escort vessels reduced to a minimum. Grand Admiral Erich Raeder, the German C-in-C, allocated relatively small resources to the building of U-boats and concentrated, instead, upon having a strong surface fleet, to be ready by 1947 or 1949 when, according to Hitler's forecast, France would have been neutralized and the time to tackle an isolated Britain would have arrived. But geographically Germany's access to the oceans remained so unfavourable in 1939 that there was little hope of surface or underwater raiders having a decisive influence by blockade. Nevertheless, German naval philosophy and strategy leaned strongly towards commerce warfare as the best way of defeating Britain and, as Doenitz put it to Raeder on 1 September 1939, '. . . the main weapon in the U-boat war against merchant shipping is the torpedo-carrying U-boat'.

Despite the Treaty of Versaille's ban upon possession of U-boats, Germany had managed, prior to 1935 when rearmament began in earnest, to keep in clandestine touch with U-boat technical and tactical developments through joint projects with Japan, Spain, Finland, Holland, Argentina and other nations. When the Anglo-German Naval Treaty of 1935 gave Germany the right to possess a submarine fleet, she had plans ready for a series of modern boats, the first of which was launched two days after the Treaty was signed. At the outbreak of war she had 57 in commission, of which 48 were ready for operations, but only 27 ocean-going types. In September 1935 Doenitz had taken command of the first U-boat flotilla and almost at once began the development of 'wolf pack' tactics by groups of U-boats directed by radio from a shore station supplied with information from scouting boats, aircraft, SIGINT and all the usual 'I' sources.

With his war experience to draw upon, Doenitz was a keen advocate of night attack on the surface as much as possible, a technique he himself had employed in action. And in May 1939 he was able to demonstrate in a convoy exercise how a U-boat pack, controlled by a pack leader on the spot, could achieve success by working in unison, on the surface, at night, remaining submerged by day.

However, he was not then aware that trials of the torpedoes with which his boats were to be armed had been, to say the least, sketchy. In a nutshell, the contact pistols fitted for direct detonation were defective, producing innumerable premature detonations or failing to function at all – a state which remained largely unknown until April 1940 when it also came to notice that the pistols had been accepted on the basis of only two trial firings. Furthermore, although the depth-keeping devices were known to be unreliable, they had been accepted by the authorities on the grounds that it was of little importance since the magnetic proximity fuse, which functioned when the torpedo passed beneath the target, would work just the same. Often it did not! In justifiable anger Doenitz could complain in April that 'there is nothing right with our torpedoes. I do not believe that ever in the history of war have men sent been against the enemy with such useless weapons.' Not only the constructors were to blame; a large share of the responsibility belonged to the Navy for not enforcing higher standards. But for the time being all torpedoes had to be set to run shallow and use the pistol only – a major tactical handicap.

With a larger U-boat fleet and reliable torpedoes, the Germans might have wrought terrible execution at the beginning of the war for the British had been extremely tardy to face up to the submarine threat. Of course, the British rebuilding programme had to take into account not only the German programme but also those of Italy and Japan, the latter of whom might not by any means be held in check entirely by the US Navy. Moreover, it was not until March 1938 that the Admiralty revised a strange policy which 'did not anticipate any use of the convoy system'. No doubt the earlier abandonment of the convoy had something to do with an unjustified belief in sonar (which was *never* tested under operationally realistic trials) and for the total lack of any convoy exercise pre-war. But it scarcely fits with the simultaneous decision in March 1938 to defer building two flotillas of destroyers, two escort vessels, three patrol vessels and four minesweepers, all of which were priceless anti-submarine vessels. With indignation the Naval Staff History states that it was 'this failure, more than any other single factor, which was to lay a heavy handicap on our fighting effort in the succeeding war'. It was far too late when, in July and August 1939, the Admiralty woke up to the threat and placed orders for 56 escorts, based upon the whaler, called corvettes. The Navy by then was committed to battle with only 180 sonar-fitted vessels of which 24 were sloops whose ocean-going qualities were unequal to Atlantic storms.

Fortunate it was for the British that the U-boat fleet was technically handicapped and that its strategic philosophy gave priority to attack upon major warships and merchantmen, to the virtual exclusion of escorts. If the Germans had been armed with a reliable, faster running torpedo and had directed attacks primarily against escorts, a situation would have rapidly been reached when Allied surface vessels were deprived of escort and therefore, in the case of merchant vessels, virtually defenceless. For at this stage, the importance of using radar to find surfaced submarines had scarcely registered and the use of aircraft to attack them had advanced but little in technique since 1918.

The state of balance of the undersea battle for the first year of war can be regarded as an expression of the balanced equation of pre-war errors by the two sides, with the emerging imbalance increasingly in the German favour mainly as the product of Allied errors leading to their defeat on land in Western Europe, as already described. Prior to the moment when the German Navy came into unexpectedly early possession of widespread access to the Atlantic, losses to Allied shipping had been caused almost as much by mines as by torpedoes. At no time had a desperate situation arisen because the U-boats had been kept in check. Although sinkings rose steadily between June and October 1940, this was more an index of improved access to open waters and the expertise of a handful of 'ace' commanders than a general advance in applied technology and technique. Doenitz tried to concentrate against convoys and, from lack of numbers, failed to achieve his goal to any marked extent until September 1940 when packs of up to five 'ace' boats sank several ships in convoys which were spotted by a patrol line of boats in the intended fashion. Yet although the first major pack attacks in October helped account for 350,000 tons sunk by Uboat, by February 1941 the rate had fallen off to less than 200,000 tons per month, supplemented by successes from surface vessels and the Luftwaffe. This was not at a decisive level. It could and should have been higher, particularly if the Luftwaffe had made an unstinted contribution.

As it had been on land, so it was over the sea. Goering prefered using 'his' force in an independent, egoistical way if he could. When asked by Raeder in August 1940 to allocate aircraft to assist U-boats in finding targets, he grudgingly sent only 15 large float planes and eight of the big four-engine FW 200 Condor which originally had been intended as a long-range bomber and as a civil air liner. The main Luftwaffe effort, he argued, was required for the Battle of Britain. Yet when that battle had been closed down it took direct intervention by Raeder with Hitler (in Goering's absence) to obtain more help from the Luftwaffe at the turn of the New Year. Furthermore, not until March 1941 was the Luftwaffe at last forced into full involvement in the blockade of Britain and made to raise its contribution to 83 aircraft. Yet only the 21 Condors committed were really effective while the 26 Heinkel medium bombers had to be withdrawn as a costly failure, and replaced by the far more efficient Junkers 88. Furthermore, aircrew were untrained for the task; navigators were inexperienced in maritime conditions, frequently losing their way and making inaccurate reports on convoy positions; pilots, in their 'lust for fame', making foolhardy, low-level attacks against ships, whose anti-aircraft armament was improved and whose overall protection was amplified by the introduction of catapult-launched fighters on merchant ships. At this point the air torpedo, dropped from a distance and hitting below the waterline, would have been invaluable (as later it proved to be in Luftwaffe hands). But senior airmen scoffed at the expensive notion, preferring the cheap bomb delivered point-blank. And Goering not only endorsed the objections but managed, in November 1940, to stop all work on the Navy's air torpedo programme and so delay development that it was early in 1942 before this weapon was at last brought into Luftwaffe service in the teeth of Goering's objections. Many would be the lost opportunities as the result of this pig-headed attitude which, like others, was based on the 1940 notion that the war was won and economies (for which Goering was politically responsible) could be made.

Only occasionally were more than half a dozen Condors airworthy throughout the first eight months of the Battle of the Atlantic in which the Luftwaffe did manage to sink 500,000 tons, a figure which would have been far higher if Hitler, as Supreme Commander, had given the highest priority to the battle against Britain's jugular vein, and insisted upon joint service co-operation. Instead he permitted the war at sea to be waged in a fragmentary, subsidiary manner and thus condoned the chronic dispersal of naval effort. The lure of Russia clouded his strategic thoughts. Loyalty to his favourite comrade, Goering, forbade interference with the Luftwaffe. Enforced involvement in the Mediterranean drew off U-boats in support of the well favoured Rommel, and increasingly condemned them to the hazardous passage of the Straits of Gibraltar.

Because the application of new technology lay at the heart of the growth and continuing success of the U-boat campaign it was essential that full support be given to it, above all in the development of much faster boats, which could remain submerged for far longer periods, the introduction of faster, homing torpedoes, and the creation of an all-embracing communications network together with a comprehensive supply of Intelligence, including SIGINT.

In 1933, Professor Hellmuth Walter had put forward a proposal for a 300-ton U-boat with a surface speed of 26 knots, a submerged speed of 30 knots and a cruising range of 2,500 nautical miles. At the heart of the project, which was based upon a cleanly streamlined hull, was a closed-cycle gas turbine engine fuelled, as eventually decided, by hydrogen peroxide. Research and development had been encouraged by the Navy but not accorded any special priority, so that it was not until early 1939 that an 80-ton boat was ordered. In early 1940 this revolutionary craft was demonstrated, with a submerged speed of 28 knots – more than three times that of the conventional diesel electric boats in service. In February 1940, Walter suggested that by sacrificing twelve U-boats from current production, he could produce within three years a fast operational boat. This was too much for Dr Friedrich Schürer, one of the heads of the U-boat Department. In conjunction with Admiral Werner Fuchs he expressed scepticism. They demanded extensive testing on land of the engine and at sea in a boat built to conventional standards, to the exclusion of Walter's proposed system, with no question of interrupting production until these conditions were satisfied. In peacetime they might have been justified. At war, when risks are an everyday requirement, they were seriously at fault. But the finger of blame should really be pointed at Raeder and

Doenitz, both of whom were aware of the project and neither of whom made a determined effort to compel the authorities to accelerate development until they had inspected the original 80-ton model in December 1941. And even then it was not until February 1942 that Fuchs was prevailed upon to sanction the construction of a test boat.

All along the enigma of Doenitz's reluctance to become involved with advanced technology is to be found. The son of an engineer, he had been caught unawares by the torpedo scandal in 1940, and there is nothing to show that he injected much urgency into the vital matter of the development of an acoustic homing torpedo which alone had the potential to attack convoy escorts. Conceived in 1934, this weapon was not tested until 1940, and was denied any special priority until 1941 when at last a special department was formed to expedite it. It was finally put into production, defects and all, in 1942. Doenitz was also tardy in recognizing the significance of radar. While the British envisaged from the start the feasibility of detecting surfaced U-boats by radar and thus eventually countering even the night attack, it was not until early in 1942 that the German Communications and Technical Divisions were asked to search U-boat's logs for evidence of enemy use of radar, and June that year before Rear-Admiral Stummel paid a visit to the Head of Naval Communications to clarify the situation and initiate countermeasures. For economic reasons, Hitler himself had discouraged advanced research on radar in 1940 when the war seemed won, but the Navy had long been in the lead in its development for ranging. Yet the Navy only heard by chance of Luftwaffe developments in radar partly because Doenitz let matters slide until the subject was thrust under his nose by the enemy. In consequence, far too little attention was paid both to detection and early warning devices, with the result that the U-boat Command, even during its 'happy times', jerked from one technical crisis to another, often without even realizing the root causes of its troubles.

Perhaps because he was absorbed with current problems in the creation of the U-boat command together with the formulation of a controversial tactical doctrine, Doenitz's vision of the future seems to have stopped at the technical level of the mid-1930s. Having little of the imaginative flair of Guderian, who adopted the present, looked into the future and conceived scenarios of radical change, Doenitz lived in the present, embracing systems shown to be feasible and fitting them into his own fixed concepts without bothering excessively about what came next. Thus he was energetic in pressing the use of the Heinkel He 177 four-engine aircraft for long-range maritime reconnaissance – and unlucky that General Ernst Udet, the Luftwaffe's Head of the Technical Office, decided that, in line with the vogue of 1938, it should be given a dive-bombing capability, and that, in accord with the late 1940 view that the war was won, long-term projects should be shelved. The He 177 was thus condemned to become one of Germany's greatest aircraft design failures, depriving Doenitz of its help until 1943. But Doenitz was wonderfully successful in obtaining the communications system he wanted as the key to centralized control of U-boat operations – and again unlucky, in a way, that this was to turn against him.

From his headquarters at Wilhelmshaven, Doenitz installed a signals network of which the British History of Intelligence remarks, '. . . for complexity, flexibility and efficiency, was probably unequalled in the history of military communication'. Through a network of transmitters and receivers on land and sea it eventually could send orders and receive a vast quantity of information concerning contacts with the enemy, convoy movements and weather. It could monitor enemy radio taffic and often decrypt a fair proportion of what it heard. For a long time, too, its own cyphers remained secure because the British failed to discover major modifications made to the original Enigma machine by the addition of an extra wheel. So with unshakeable confidence the Germans chattered on the air, Headquarters progressively extending its control to the point at which, in 1943, it was sending detailed instructions to each boat as to task, destination, course, information about the enemy and weather forecasts. In parallel, the U-boat commanders more and more broke radio silence in order to report enemy movements, the weather and, with increasing frequency (perhaps to boost their morale and ego) boasting of success.

Of course, radio communication was essential to Doenitz. There was no other way of making the maximum use of his forces at sea. And until the enemy discovered how to decrypt Enigma the only value to be obtained by the British from intercepts was boats' location by DF, coupled with information from agents who reported the coming and going of boats from the ports. The Germans were perfectly well aware of all this, but underrated the DF threat because they assumed it would only come from shore stations, with resultant delay in transmission to ships in action at sea, and would not be exact. What they failed to take into account was the invention in France and Britain of radio direction-finding equipment which could be carried in ships to pick up short-wave radio signals and pin-point their place of transmission with great accuracy and speed. By January 1942 the British had a practical set in service with which it was possible for convoy escorts and hunting groups to acquire and evaluate the U-boat in their immediate vicinity without the slightest delay, provided that their operators heard the signal and were good at their job.

Naturally the Germans were aware of the possibility of Enigma's decryption but only very slowly alerted to its actuality. It was one of the weaknesses of their system that allowed isolated ships to take to sea the full monthly settings of Enigma keys and those of other codes which were in general use for both surface and underwater craft. Only surface raiders, indeed, had unique keys because of their vulnerability to capture. Other vessels, even such sprats as the trawler *Krebs*, it was assumed would destroy their Enigma and their codes if threatened at sea. But *Krebs* was caught inshore in unusual circumstances on 4 March 1941 by a commando raid on the Lofoten Islands, and not, as the Germans were made to believe, totally gutted. True her Enigma machine was 'ditched' but from her lockers a specially briefed boarding squad had seized a spare set of wheels and sufficient material for reading not only a month's messages preceding her capture but those for the next two months.* Of far greater importance, they provided vital clues as to the working of the German system with useful leads for future analysis, together with invaluable Intelligence about the exact location of various German weather ships at large in the Atlantic, each with its Enigma machine and codes for the capture. One of these 'cops', *München*, was picked up off Iceland, complete with April and June settings (but less her Enigma machine) on 7 May.

Two days later the convoy escort destroyer, *Bulldog*, managed one of the luckiest and most valuable 'cops' of the war in the aftermath of the forcing to the surface of *U 110*, under the experienced Kapitän-leutnant Julius Lemp. According to the strictest of standing orders, Lemp set the scuttling charges prior to ordering 'abandon ship' and

---

*Insight into the naval Enigma might have been obtained in April 1940 when the patrol boat *V2623* had been captured off Norway. Unfortunately there were no standing instructions for procedure in such cases, with the result that *V2623* was thoroughly looted before search and only a handful of invaluable documents could be recovered.

CRITICAL FLAWS

▶ British and German pre-war failures to attach due importance to underwater warfare and its ramifications.

▶ German failure to give priority to attacks upon escort vessels and Goering's reluctance to allocate sufficient aircraft in support of the Battle of the Atlantic.

▶ The German moratorium of 1940 on several key technical developments, including radar.

▶ The carelessness of both sides in electronic discipline.

jumped last of all into the water. To his dismay the charges did not detonate. Worse still, as the enemy closed and he knew he could not return on board, the realization dawned that he had disobeyed orders by failing to throw overboard in weighted bags the Enigma and his codes. There is evidence to suggest that he deliberately allowed himself to die in the icy waters rather than be captured. Hardly daring to breathe for fear of accidentally setting off the charges, a boarding-party searched the boat and found the Enigma and all the code books intact, including two special codes of an unknown type. These, plus charts and several items of machinery for investigation, were laboriously transferred by whaler to *Bulldog* without being seen by the enemy or a nearby convoy. Through the simplest of human errors a defeat far transcending many large naval engagements had been inflicted on the Germans. At a stroke the British, with further material from another captured weather ship, *Lauenberg*, on 28 June, were able to reconstruct future editions of the new codes and delve into the secrets of the Naval Enigma machine against the day when the seized July keys expired and the Bombes and cryptanalysists would have to take over again. They were also able to acquire deep insight into the fabric and inner workings of Doenitz's command, so that even when Ultra failed to decypher signals it was sometimes possible to divine German intentions on the thinnest of meagre evidence. They could also check the quality of German Intelligence and detect when British codes were being penetrated in due time to make changes which would baffle the Germans – a luxury denied the Germans because the British were more careful with their security.

Nevertheless a point would be reached at the end of 1941 at which, on the face of it, Doenitz could convince himself that the battle was moving his way. The statistics of sinkings, after all, told their own tale and Doenitz, as all good leaders should be, was an optimist even if, in indulging that optimism, he slipped into self-delusion. Moreover, with Hitler's formal declaration of war against the USA on 11 December, four days after the Japanese had struck at Pearl Harbor and begun their advance into South-East Asia, it was now possible to attack a proclaimed non-belligerent nation which for more than a year had been openly supporting the British while hiding behind a bogus neutrality. And this opportunity he relished.

9

PENALTIES FOR THE UNIMAGINATIVE
The Battle of the Atlantic, Final Phase

Just as, in 1917, Sir John Jellicoe had exaggerated the ramifications of implementing the convoy system, his adversary, Admiral Henning von Holtzendorff, Chief of the German Naval Staff, overestimated the material effects of introducing unrestricted war against commerce while underestimating its political consequences. Arguable as it was that the sinking of 600,000 tons of shipping per month and the dissuading of 40 per cent of neutral shipping from using British ports would force Britain's withdrawal from the war, the difficulties of achieving this target and the dangers of provoking an indignant USA into entering the war were too lightly discounted. For these reasons the U-boat campaign had failed and America's entry into the war ultimately proved decisive in adding much needed strength and encouragement to the Allied cause. It was therefore flying in the face of history for Germany to delude herself that a similar formula would work in 1941. Indeed, so much did Hitler fear the consequences of unrestricted U-boat warfare that he handicapped his commanders with a hedge of restrictions against sinking 'friendly neutrals' and ships of the USA in certain prescribed waters, notably those of the Western Atlantic. In these circumstances the magic target figure of 700,000 tons sunk per month and exclusion of neutral shipping from Britain was virtually unattainable, and became the more remote once the USA began escorting convoys from Iceland and Greenland in July 1941 and attacking U-boats if they interfered. The torpedoing of the US destroyer *Kearney* and the sinking of the *Reuben James* in October (when barely 100,000 tons were sunk) merely highlighted the deteriorating German situation and the overshadowing threat.

So Doenitz had his head in the sand when he welcomed the opportunity to release his commanders from restrictions and with glee ordered them to concentrate their attacks upon America's eastern seaboard. Moreover, he was reacting evasively to the increased deterrent from much stronger Allied defensive measures (actuated by improved air cover, provided by escort carriers, more escorts and the new 1.5-metre radar set which could detect U-boats on the surface by day and night) by switching from hard battles in the eastern and central Atlantic to the softer options on the western side. He was merely postponing the day of reckoning in order to garner easier sinkings to boost the U-boat score sheet. The grand total of Allied losses, in all theatres of war, including the Pacific and Indian Oceans at the height of Japanese depredations were thus made misleadingly impressive:

Month 1942	By U-boats in Atlantic (000 tons)	Total from all causes from every theatre (000 tons)
January	190	420
February	290	680
March	350	834
April	280	675
May	425	705
June	405	834
July	190	618

Successes of the February to June magnitude made it admissable to minimize the radar threat and temporize over development of the Walter fast submarine. It could be argued that the number of U-boats coming into service far exceeded losses and, along with a steady increase in the force available, promised still greater triumphs by sheer weight of numbers. What Doenitz overlooked in December 1941 was the known principle (well demonstrated by the Germans already) that superior technology has a nasty habit of upsetting sheer weight of numbers and that indifferent foresight by both sides might eventually have a neutralizing effect.

Logistically U-boat Command was inadequately prepared for sustained operations off the American coast. In the immediate aftermath of the sinking of the battleship *Bismarck* in May 1941, all but one of the supply ships at sea to support surface raiders and U-boats were caught – with hardly any assistance from Ultra, but to the concern of the British authorities who worried that so swift a clean sweep might arouse German suspicions about the compromise of Enigma. But the Germans found other reasons to explain their losses and, in any case, believed unswervedly in Enigma's impregnability.

Content with existing arrangements, Doenitz had not pressed hard for the construction of the Supply U-boats which had been projected pre-war. *U 459* was not laid down until November 1940, not launched until September 1941, was found deficient in handling capabilities and not ready for operations until March 1942 – the first of several such boats to extend the voyages of the long-range Type VII and Type IX U-boats. But the initial allocation of combat boats to this promising mission was also tardy and niggardly. In addition to the U-boats sent into the Mediterranean to help Kesselring and Rommel, Hitler was insisting upon witholding 20 more to combat the Allied invasion of Norway which his intuition told him was imminent – an intuition sedulously fed by Britain's persistent attention to that area for commando raiding, interception of surface raiders on their way to sea via Arctic waters, and operations related to convoys to Russia through Murmansk. From a total of 256 operational boats, Raeder initially released for Operation 'Paukenschlag' a mere half dozen and their departure was delayed until 2 January 1942. So few in number, there was no question or, as it turned out, any need to operate as a pack. But they did not get to work until the 13th. Unexpectedly, however, the commanders found themselves in what became known as 'The Second Happy Time', in which they could take their pick of hundreds of individual unprotected ships voyaging out of convoy as if there were no war in progress at all.

Whether or not the US C-in-C, Admiral Ernest King, was averse, as has been suggested, to playing second fiddle to the Royal Navy and felt he had had nothing to learn from 'a bunch of limeys', is debatable, though plenty of people were ready to testify to it, even in the prestigious US *Navy Review*. It could have a bearing on why the U-boats had an almost free run off the coast of North America from January until June, although it must be remembered that King, a bully with a bad temper, was violently anti almost anything or anybody – including the US Army or any form of joint planning organization – that crossed his path. Nearer to the point lies the fact that King, who had but recently relinquished the appointment of C-in-C, Atlantic Fleet, with responsibility for these waters, had turned his back on the convoy system on the grounds of paucity of escort forces available. His theory was that 'inadequately escorted convoys were worse than none at all'. It was not entirely his responsibility that a handful of coastguard cutters, converted yachts and armed trawlers (provided by the British) were facing the music because the US Navy, like the Royal Navy, had given low priority to escort vessels. Or that they were building a number of inferior submarine chasers. That must be laid at the door of a mistaken concept of modern naval warfare based upon a misreading of history and poor operational research. But why King had not drawn up contingency plans for a general defensive system, including the convoy system, before the war is beyond comprehension. And why both he and Vice-Admiral Adolphus Andrews, the Commander, Eastern Sea Frontier, persisted in their opinions when, night after night, ships silhouetted against the unextinguished lights of the American shore were being sunk by U-boats with impunity, was ridiculous. How was it that the crews of the 268 US Army aircraft available were not trained for maritime duty and their patrols not co-ordinated with the 173 surface craft of various kinds? Why did not Roosevelt bring more pressure to bear on what was a political matter, and how was it that when Andrews pleaded for fifteen of the considerable force of destroyers available, King released only seven? In answer to these questions it must be noted that Roosevelt usually handled King with kid gloves and that Andrews invariably was bullied into submission by King. But that does not excuse Andrews for having those seven destroyers dashing backwards and forwards from one sinking to another, without making a single U-boat kill, instead of hunting systematically. For most of this sorry state of affairs, allied to inter-service rivalry, King must shoulder a major share of the blame. Not only were the Navy and the Army at odds on a whole range of subjects, but the Navy was unprepared because, as the US Official Historian, Professor Samuel Morison, has pointed out, 'No scientific method of search had been worked out. US destroyers were then so ill-fitted for search and so imperfectly trained for attack that to use them as a roving patrol was worse than useless.'

It was worse than useless because it dispersed the attack upon U-boats from where they could most easily be found – in the vicinity of convoys. Instead they roved in shipping lanes to a fixed timetable, which the Germans came to learn, thus enabling them to evade the patrols. Yet in this traditional eagerness of the Americans for offensive action may be found the underlying reason for their unwillingness to take what appeared, to King and Andrews, to be defensive measures. Which in turn revealed the fundamental flaw in reasoning which ignored the wisdom of their own Admiral Sims who, during the First

World War, had convincingly argued. 'If we concentrate our shipping into convoy and protect it with our naval forces, we will therefore force the enemy, in order to carry out his mission, to encounter naval forces . . .' In other words in using the convoy as an element of offensive strategy.

The US Navy had ample warning of the oncoming German attack supplied to them by British Intelligence from SIGINT. But when, within a month of the offensive's start, the Germans introduced a brand-new, four-wheel Enigma machine, the Bombes, which were geared only to deal with the three-wheel type were totally baffled.[*] Vital information began to dry up. Not one U-boat was sunk in American waters during the first quarter of 1942. In mitigation it can be claimed that King was being loyal to Andrews in supporting a rigid standpoint which King had himself foisted upon him; and that his tardiness in reacting to the gravity of the Atlantic threat was the result of giving priority to the Pacific theatre of war where the naval battle balance had swung the Japanese way as they overran vast and vital strategic areas. Yet doggedly, and with political insensitivity, King continued to veto the essential change to the convoy system while a losing battle was played out nightly, witnessed by American people on shore whose horror became a public outcry. A toll in February of 65 ships sunk in American waters (out of 71 in the entire Atlantic); nearly all of the 86 lost in March and a further 69 in April (when the first U-boat was sunk) could not be laughed off. Nevertheless, it was not until mid-April, after night sailings were banned (with serious disruption of trade) that a slackening of losses took place. Whereupon Doenitz switched his boats to the Gulf of Mexico and the Caribbean where they continued their depradations with devastating zeal throughout May and June.

At last, in the middle of May, King gave approval to start a full convoy system, a month later, blandly writing in a letter to the Army Chief of Staff, General George Marshall: 'I might say . . . that escort is not just *one* way of handling the submarine menace; it is the *only* way that gives any promise of success. The so-called patrol and hunting operations have time and again proved futile.' Maybe it was that, by the time King wrote that letter as if he had known the answer all

---

[*] A German operator's erroneous use in December 1941 of the fourth wheel followed by a correction on the extant three-wheel machine was the first insight the British obtained of this machine, although an initial warning had been received in June 1941.

along, the tension in the Pacific had relaxed after the drawn carrier battle in the Coral Sea in May and the rout of the élite Japanese carrier force at Midway on 3–5 June. As likely as not it was the result of public outrage and an implied threat from Marshall who had expressed his fear that the losses '. . . will cripple our means of transport . . . to exercise a determining influence on the war'.

Soon the convoy antidote cut losses. Although the U-boats sank 752,000 tons in American waters in May and June, by July their commanders were reporting either empty waters or fiercely defended convoys. At once Doenitz, who rarely discouraged his men by persevering with profitless missions, pulled them back for a renewal of the struggle in mid-Atlantic. The defeat would have come earlier if Admiral King, the product of a Navy well-educated by teachers such as Mahan, Fiske and Sims, had paid more attention to history. Better still if, with a more open and flexible mind at the beginning, he had experimented with one or two convoys (as the British had been prevailed upon to do in 1917) just to see how they fared. But as Air Marshal Sir Hugh Dowding, the technically-minded victor of the Battle of Britain, happened to be writing at that moment (with examples) in the chapter of his book headed 'Why are senior officers so stupid?':

'One thing which always amazes me is the apparently innate repugnance of senior officers to settle by controlled experiment questions which can be so settled.' Maybe, as Brigadier Dykes, the British Secretary to the Combined Chiefs of Staff in Washington, wrote about King, he was 'a man of great strength of character with a very small brain'.

The resumed battle elsewhere in the Atlantic began to swing the German way. Unlike the game of chess, in this deadly contest the number of pieces on the board increased and their power fluctuated as the result of technical enhancements of which the other side was frequently ignorant. The true balance of forces was constantly concealed from the players. Often the mistakes made were unwitting and unreported. Quick to recognize that the gradual spread of Allied air power with carrier-borne and long-range four-engine aircraft, with new improved depth-bombs, would soon cover the entire Atlantic, the Germans belatedly began to improve U-boats' anti-aircraft armament to enable them to fight back on the surface. Swift, in 1941, to appreciate the threat posed at night by the British 1.5-metre radar in

Right: Hitler confers with Goering (both seated) on 21 May 1940, when the decision to invade England was fatally deferred. The hierarchy responsible for many another fatal error – such as leaving Dunkirk to the Luftwaffe, starting the invasion of Russia and for the belief that Hitler was the Saviour of Germany – are also present; from left to right, Generals Jodl and von Brauchitsch, Admiral Raeder and General Keitel. (Author's collection)

Below: Stalin (left), who made the fundamental mistake of believing that Hitler would not invade Russia, with Roosevelt, whose unpremeditated announcement of the policy of Unconditional Surrender at Casablanca in 1942 did much to intensify and extend the war. (Imperial War Museum)

Right: Von Rundstedt (left), whose abiding over-respect for the already-defeated French and underestimate of the power of mechanization – as epitomized by Guderian (right) – contributed largely to the failure to prevent the evacuation from Dunkirk, which led to so many more German mistakes in the campaigns to come. (Guderian)

Right: Wavell (left), whose decision to invade Greece prevented exploitation of the victory over the Italians in Cyrenaica to seize the remainder of the North African coastline. He is seen here with Auchinleck (right), who tried to succeed where Wavell failed in North Africa, but whose errors in the selection of commanders and whose unwieldy execution of command led to so many defeats in 1942. (Imperial War Museum)

Right: Kesselring greets Cruewell in the aftermath of the German defeat in Cyrenaica in 1941, for which Rommel, watching from the background, was very much responsible, owing to his rash tactics. (Kesselring)

Below: Kesselring trying unsuccessfully to persuade Hitler and Mussolini that the capture of Malta was of far greater strategic importance than the capture of Cairo. Keitel, the lackey of Hitler, looks on. (Kesselring)

Above: Before Gazala, Ritchie (centre, with pipe), with Norrie to his right and Gott to his left, attempting ineffectually to coordinate the plans dictated by Auchinleck from Cairo. (Imperial War Museum)
Below: Freyberg, for whom the problems of command in Crete in 1941 were 'too big', sits in the back seat with Churchill who, as

Prime Minister, had to make the best he could of the situation bequeathed to him in 1940 by his predecessors. Up front sits Montgomery who, under less pressure than *his* predecessors, ma fewer errors than them in helping to deliver the victories Churchill demanded. (Imperial War Museum)

Right: Doenitz (centre), who never managed to harness the technology necessary to make the U-boat campaign sufficiently effective, flanked by Armaments Minister Speer (left), whose directive to make full use of Germany's industrial capacity came too late, and by Jodl, whose sycophantic loyalty to Hitler at OKW merely condoned the numerous fundamental errors of his master. (Imperial War Museum)

Right: Harris (left), the apostle of area bombing, who lost the battle of the night skies above Berlin, with Eaker (centre) and Spaatz (right) who eventually corrected the original American misconceptions by winning the fight with accurate daylight bombing over Germany. (Imperial War Museum)

Right: Eisenhower stands between Arnold, the Commander of US Army Air Forces, King, the Chief of US Naval Staff, and Marshall, Chief of US Army Staff. Each, at the head of so vast an enterprise as the American war effort, was to make his share of mistakes, but none among them allowed more damage than King by his refusal to adopt the convoy system in the Atlantic until far too late. (Imperial War Museum)

Above left: Brereton, who was denied sufficient time to study the Arnhem operation and who permitted his subordinates to reject coup de main attacks on the bridges, thus contributing substantially to the ultimate failure. (Imperial War Museum)

Below: Horrocks and above right Browning (left with Gavin), the tw Corps commanders who, in action, erred by not insisting upon the need to seize the vital bridges at Nijmegen and Arnhem, regardles of risks to security. (Imperial War Museum/US Army)

Above left: Yamamoto, who gambled on a complete naval victory to win the war and who lost because of his own defective planning and the omissions of his senior commanders.
Above right: Nagumo, whose uncompleted tasks at Pearl Harbor and Midway hastened the eventual doom of Japan.
Below left: Fukudome, whose adherence to an outmoded air

defence doctrine at Leyte Gulf doomed the Japanese Battle Fleet to destruction.
Below right: Kurita, whose indecision at Leyte Gulf denied him the fleeting opportunity to wreak havoc among the American Amphibious Force. (All Official US Navy photographs)

Above: The American admirals, who were not innocent of a few tactical errors themselves, but who took full advantage of the far more serious Japanese mistakes to win the vital battles – Nimitz (far left), whose strategy was sagacious; Fletcher and Spruance (respectively third and fourth from left), whose handling of the aircraft carriers at Coral Sea and Midway assured ultimate victory in the Pacific. (Imperial War Museum)

Right: Halsey, whose lust for glory almost led to disaster at Leyte Gulf. (Imperial War Museum)

conjunction with searchlights, they responded too late in August 1942 with a detection device called Metox, and might have done so a lot earlier if experienced U-boat commanders of surfaced boats had not persisted in believing that usually they sighted an enemy aircraft before it sighted them, or thought they had been surprised because a look-out was slack. Yet when it came to the fundamental question of the German Navy winning the Battle of the Atlantic outright, Doenitz brushed aside as impossible President Roosevelt's announced intention to build 10 million tons of shipping a year which, with the output of British yards, would post a new impossible target demanding 1.3 million tons sunk each month to match. That was a deliberate mistake since to admit the danger would have undermined everything the Navy and, above all, U-boat Command, stood for as war-winning organizations.

Wheel and deal as Doenitz would to sustain a campaign which for ever stood on the brink of defeat, as a combat-experienced submariner himself he was as true as possible to his crews. While demanding from them the ultimate sacrifice, he would never readily throw away their lives by sending them on unjustifiably futile missions. He kept close touch with commanders, meeting them as often as possible, ensuring that they were supported in every way before they sailed and that they were convinced of the value and feasibility of their tasks; greeting them on their return with a heroes' welcome at the quayside followed by a good leave. Between times providing the best possible accommodation, food and drink together with attention from the German 'signals girls and carbolicy nurses' and those attractive ladies from the conquered nations who were prepared to collaborate. But although pack tactics against convoys continued to win distinguished successes in the aftermath of the 'Second Happy Time', Doenitz was not to know that this was merely an interlude created by the inability of the Allies to break the four-wheel Enigma's key. Nor was he aware of the impending arrival into service of new, deadly weapons, some of them beyond German expectation.

With what facility fortune could swing against the German Navy was demonstrated during the overture to the 'surprise' Allied invasion of French North Africa at Casablanca, Oran and Algiers on 7 November 1942 – Operation 'Torch'. For surprise should not have been allowed if the extraordinary quantity of information available to the Germans about 'Torch' had been correctly applied. Indeed, the sheer volume and diversity of Intelligence may well have been the reason for German misinterpretation or their failure to pick the convoys' real objectives as they were detected closing in upon Gibraltar in October. Rumours and prophesies postulating anything from a major landing in Sicily, Tripolitania (in the rear of Rommel's hard-pressed army at El Alamein) or the Aegean were rife. The prospects of another Malta convoy found strong favour with Kesselring but an Italian guess that it *would* be North West Africa was briskly rejected by the Germans as a matter of arrogant course. It was a luxury, indeed, that the Allies were able to read most of these forecasts via SIGINT and be reassured that not one among them was quite right. They might have been happier still if they could have read the Navy Enigma and known that the German Navy and U-boat Command discounted a major invasion because it was 'militarily impossible'.

While uncertainty remained the keynote at most Axis headquarters, with not one commander or staff prepared to state an unequivocal opinion, the German Navy, on the basis of two convoy sighting reports at sea and a report from Gibraltar that the shipping there included only two troopships and a few landing craft, pronounced with assurance on 4 November that it was merely another Malta convoy assembling. So, with that in mind, Doenitz sent the Atlantic U-boats on a wild-goose chase searching for convoys following the normal north–south movement pattern in that part of the ocean, and at Hitler's instigation deployed the Mediterranean Flotilla (reinforced by five boats diverted from the Atlantic) in defence of Sardinia and the approaches to Malta. In consequence, none of the convoys heading for Gibraltar from Britain and the USA were seriously molested and even after the convoys for Oran and Algiers entered the Mediterranean, they enjoyed a virtually free passage.

Numerous were the reasons for this cardinal error by Doenitz. His Intelligence branch was denied useful SIGINT because the Allies had changed their cyphers shortly before mounting 'Torch' and his cryptanalysts had not yet broken it. Also, clever diversionary routing of the convoys founded on SIGINT and DF and the mass of contradictory rumours spoofed commanders and staffs. But they might have been a lot more receptive to the truth had they not, the previous March, closed their minds to the possibility of a so-called 'Second

Front'. In the aftermath of the memorable British commando raid against Saint-Nazaire, which permanently deprived the Germans of the one dry dock on the Atlantic coast capable of taking the battleship *Tirpitz* and nearly denied them the use of the new submarine pens, the post-operation report had concluded: 'Successful landings on a large scale . . . may still be ruled out'. And this opinion had been reinforced by the débâcle of the raid against Dieppe in August which had thrown light on weaknesses in the Allied amphibious capability in Europe. So, conditioned against a major invasion, reaction was mis-guided and slow from a command and a defence caught off balance. It was two clear days after the landings before the first U-boat 'with excessive caution', arrived off Casablanca – and unfortunate for the Germans that its commander happened to be the only U-boat commander ever to be tried for cowardice during this war. And it was 24 hours before boats in the Mediterranean tackled the mass of shipping off Algiers and Oran, where they met such stiff resistance that only two ships were sunk by U-boats in the anchorages. It was the Luftwaffe torpedo aircraft which did the most execution by sinking at Bougie, for example, 75 per cent of nearby Allied assault shipping for the loss of only six aircraft, thus demonstrating how serious had been Goering's 1940 mistake in crabbing this kind of attack.

Although the tally of U-boat successes and the magnitude of their effort would continue to grow in the ensuing five months, their failure to make the slightest impression on the first major Allied invasion was a defeat of immense importance. In May 1943 the direct sea route through the Mediterranean would be reopened with enormous economies in Allied merchant shipping and a significant improve-ment to their naval forces' strategic and tactical flexibility. But of vital psychological importance, the U-boats, the 'war decisive weapon', suffered a major set-back as an anti-invasion weapon. Even when at last they did enter the shipping transit areas they were so keenly hunted that their losses exceeded their sinkings. It was the failure to intercept at all which rankled most, the German Intelligence staff, Hitler, Raeder and Doenitz having fallen into the same sort of incredulity trap which had snared the French in 1940 in connection with the Ardennes; deluded Wavell over the chances of Rommel attacking in March 1941; caught out Stalin over the prospects of a German invasion of Russia in June 1941; and amazed Rommel in the matter of how the British would deploy their armour at Gazala. And even as Doenitz was hearing that he was to succeed Raeder when the latter resigned after a bitter row with Hitler on 30 January 1943, the temptations of yet another bout of 'incredulity' were infiltrating his mind.

Mistakes by the hundred would inevitably be made in the execution of orders and missions at the lower levels of command on land, in the air and on the sea. The propensity to err increased in direct proportion to the quality of Intelligence supplied. Whatever mistakes the British may have made in the war at sea – including such celebrated aberrations as the dispersal and consequent ravaging of Convoy PQ 17 to Russia in June 1942, due to mishandled Intelligence and inept command at the top in the Admiralty (which will not be detailed here) – there was never the slightest reservation in their minds, or of the Americans, concerning the vital importance of Enigma decrypts in relation to the Battle of the Atlantic. Calling with over-restrained emphasis for 'a little more attention' to be given to cracking the four-wheel Enigma, the Admiralty, on 2 November 1942, stressed that this was the one campaign which the cryptanalysts in Britain were not influencing to any marked extent and that it was the only one in which the war could be lost unless they did help. This should be read in the context of initial delay in 1941 to starting the design of 'a high-speed four-wheel Bombe'. Pressure of work and staff shortages very properly diverted priority to three-wheel Bombes which were solving a mass of other different and vital cyphers. But, for a variety of organizational reasons, several more production delays had taken place both in Britain and America. To cut a long and, at times, sad story short, the day at last dawned in December 1942 when the first laborious breach in the Navy's four-wheel Enigma was made and from then on a slowly increasing number of decrypts were produced. To begin with it was in fits and starts, the service often suffering from several days' delay, although occasionally aided by German incompetence when, for example, their operators were issued with settings only for the three-wheel machine and had to set the fourth wheel at neutral, thus obligingly simplifying decryption. Not until August 1943 could it be said that Allied decryption matched that provided against the German Army and Luftwaffe codes. Yet whatever was received added just that much extra to the combined contribution already coming from a whole catalogue of new weapons and techniques.

As already mentioned, aircraft from escort carriers, as well as long-range bombers, were beginning to fill the mid-Atlantic 'gap' beyond the range of shore-based machines. Their full effect, however, could not be realized until they were able again, post-Metox, to detect and kill U-boats at night. Their ability to do so depended upon centimetric radar which had been made feasible in 1940 by the brilliant invention in Britain of the powerful cavity magnetron valve by Dr J.T. Randall and Mr H. A. Boot. As first fitted to a few corvettes in the summer of 1941, the ASV Type 271 radar, with the magnetron valve, had the ability to detect surfaced submarines at 10 miles range (and a periscope at 1,300 yards). It immediately produced results with increased sightings and attacks. But the additional beauty of centimetric sets was to be found in their comparative compactness, their very small aerial array and the inability of Metox to detect their signals. When fitted to Wellington bombers at the beginning of 1943 and calibrated with the already proven Leigh Light searchlight, a formidable weapons system came into operational service on 1 March at the very peak of U-boat endeavour. The U-boat fleet had risen to a strength of 240 which enabled Doenitz to keep more than 50 at sea at once, supplied by a flotilla of fourteen 'Milch Cows'. By sheer weight of numbers and cleverly co-ordinated pack tactics, the toll of sinkings was rising remorselessly. In December 1942 the score was 61 ships sunk, including 19 in convoy; in January, due to bad weather, only 15; but in February sinkings shot up to 48 while in March, the month in which the greatest ever convoy battle took place (see below), the total was 105, 72 of them in convoys alone. And in those four months, losses of German and Italian submarines amounted to 8, 9, 22 and 16.

The convoy battles were at their most complex as U-boat packs, escort vessels and specially formed hunting groups equipped with the latest radar, sonar and depth-charges, milled around the columns of ponderous merchant vessels. Although the spaces between vessels had to be widened to counter a U-boat technique of blindly firing a salvo of torpedoes into the convoy (called 'browning') in the hope of hitting one or two, and, after 8 December (when two U-boats collided with the loss of one while attacking) packs were restricted to 13 or 15 boats only, concentrations in space and intensity of action progressed unchecked. The increased use of HF voice radio between escorts certainly simplified and speeded reaction and co-operation between hunting vessels. Yet many instances of escorts becoming disorganized when coping with pack attacks were recorded. On the other hand, the strain upon U-boat commanders induced by the need to stalk and attack a convoy, in conjunction with other boats, over a period of three or four nights, was also tremendous and invariably impaired efficiency, to the hazard of their vessels. Moreover, while Allied air intervention in the battle was rising to a crescendo, the Luftwaffe played a miserably small part, notably since fighters from escort carriers were such a deadly threat.

Bearing all these factors in mind, the story of the crucial battles of the March convoys has emphatic significance, notably in the light of Doenitz's concentration of no less than 50 U-boats in mid-Atlantic. There have been many accounts of this struggle of which Jürgen Rohwer's book of 1977 is probably the best in details, despite a few unavoidable omissions concerning SIGINT which have been made good by the publication in 1984 of the British Official History of Intelligence, vol 3, part 1. The map on pages 136–7 illustrates the pattern of convoy movement – the northerly and southerly routes connecting the USA and the United Kingdom and the routes from Gibraltar to the United Kingdom and to the USA. It shows how a stream of convoys at regular intervals followed these routes, some moving faster than others, passing one another in mid-ocean and frequently changing course because of enemy action, weather or the danger of icebergs. Also shown are the U-boat packs, either on their way to and from home ports, or in the extended patrol line combing the paths of convoys whose approach on a known course was unfailingly predicted by the German B Dienst Service listening to and reading the Allied convoy code. And finally the U-boats closing in on their prey, guided to the feast by U-boat Command acting on reports from a 'contact-keeper' U-boat.

As usual the common denominators were the weather and the sea. Only the submerged U-boat could temporarily escape rough weather and throughout this period, as a series of troughs and depressions crossed the Atlantic, there was never a calm moment. But from poor visibility due to mist, rain or snowstorms there was no relief for anyone. Also as usual, the action was continuous. As one convoy moved out of the reach of the U-boat packs or bombers, another took its place while the packs were reshuffled but remained, nevertheless, constantly in being at fluctuating strengths. For example, when on the 5 March Convoys HX 229 and 229A were assembling at New York, the slower SC 122 was already at sea and UGF still further outward bound on its way to Gibraltar. Convoy HX 228 off Newfoundland was heading into immediate danger and SC 121 was engaged in a stiff fight against two packs south of Greenland with still more U-boats being directed to establish a patrol line ahead of its anticipated course. And simultaneously ONS 169 was diverting round a located patrol line while a series of quite separate and continuing engagements took place in the Bay of Biscay and off Portugal.

When shown like this the 'chess-board' appears to be neatly squared off, but in fact it had many indistinct edges. In the train of each convoy were stragglers suffering damage from weather, enemy action or mechanical breakdown. Shepherding them when possible were a few tormented escorts who occasionally stumbled by DF, radar or sonar, upon a lone U-boat which had fallen behind the pack in search of stragglers, or had been so harassed by attack that it had been unable to keep up with the convoy ahead. At the periphery of the battle, control was at its loosest and intuition often reigned supreme. Across the scene as a whole, in which there was perpetual interaction of one group against another, it was almost impossible precisely to declare how many upsets came from genuine error or how many from pure mischance. Here a few characteristic incidents must suffice.

There was, for example, the decision to keep the escort carrier USS *Bogue* and her two escorting destroyers too long within Convoy HX 228 for fear she might be lost, thereby inhibiting her ability to launch and receive aircraft. This deprived the convoy (and herself) of the air weapon so desperately needed, which was her *raison d'être*, and for which reason she had had instructions to act independently but within the *vicinity* of the convoy.

Navigational errors on days when it was impossible to shoot the sun (and U-boats were forced to remain submerged) were commonplace. On one occasion *U 600* and *U 468*, harried by escort vessels, were duped into reporting ON 170's course wrongly and plotting it a good 40 miles from the true position, with the result that this convoy avoided trouble and the U-boats were sent off in the wrong direction. So too did simple clerical, coding and decoding errors have a distractive effect. Convoy HX 229 was deprived of the cover of a long-range Liberator bomber for some hours when the DF signals personnel of HMS *Volunteer*, overburdened by other tasks and unfamiliar with the

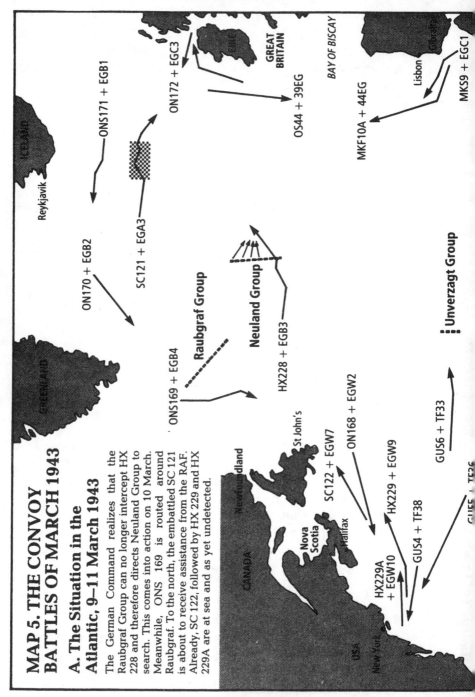

MAP 5. THE CONVOY BATTLES OF MARCH 1943

A. The Situation in the Atlantic, 9–11 March 1943

The German Command realizes that the Raubgraf Group can no longer intercept HX 228 and therefore directs Neuland Group to search. This comes into action on 10 March. Meanwhile, ONS 169 is routed around Raubgraf. To the north, the embattled SC 121 is about to receive assistance from the RAF. Already, SC 122, followed by HX 229 and HX 229A are at sea and as yet undetected.

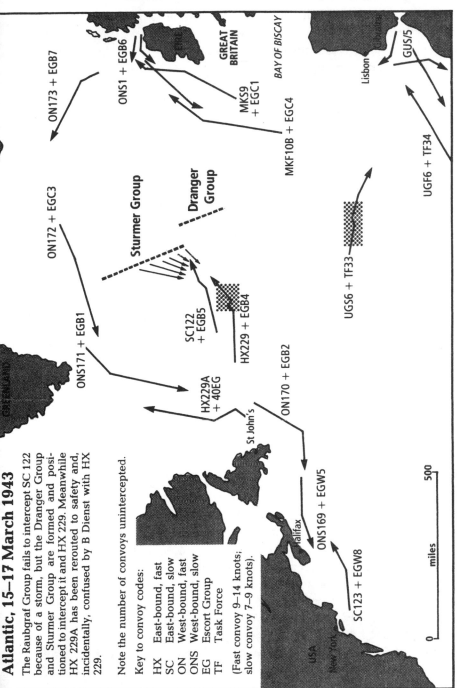

Atlantic, 15–17 March 1943

The Raubgraf Group fails to intercept SC 122 because of a storm, but the Dranger Group and Sturmer Group are formed and positioned to intercept it and HX 229. Meanwhile HX 229A has been rerouted to safety and, incidentally, confused by B Dienst with HX 229.

Note the number of convoys unintercepted.

Key to convoy codes:

HX   East-bound, fast
SC   East-bound, slow
ON   West-bound, fast
ONS   West-bound, slow
EG   Escort Group
TF   Task Force

(Fast convoy 9–14 knots; slow convoy 7–9 knots).

ON173 + EGB7

ONS1 + EGB6

GREAT
BRITAIN

EIRE

BAY OF BISCAY

Lisbon

GUS/5

MKS9
+ EGC1

MKF10B + EGC4

UGF6 + TF34

ON172 + EGC3

Sturmer Group

Dranger
Group

UGS6 + TF33

ONS171 + EGB1

SC122
+ EGB5

HX229 + EGB4

GREENLAND

HX229A
+ 40EG

St John's

ON170 + EGB2

ONS169 + EGW5

Halifax

SC123 + EGW8

USA

New York

0   500

miles

equipment, sent a bearing to the aircraft which was 180° wrong. As a result, two U-boats were able to position themselves unseen on the surface in daylight and torpedo two ships.

The outstanding impression in the narrative of these battles is that of the number of failures on the U-boats' part compared to their successes. Repeatedly we read of their being attacked, occasionally damaged and chased off. Time after time torpedoes were fired and either missed their targets or failed to detonate – a success rate of 38.8 per cent is quoted by Rohwer. Sometimes a lucky commander scored several hits with one salvo. In the majority of cases the U-boats never engaged at all. Regularly when they did, they exaggerated the result. On the other hand, over-estimates of local U-boat strength by the hard-pressed escorts not only caused deep depression in the Allied Commands in the USA and Britain but, due to their inaccuracy as revealed to the Germans through decryption, encouraged the Germans to believe Enigma was still secure.

The furious convoy battles of March with their heavy losses, which caused the British Admiralty to fear that convoys were no longer an effective form of defence, were rated as victories by the Germans who exaggerated their successes. Yet of the 150 merchant ships sailing in Convoys SC 122, HX 229 and HX 229A, only 21 (and no escorts) were sunk, despite the efforts of 44 U-boats over a period of five days. True only one U-boat was sunk. On the other hands only 15 were involved in sinking, in 7 cases shared. At the same time in the month, when 72 ships in convoys went down and numerous other actions took place, a sense of proportion was needed. A great many convoys of many hundred ships got through almost if not entirely unmolested – a situation brought about, in part, by concentrating too many U-boats against the SC 122 and HX 229 convoys to the exclusion of others. Yet this was the highest concentration the Germans could manage and was unlikely to be exceeded even if the current favourable ratio of losses to construction continued. So when would the victory come?

Within a month, of course, it would appear to the Allies that the gloom of March was only a passing cloud. By then it was the turn of Doenitz to ask fundamental questions. Why in April, a month of better weather, were only 25 ships in mid-Atlantic convoys sunk and 16 U-boats reported missing? It had surely to be understood that when enemy ships and aircraft infallibly homed-in on surfaced boats; and when a pack of 15 boats, for the loss of one and damage to three others in three days' battle, could sink only two ships, something was fundamentally wrong. Yet Doenitz who, in the aftermath of the great March convoy victories, had congratulated everybody on being so well trained, now agreed with those who placed the blame for the April set-backs upon 'inexperienced commanders' and, of course, the weather.

Because of this atmosphere of blind optimism, nurtured as it was by Doenitz's attitude and the lack in his organization of a research branch which could collate and analyse reports, the holocaust of May came all the more as a shock. Scarcely a day passed without at least one U-boat failing to make signal contact; on each of five days three boats went missing and one day, four. By the end of the month the grim total of losses had risen to 46. Stunned, and realizing that his crews' morale was cracking together with their unwillingness to tackle fiendish defences, he temporarily pulled his boats back while countermeasures were devised and the new weapons, belatedly expedited in 1942, were rushed into service. The errors of the past were catching up fast with Doenitz and his packs, since it was not simply sheer enemy numbers and a suspected new radar that was doing all the damage – contributory as they certainly were.

As Doenitz discovered when he became C-in-C, Raeder had not put all the drive he might behind the production of armaments and electronic equipment for the U-boats. For Raeder, of course, always yearned for a balanced Navy and, indeed, his resignation came about as the result of a row with Hitler in an attempt to keep surface raiders in being. As C-in-C, Doenitz naturally favoured the U-boat arm and took credit for immediately urging on scientists and industry the need to concentrate upon priorities for them and, at last, to co-ordinate their efforts. That he had failed seriously to attempt to do this prior to becoming C-in-C, is just another symptom of his own short view of the future and his lack of imagination; this rubbed off on his exceedingly small staff which, as an Allied investigator remarked after the war, 'carried the stamp of his (Doenitz's) personality'.

Doenitz's unwillingness to employ a larger staff may, indeed, be traced to the inherent inability of nearly all German leaders to share their burdens more widely. Educated in the habits of autocracy and the cult of the all-discerning deity, they were deprived of adequate support because, long before 1940, the virtues and advantages of supreme individuality in command had been eroded by the pace and extent of progress which called for many more specialists to deal with the complexities of new technology through expanded and sophisticated organizations and methods. Correctly appreciating that a principal cause of their defeat was sheer weight of Allied numbers and the air threat (about which they could now do very little), the German scientists and technologists compounded the errors of their military masters. It is not unfair to say that, in their investigation of known or suspected Allied weapons, they were conditioned by the measures of their own difficulties, successes and failures in similar fields of research and development. For example, because they were suffering from considerable problems in producing a so-called anti-escort, homing torpedo, they did not give sufficient attention to countermeasures against such a weapon. So the contribution made by an American air-launched homing torpedo in adding three kills to the May holocaust was that much simpler to achieve – and opened a new phase in U-boat sinkings which the Germans suspected but of which they, as yet, were unaware.

German studies of the detection by radar threat stopped short of a searching investigation into centimetric radar for the simple reason that the scientists rated it 'impossible'. From their own studies of this obviously highly desirable project they concluded that generation of adequate power for a compact set was unfeasible. Therefore they assumed that the Allies had reached the same conclusion! Of course, British scientists had adopted a similar position when considering German radio beams in 1940 and, fortunately for Britain, had been overruled by a simple practical experiment (as will be mentioned again in the next chapter). The irony was that the Germans had had in their possession since the end of March 1943, an example of the key to the problem, a magnetron valve. But like the British in Egypt in 1941 when, for months, they had in their possession examples of German face-hardened armour, they did not look closely enough at their capture, despite their belief that enemy radar was at the root of their troubles at sea. Obstinacy and arrogance are not the prerogative of statesmen, politicians and military leaders. Scientists have their share of those vices, along with gullibility. The German scientists, whose knowledge and pursuit of infra-red technology was well advanced, took it for granted that their opponents must be following a similar line of investigation, but, it was hoped, somewhat in arrears. And the British, aware of this, deliberately and obligingly encouraged them.

Brilliant as the German scientists were in individual prowess, team effort suffered from their tendency to work in watertight compartments. The magnetron valve might have been evaluated earlier if the specimen available had been found in an aircraft employed in the war at sea. But the one recovered from the H_2S set in an RAF Lancaster bomber, which came down in Holland, belonged to Bomber Command and was used to identify targets on land. The Germans simply did not attach sufficient importance to the valve at this stage, although they suspected its purpose. Instead they wasted the summer and autumn chasing shadows, developing a lower frequency radar detector called *Wanze*, which naturally proved useless, and giving lower priority to *Naxos* which scanned the higher frequencies.

At the same time, they handicapped their sailors further in August by abandoning Metox on the evidence of a quick-witted captured RAF pilot who, when asked how the Allies detected U-boats, replied (off the top of his head) that they hardly ever used active radar for homing but instead utilized the radiations from Metox which, he claimed, could be picked up at 90 miles by an aircraft flying at heights of 825ft and 3,300ft. Despite recent investigations, which played down the danger of *Metox* radiations, the Germans swallowed this yarn, attaching great importance to this one statement because information from prisoners was regarded as almost the only valuable Intelligence available. Pathetically, it was concluded: 'Even if this is a deliberate attempt to mislead us, especially as the alleged range seems improbable and could only be achieved by a very sensitive receiver, the statement must be accepted as true . . .' As a result *Metox* was abandoned and the U-boats were deprived of their only anti-radar aid. And Doenitz naïvely and sweepingly reported to Hitler that 'the deplorable and disgraceful matter of the Metox radiations . . . explains all the hitherto mysterious and inexplicable phenomena, such as the enemy's circumvention of the U-boat dispositions and our losses in the open sea . . .' If ever a man looked for technological panaceas it was Doenitz!

Breaches of security, via Enigma, the Germans ruled out, despite their own persistent successes in June 1943 in reading, with three days' delay, the Allied convoy code. The Navy's Director of Signals, through B Dienst, provided evidence to show that the enemy could not have decrypted Enigma. A further examination of the machine by Generals Fellgiebel and Martinez (respectively Chiefs of Wehrmacht and Luftwaffe Signals) produced similar comforting answers. But they did not check the machine's wiring and they delegated the investigations to the self-interested experts who made the machines instead of handing it to independent experts and cryptanalysts who might well have brought fresh and educated ideas to bear in detecting vulnerabilities. This maladroitness helped seal the fate of the 'Milch Cow' supply boats, among many other U-boats at sea. For although the British objected to attacks upon them at their refuelling rendezvous points for fear of alerting the Germans that Enigma had been compromised, Admiral King and the Americans had their way. In fact decrypts supplied only a portion of the dossier assembled against the 'Milch Cows', and the fate that overtook 10 of the 12 in service between 15 May and 4 October 1943 was the product of a combination of radio intercepts, DF and circumstances which did not provoke the Germans into a further re-examination of Enigma.

The loss of 17 U-boats in June and 46 in July (with no less than seven on the 30th) reduced operational U-boat strength to 207 in this month when, for the first time, Allied construction of merchant ships exceeded sinkings. This drove the German U-boat leaders into a panicky desperation which translated itself into a further succession of errors, some of them bordering upon the ludicrous. When, for example, the essential U-boat tactic of keeping up with or overtaking convoys by day on the surface became imperilled by repeated air attacks, which *Metox* did not detect, a policy of fighting it out on the surface with batteries of light anti-aircraft guns was adopted. Quite apart from introducing instability and handling problems in the boats, this tactic laid them open to easier detection and attack from surface as well as air units, the latter benefiting in May by the initial use of rocket projectiles which enabled them to stay beyond the AA guns' reach. A few aircraft were shot down, but the shoot-out game soon proved far too costly and was tacitly abandoned.

Characteristically of the German naval technical world, development of improved torpedoes, above all the acoustic kind, had been lackadaisical — and in the case of the latter confused and diluted by working on too many separate projects. Not until February 1943 was *Falke*, the slow, 20-knot torpedo, the first German acoustic type, ready for trial. It was used with success against a convoy on 16 March and released for full service on 1 July despite its deficiencies. The more promising *Zaunkönig* (known as Gnat to the Allies) with its designed speed of 24.5 knots to fulfill the anti-escort role, was much further delayed because its proximity fuze (like most German contact fuzes) was unreliable – premature detonations occurred in keel wash. In May 1943 Doenitz was told it would not be ready until 1944 – but the pressure of losses compelled him to insist upon readiness by 1 October – a date he advanced to 1 August on 13 July as U-boat losses reached appalling heights.

Zaunkönig, virtually superseded *Falke* and made its début on 20 September in a 3-day action against two convoys. According to delighted U-boat commanders it was an enormous success. For the expenditure of 24 *Zaunkönig* in addition to many more of the conventional torpedoes, they claimed to have sunk twelve escorts although, in fact, it was only three together with six merchantmen, and one escort damaged. Over-claiming was of course, inevitable from fully submerged boats which fired blind. As the German account *U-boat Warfare in the Atlantic* so well puts it: 'Propeller noises, asdic impulses, torpedo and depth-charge detonations, sinking noises and foxers presented the naked ear with a peculiar, but often impressive, cacophony of sounds. The difficulty of drawing the correct conclusion from these confused noises, in a skirmish with a destroyer and in the vicinity of a convoy, can only be appreciated by one who has experienced it.'

Yet within 16 days of *Zaunkönig*'s appearance, the British had issued the first countermeasure, a towed, noise-making device called 'Foxer' which did much to nullify the new torpedo's effect and, by its horrible noise, terrified several Germans who heard it. For something like *Zaunkönig* had been long expected by the Allies, and its antidote had been developed in parallel with work on their own acoustic torpedoes. Gullible as ever, Doenitz and his staff, together with scientists who despised their opponents, discounted 'Foxers' and, eager for a shaft of brightness in the gloom, happily and for several months, accepted superficial evidence as proof of success and continued to waste effort on weapons which largely had been mastered.

The remedies and gadgets the U-boat command was playing with in 1943 came too late and were doomed to impotence – such devices as Aphrodite, a hydrogen-filled balloon with aluminium foil, and *Thetis*, a buoy with a long spar, both intended to confuse radar, provided useless palliatives for an out-moded weapon system, the slow submarine. The fact of the matter was that the U-boat with which the Germans had started the war had reached the fullest extent of its operational life from which no amount of modification could rescue it. To survive against the sophisticated weapons which the Allies had urgently built and deployed against it, the U-boat had to be made to run much faster, be given a far deeper diving capability and the ability to stay submerged longer, and be made to run quieter in order to outpace the enemy, evade him and neutralize his weapons. In the fast, Walter boat, with closed-cycle engine and streamlined hull, the Germans long ago had been presented with a solution to these problems. Had it been brought into service by 1943, in conjunction with the schnorkel breathing mast (invented by a Dutch naval officer, Lieutenant-Commander J. J. Wichers, in 1933 and also fostered by Walter) the scales might well have tipped against the Allies in mid-summer of that year.

But not only was Doenitz's call in September 1942 for a hastening of the proven Walter boat a typical product of too long delayed concern over losing a battle, it reached a U-boat building industry still divided within itself. Factions supporting competing concepts of power plant, hull, layout and performance vied for favour instead of being directed by a central agency to collaborate on one or two approved designs. Calls for test models were reiterated. Even after the Navy had at last fixed upon the specification and production of an operational Walter boat in October 1942, it was lured in March 1943 to approve construction of a test model of the rival Deshimag's Daimler-Benz closed-cycle engined boat, despite the knowledge that building facilities were already working to capacity. In this way the Navy and its exclusive, accredited suppliers fiddled, as the sailors, confronting a resurgent enemy, approached their immolation. Yet even in April 1943, when Doenitz managed to persuade Hitler to transfer U-boat construction from the traditional Naval control to that of the Armaments Ministry, under Albert Speer, his aim was merely to boost conventional production from 30 to 40 a month to replace current losses. Not until August 1943, however, would an automotive production engineer, Otto Merker, be brought in to promote mass construction of the chosen mainstay U-boat, the Type XXI. But Type XXI, which utilized the Walter streamlined hull and could achieve only short bursts of high speed through increased battery loads, introduced as many technical problems as the Walter design, of which the projected, large type was excluded from production and only 28 of

---

CRITICAL FLAWS

▶ German failure to appreciate the extent of the enemy technological threat – in effect, a tendency to despise their opponents, particularly in the field of radar.

▶ The dilatory introduction of supply U-boats.

▶ King's rigid rejection of the convoy system.

▶ German misappreciations leading to failure to detect the objectives of Operation 'Torch'.

▶ British delays in building a Bombe to decrypt the four-wheel Enigma machine.

▶ Doenitz's inflexibility in facing up to several fundamental problems, allied to employing too small a staff of too narrow a scope.

▶ German failure to give priority to the development of fast U-boats.

---

the small, coastal Type XXIII ordered. Overall production of the older boats, fitted with schnorkel, would soar in 1944 but still it was hard-pressed to keep pace with losses and inevitably obsolete U-boats would be hunted down and destroyed taking good crews with them.

Inevitably, too, in the nature of over-hasty development of a new system which Doenitz seems hardly to have understood, the Type XXI, constructed in large numbers as they were, remained tied up in dock with a host of defects and never entered operational service. But seven of the small Type XXIII, conventionally powered by diesel/electric motors but based on the rejected Walter Type XXII stream-lined hull, did see action and, with their submerged speed of 14.5 knots, managed in 1945 to sink five merchant ships off the English coast without loss. They thus demonstrated their potential and indicated what might have happened if Germany had acquired larger Walter 26-knot U-boats two years earlier.

As a monument to the German Navy's lack of imagination and foresight in the application of advanced technology to U-boat warfare (the only available means of bringing Britain to her knees after the failure to invade in 1940), the Walter boats stand supreme, with

Doenitz as the architect of that incompetence due to his obstinate maintenance of an out-dated mode. And his epitaph is perhaps best expressed in the celebrated and doleful admission to Hitler at the beginning of 1944, when the scientists and the *Naxos* detector were at last proving the fallibility of them all: 'It seems all our previous ideas about British location were wrong: it was the 10cm radar . . . which caused all the German losses'. Thus indicating that, while getting closer, he was still well adrift from the whole truth.

For the Germans never came to appreciate the significance of the Allied capability to DF the U-boats HF signals at sea which were the principal source of on-the-spot Intelligence to the hunters. As a result, the U-boats went on 'chattering' once they had made contact with a convoy and were repeatedly detected, harassed, driven off or sunk, often before their attacks began. Yet from April 1943 onwards the German radio monitoring service had detected and reported this, only to be brushed aside by those of narrow vision, at U-boat Command and elsewhere, whose obsession was with the radar threat.

There is no question, or evidence, that the HF/DF problem was deliberately excluded from serious consideration, but full realization of the extent of the danger and the need to take countermeasures would have been heartrending to Doenitz. At a stroke the founda- tions of centralized control of the U-boat packs would have been disrupted. No longer would he have been able to play maritime chess. The slow U-boats, acting in uncoordinated silent loneliness would have been blinded and baffled. Until faster boats with vastly improved torpedoes were available, the campaign would have been in limbo. As it was, scores more U-boats continued to meet their doom until the end of the war.

10

THE PRICE OF INITIATIVE
The Japanese Intervention, 1941

In the spring of 1943 the boot changed feet. Except by the acquisition of some miracle weapon of quite devastating capacity – such as swarms of uninterceptible rockets delivering thousands of tons of high explosive on Allied cities and installa-tions, or a nuclear bomb of quite unimaginable destructive power such as had been hinted at more than once by scientists – the Axis powers were doomed to defeat. So far as Germany, Italy and Japan were concerned the choice was either a discreet with-drawal from the war or fighting to the death. To the Allies it was a matter of ending the business as quickly as possible commen-surate with the least cost in lives and to their own property. Deprived of the initiative, the Axis would increasingly make more forced errors under the pressure of events and their own shortcomings. The Allies had to strive to eliminate mistakes in the exorbitant search for an economically reasonable solution. Yet by spring 1944 the expense to both sides was becoming more apparent as the complexities of an evolving world situation were revealed and earlier miscalculations exposed.

The struggle in Europe continued at Hitler's insistence, the German people supporting him out of a propaganda-guided mis-conception that, somehow or other, his genius would find a way out of the corner into which his initial errors had driven them. With each set-back their sense of hopelessness was moderated by the balm of lies poured down their throats by Joseph Goebbel's Propaganda Ministry. As intensifying Anglo-American air attacks ravaged their cities with unimaginable ferocity, the people took shelter in ever-increasing apathy, seeming to stare through the desperation of their problem without recognizing its full portent. As the Russians drew nearer to Germany's pre-war frontiers in the east and the Allied armies landed in Sicily in July and then Italy in September 1943, that unhappy country withdrew from the Axis and yet found herself embroiled more fiercely than ever in an imbroglio of destruction and hatred. Above Western Europe the air battles raged as the moment for a mighty Allied force to land in France approached.

The Japanese arrived at a similar plight by another route and for psychologically different reasons. How this happened will be described in far greater detail in Chapter 14. At this point it is merely necessary to say that a majority among the Japanese people believed, for traditional and historic reasons in their invincibility (*Neikon Seishin*) – a state of mind created, at source, by a society whose means of expression, intercourse and political system were unique. Midway in development between the old feudalism of bushido and modern Western industrialization and military method, the Japanese politico-military leadership, because it was more profoundly influenced by past philosophies and achievements than present realities, went to war in the calculated knowledge, as stated by their Naval C-in-C, Admiral Yamamoto Isoroku, to Prime Minister Konoe in September 1941: 'If you insist on my going ahead [with war] I can promise to give them [the Americans, British and Dutch] hell for a year and a half, but can guarantee nothing as to what will happen after that' – an expression of doubt which was decisively complemented by the Naval Chief of Staff, Admiral Nagano Osami, when he told the Emperor: 'The government has decided that if there is no war, the fate of the nation is sealed. Even if there is war, the country may be ruined. Nevertheless a nation which does not fight in this plight has lost its spirit and is already a doomed nation.'

In Japanese eyes, therefore, the decision to extend the war they had started against China in 1937 was correct, just as it had been correct in the eyes of their militaristic government to initiate hostilities against China as a natural consequence of Japan's expansionist destiny. Her inadmissable mistake had been subsequent opportunism which led her to reach for dominance of the Western Pacific with a bellicosity which was bound to arouse American and British resistance. It was foolhardy to occupy French Indo-China after France's fall in 1940, and to ignore American warnings along with every indication that, in due course, two powers of vastly superior industrial potential would be provoked into curbing Japan's bellicosity, making it impossible for her to pull back without irredeemable loss of face.

Yamamoto's calculation of 18 months' hell for the Allies was based on the level of Japan's oil stocks and the rate at which they would be run down in time of war unless replaced from sources under her own control. The progressive imposition of economic sanctions by the USA since September 1940 and her joint action with Britain to freeze

CRITICAL FLAWS

▶ Japanese arrogant underestimation of American capacity
and determination which connived at her dangerous
gamble of conquest in the Pacific with inadequate
resources.

Japanese assets in July 1941, simply made action to seize sources of
production in The Dutch East Indies and Burma the more necessary.
His military mistake lay in the belief that a single great naval victory
had the potential to decide a war, a concept quite recently lodged in
Japanese philosophy as the result of two great naval occasions when
they had routed the Chinese fleet at the Battle of the Yalu River in
1894 and annihilated the Russian fleet at Tsushima in 1905. In order to
repeat these triumphs so completely as to cripple America and Britain,
Yamamoto knew that the blow would have to achieve total surprise
against an opponent who happened to lie fully concentrated and
complete in, at the most, two localities. It was a most exacting
intention and a gamble with his nation's future. For Yamamoto, a
compulsive gambler to whom games of chance such as *shogi, go,
mahjong*, cards and roulette were said to be more important than food
and drink, had been unable to control this flaw in his character when
it came to planning the crucial decisive battle against his attack on the
USA. The proposed attack on Pearl Harbor, by the very nature of the
highly secret but easily detectable approach of the Japanese carrier
squadron towards Hawaii, the dependence almost wholly upon air
attack to deliver the knockout blow and the need to destroy all of a
variety of vital targets within a very short period of time, was
inherently a gamble even if only the effects of uncertain weather were
taken into account.

Like most major Japanese war plans, the Pearl Harbor raid was
complicated and very dependent upon perfection of execution. It also
relied upon excellent security and Intelligence about the enemy —
who would obligingly comply with Japanese assumptions concerning
his reactions! Which was asking far too much especially since,
unbeknown to the Japanese, the Americans for some time had been
reading their diplomatic codes and were aware of an approaching
clash, though at a place and a time as yet unrevealed. Prior to the

attack, the Japanese had been informed by their agents in Hawaii that both enemy carriers had left harbour for the weekend, an unusual practice which gave rise to suspicions that the plan was disclosed – and was, indeed, a precautionary measure on the American part. Above all, the Japanese were unaware that only half the American aircraft carrier force was present in the Pacific when the raid was launched on Sunday, 7 December 1941. Neither did the Japanese place sufficient emphasis on the value of American submarines, or the importance of the dockyard's machine shops and the oil storage tank 'farm', relegating these installations to a third strike after the battle-ships, carriers and cruisers had been sunk. With the result that they were left intact when Admiral Nagumo Chuichi cancelled the third strike for fear of unacceptable losses from air attacks from enemy shore- and carrier-based aircraft known to be still at large. A keener supporter of battleships than aircraft carriers as the supreme instru-ment of decision at sea, Nagumo was content only to have destroyed the enemy's battleship force. He declined to gamble further having won a large prize, though without breaking the bank. Thus weapons, facilities and supplies, which were vital to the US Fleet's rapid recovery, were left in being to hasten the day of retribution.

Essentially, though, neither the Germans nor the Japanese managed to appreciate the global nature of the war upon which they were embarked, or how well their enemy both understood it and managed to adjust the balance of forces required at each vital spot. There was no genuine joint planning between Berlin and Tokyo, no attempts to co-ordinate efforts to mutual benefit as was practised between Washington and London. As a result, defeat of the U-boats in the Atlantic was as much a victory over Japan as it was over Germany while the priority given to preponderance of effort against Germany was merely a matter of degree, delaying only by a few months the ultimate crushing deployment against Japan. And nothing Japan could do, in the aftermath of defeats at Midway and in the Solomon Islands in 1942, would deflect Allied forces from the bombardment of Germany and the prosecution of the greatest ever amphibious operation, in 1944. Simply, it was left to the Allies to make the fewest possible mistakes in bringing the war to a conclusion.

11

MISCONCEPTIONS OVER GERMANY
Bomber Offensive in Europe, 1940–1943

In a demi-official letter written to HQ Bomber Command on 3 November 1944, Air Vice-Marshal Donald Bennett, AOC the RAF Pathfinder Force, recalled the reluctance of a couple of crews, the only ones in his experience, who 'balked at the jump' when asked repeatedly to attack targets for which they had no enthusiasm. He cited the sustained attacks on Essen in 1943 and Berlin in 1943/44, emphasizing that against Berlin many crews did not press home attacks and that large numbers of 4,000-pound bombs and incendiaries had been dumped in the North Sea and over Denmark. He might have added that an increasing number of Allied aircraft were cluttering up airfields in Sweden where their crews had landed and been interned, ostensibly after losing their way or being damaged. And of course the subject of Lack of Moral Fibre in aircrew was a matter of concern under constant study. This had been the background of uncertainty against which the Allied air forces, but above all Bomber Command, approached their supreme endeavour to win the war by bombing the heart out of Germany and establishing air power as the absolute arbiter in war.

The Allied bomber offensive, which reached one of its peaks in the attacks on Berlin between November 1943 and March 1944, was a product of the Casablanca Conference in January 1943 at which President Roosevelt, Prime Minister Churchill and the Combined Chiefs of Staff of the USA and Britain had, among other objectives, established a formula for ending the war. First priority was accorded to winning the Battle of the Atlantic; an invasion of southern Europe in 1943 after completion of the conquest of North Africa was decided; in addition, resources were allocated to supporting Russia and strengthening the assault upon Japan in the Pacific and Far East. Germane to everything was Roosevelt's unpremeditated announcement at the press conference that the Allies would insist upon unconditional surrender from the Axis powers, a careless remark which initiated a policy liable to prolong the war since it provided the enemy with the chance to make propaganda designed to stiffen their own people's determination to fight to the bitter end for fear of extinction. At Casablanca the brutality of war was stimulated and symbolized in its totality by the adoption of what became known as the Combined Bomber Offensive – the Directive to the RAF and the US Army Air Force to attack the full range of economic, military and political targets in Germany. Specifically mentioned was Berlin '. . . which must be attacked when conditions are suitable for the attainment of specially valuable results unfavourable to the morale of the enemy or favourable to that of Russia'.

The concept of winning a war by an independent bomber offensive had been embraced far more closely before the war by Britain than it had by America – or Germany, for that matter, as mentioned previously. In the 1930s Britain looked on a strong bomber force as a deterrent to bombing attacks on the mother country, while Germany played down that concept because of lack of resources and in the entirely correct belief that sufficient accuracy in finding and hitting could not be achieved with the technology available. As for the USA, it vacillated until 1938 when Roosevelt put his weight behind an expansion of the Army Air Corps and the creation of four-engine bomber groups in addition to formations dedicated to support of the Army. To begin with, in the knowledge that accuracy was best achieved in daylight and the belief that heavily armed, fast bombers could outfly and outfight fighter aircraft, the apostles of the independent concept staked their claims, upon the omnipotence of the bomber. But as already shown in this book, the daylight bomber was extremely vulnerable to fighters, unless escorted by its own fighters, the speed and performance gap between the two categories of aircraft having been dramatically widened with the supersession of the biplane fighter by the monoplane in the mid-1930s. The defensive characteristics of compact bomber formations, even those fitted, as the British were, with power-operated multi-gun turrets, were quite inadequate. Therefore the misnamed earlier American Flying Fortress of 1940, without turrets, was at a hopeless disadvantage.

When Britain stood her ground alone, from June 1940 to June 1941 and, until the invasion of Sicily in July 1943, could only bring direct pressure to bear upon the Axis in Europe by the exercise of air power, she found herself restricted in that endeavour by the vulnerability of the bomber. Daylight pin-point attacks against targets in Germany from low level, beyond fighter cover, were attempted and proved expensive – as precisely had similar attacks by the Luftwaffe on England. Long-range attacks by night made a lot of noise, and were extolled by Bomber Command and British propagandists, but achieved little else. As an article of faith the attempt was splendid, but as an instrument of precision destruction it was quite ineffectual since it had not been properly thought out before 1939. For this lapse many politicians and military leaders were to blame. One of the underlying reasons was shortage of economic and industrial resources; another, the divisive influence of inter-Service squabbles. The world and Britain were recovering from recession. Rightly the Royal Navy demanded air support for nearly all its operations, as did the Army. Self-righteously, a dedicated lobby of RAF officers struggled for the preservation of their newly formed Service and its promotion to that of a decisive weapon in its own right and, as one facet of their battle, grossly exaggerated the bomber's powers of destruction.

Virulent in his opposition to navy and army requirements (besides those of certain RAF commands) was Group Captain Arthur Harris who became Deputy Director Plans (DDP) at the Air Ministry in 1934 with the task of helping formulate policy and the specifications of aircraft required for its fulfilment – above all fostering the concept of the long-range four-engine bomber with a large bomb load. But as Group Captain Bennett discovered when he took over as DDP in 1937 '. . . we appear to be neglecting practical research and experiments . . . on the type of bombs and tactics which will bring about the destruction with the least expenditure of effort on each type of target'. Possibly, too, this was what Dowding had in mind four years later when he wrote of resistance to controlled experiments and what Dr R. V. Jones meant when he later wrote that he discovered in Bomber Command a resistance to science, noting the contrast with Fighter Command when commanded by Dowding. It was Jones who, in 1940, despite the scepticism of scientists and airmen, had managed to demonstrate by a practical investigation that the Germans were using radio beams as an aid to finding and hitting targets in England at night. Dowding, when told of this, instantly gave the order to 'jam', with the result that German efforts in the radio war were persistently frustrated thereafter.

Destroying the target with the least expenditure of effort was not the only aspect of a bomber offensive that had not been tackled.

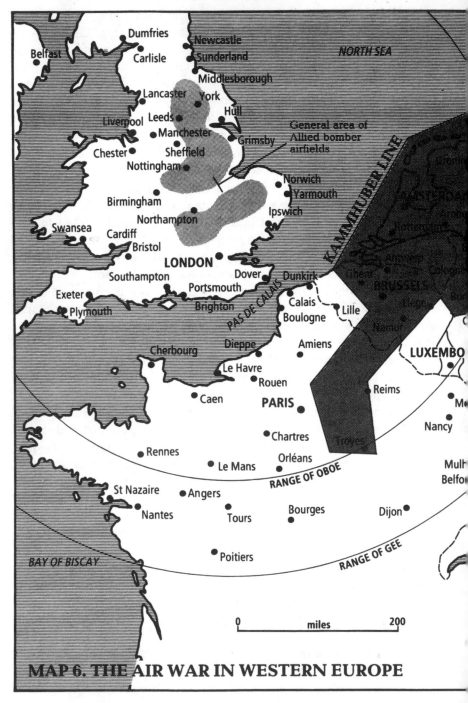

MAP 6. THE AIR WAR IN WESTERN EUROPE

The operational research needed to assess how much explosive was required to destroy each target had not been scientifically measured. Emotive events, such as the destruction of Guernica in Spain by German bombers in 1937, plus a tendency to include in calculations the worst effects of explosives without excluding nullifying factors, led to a progressive accumulation of 'evidence' by the RAF that far exaggerated the damage which might be caused in any set of circumstances. Unsubstantiated crystal-gazing of this kind inevitably had political effects through terror. It terrified politicians who were faced with crucial decisions in diplomatic bargaining with the Axis and made them susceptible to dubious and false impressions, leading to incorrect calculations of risk. And it strengthened the hands of sincere disarmament movements thus weakening defensive measures against the Axis threat and encouraging the dictators. But at the root of RAF confidence in its ability to carry out an effective night bombing campaign over Germany lay the belief that astro-navigation and dead reckoning were assured methods of finding the target. While at the root of US Army Air Corps thinking resided the self-assurance that the latest, much more heavily armed Flying Fortress could fight its way through and hit the target with deadly accuracy using the Norden bomb-sight: they had done it on exercises in ideal conditions. 'What more could one ask for?' they would say.

Harris, in his capacity as Deputy Chief of Air Staff, is quoted by Dr R. V. Jones, as minuting in February 1941: 'We use no beams ourselves but we bomb just as successfully as the Germans bomb, deep into Germany.' This was an astonishing if biased claim, not simply because there was already considerable suspicion via Intelligence sources that the RAF might not be hitting its targets, but because Harris himself, as a vastly experienced night fighter pilot from the First World War, knew all about the difficulties of flying and navigating in a hostile sky at night, and who was surely aware that even in peacetime exercises in 1939, in *daylight* above cloud, navigation by dead reckoning was lucky if it brought an aircraft within 50 miles of its target. Furthermore, Luftwaffe night bombing accuracy, with or without beams, was nothing to boast about.

Time and again enthusiastic RAF claims of targets hit and destroyed were belied by Intelligence reports. Belatedly, and in the face of Bomber Command objections, D. M. B. Butt (an impartial civilian working as secretary to Professor Frederick Lindemann,

Scientific Adviser to the Minister of Defence, Winston Churchill) produced enough evidence from air photographs to show that targets were only occasionally being hit – the cameras having been installed in bombers, incidentally, against opposition from aircrew who resented aspersions that they were falsifying their claims. In August 1941, Butt reported that, on by no means complete photographic evidence, only one third of the bombs dropped got within five miles of the target and that over the fairly heavily defended Ruhr only one tenth of the bombers had got within five miles of the target. The debate which ensued between Churchill, a somewhat deflated Air Staff and the scientists did yield results, but it also drew from the Air Staff an admission that its pre-war exaggerations of damage likely to be inflicted had been 'crystal-gazing'. Which was all very well, but, as Winston Churchill reflected in a pungent minute to Air Marshal Sir Charles Portal, the Chief of Air Staff (CAS), that this picture of air destruction had led to a gross waste of effort in making provision for casualties from air raids, had played a part in depressing statesmen responsible for pre-war policy and had played 'a definite part in the desertion of Czechoslovakia in August 1938' – and more besides.

Let it not be thought that in 1939 the Germans were well prepared to resist a night attack upon their country. It was not until June 1940, after bombs had fallen on the Ruhr in May, that they formed their first night fighter squadron and September before the first radar installation to track bombers was introduced. In August 1939 the idea of air raids upon Germany had been dismissed as 'fantasy' and Goering had claimed that no enemy bomber would penetrate the Ruhr defences – which comprised searchlights directed by sound locators and guns which expended several thousand rounds per aircraft shot down, the ratio widening with height up to maximum range at 30,000 feet. The rapid development of air defence zones by General Josef Kammhuber, with its initial concentration upon defence of the Ruhr, was followed by progressive extensions to more key centres, and finally their incorporation in the famous 'Kammhuber Line' which was an integrated radar and radio system controlling searchlights, guns and, above all, fighters. But as with everything else in the euphoric winter of 1940/41, when ultimate victory seemed just round the corner and when RAF bombing was merely an inconvenience, Goering and Udet, with Hitler's blessing, retarded radar development. It took a personal request by Kammhuber to Hitler to obtain permission to develop what the former considered the key to night fighter interception of bombers – airborne radar. Otherwise the first sets would not have been ready, as they were, by early 1942, on the eve of the RAF making more accurate attacks by night and the US Army Air Force preparing to begin its daylight assault on Germany later that year.

It is a hallmark of the development of British radio and radar navigation and bomb-aiming equipment that the motivating impulse came from the scientists and rarely at the request of Bomber Command whose officers tended, in fact, to resist their introduction. GEE, a radio navigation device based on synchronized pulses from master stations, had been proposed in 1938 and turned down, without sufficient examination, because it was considered not only too short in range but, in Bomber Command's view, unnecessary. The Butt Report, with its emphasis on faulty navigation, produced an official change of heart even though the die-hards still rated such aids as 'adventitious'. There were indeed, officers in Bomber Command, led and encouraged by Harris, who indulged in exotic words and phrases when bent upon denigration of something not invented by them. But when Harris took command of Bomber Command in February 1942, with an available force of about 300 bombers, GEE, with its maximum range of 400 miles, was the key to any success he might achieve until the Germans identified and jammed it. It had been tried out operationally on a small scale since August 1941 and had proved successful. On 8 March, against Essen under Harris's control (but not at his instigation) it was to be central to the introduction of a new technique for guiding a major bomber force. GEE-equipped aircraft were to mark the target with flares. The target was then to be illuminated by incendiary bombs also dropped by GEE aircraft. Finally the main force would deliver high-explosive bombs on the fires below. Basically it was a method first employed by Kesselring against Coventry in November 1940 using radio beams to guide the flare markers. It would constitute the framework of nearly all massed formation attacks by the RAF at night for the duration of the war and be the foundation of what was called 'area bombing'.

But GEE was of little use as an aiming device. For that task the Telecommunications Research Branch had on offer H_2S (the centimetric running mate of ASV Mk III which was to prove such a threat to U-boats) and Oboe. H_2S was a centimetric radar set which scanned downwards from an aircraft to present on its cathode-ray tube (CRT) a moving map of the terrain in sufficient detail, for the most part, to navigate by. It could not be jammed. It came about in November 1941 as the result of discussions revolving around the Butt Report and the need to improve navigation. Despite set-backs, including the crash of the trials aircraft carrying the prototype set with the loss of five scientists involved, it was ready for its first operation against Hamburg on 31 January 1943 and scored a brilliant success. As a report on the trials explained, H_2S made possible blind bombing through cloud comparable to the best results produced in perfect visibility.

Oboe was quite different from H_2S in that it was a radio device capable of receiving a signal at the intersection of two beams which told the aimer when to release his bombs in order to hit the target. It made accurate bombing possible out to a maximum range of 300 miles. Also a product of the Telecommunications Research Establishment, its initial reception by the Air Staff, when first put to them in June 1941, was cool but not entirely negative. As a result, development took place quickly enough to have an operational model in service by December 1942. Not, however, so much to aim bombs but, instead, at the request of Bomber Command, to drop coloured indicators to mark targets more precisely than ordinary parachute flares. Like GEE, Oboe was vulnerable to jamming but, unlike GEE (a model of which soon fell into German hands, and against which jamming measures were taken within six months of its introduction) Oboe remained free of jamming for nearly a year. This was partly because it did not fall into German hands for some time, partly because the Germans did not associate its signals with bombing raids, also because it took German technologists five months to produce a satisfactory jammer – a very expensive delay.

Directive No 22, which the Air Staff issued to Harris upon his appointment as C-in-C, Bomber Command, placed emphasis upon area attacks, founded upon GEE, against major industrial cities in Germany with the intention of focusing 'on the morale of the enemy civil population and in particular of the industrial workers'. But at that time and, indeed for most of the war, Intelligence concerning German morale and her economy was sketchy and conflicting without giving the slightest indication of weakness which, in any case, would be affected by such matters as reverses in Russia. The Directive laid down that targets vital to the war at sea and in other countries would also at times have to be attacked, along with harassing attacks upon Berlin. And although Portal, the CAS, laid emphasis upon area bombing, attempts at precision bombing of specific targets were not ruled out. What the Directive did not suggest was any notion that Bomber Command was to seek a decision on its own. Its role was complementary to the total war effort and its co-operation with the other Services was expected.

Yet from the start, as Harris expanded his attacks with an increasingly powerful force, he implied that winning the war by bombing was his underlying aim. Repeatedly he indulged his characteristic opposition, amounting sometimes to paranoia, to the other Services or any person or organization if ever they attempted to divert him from that aim or subtract resources from his Command. The year 1942 was to be one of growth in which the numerical and technical strength of Bomber Command was built up. With the aid of GEE and improved organization and training, the technique of concentrating a stream of bombers in time and space consistently to find and hit their targets was developed. A very complicated method was forced upon Harris by the increasing success of Kammhuber's defence, in which radar-directed fighters, anti-aircraft gun concentrations and decoy fires were not only deflecting crews from their task but inflicting a rising percentage of losses. The much-trumpeted One Thousand Bomber raids on Cologne, Essen and Bremen in May/June 1942 demonstrated the technique's feasibility without inflicting immense damage on the latter two targets, due to dispersal of the bombing. They took place at the expense of dislocation in the Command because of the effort to scrape up so many machines, many of which were obsolescent. Nor were the defences swamped, as intended, nor the loss ratio decreased.

The remainder of 1942, indeed, was a tale of steadily mounting Bomber Command activity matched by steadily improving Luftwaffe night defence. With each step forward by Kammhuber, a corresponding response had to come from Harris in order to keep one jump ahead. More flexible than Doenitz, Harris now encouraged fore-sighted electronic aids and looked with favour upon Operational Research which initiated improvements to methods without detracting from his aims. His widely known opposition to a Pathfinder Force, consisting of expert crews to find and mark targets ahead of the arrival of the less experienced main body of bombers, was mainly a matter of degree and did not long prevent the formation of that élite body, at the insistence of Portal, in June 1942.

The first attack by a formation of US Flying Fortresses in daylight on Rouen in August 1942 added diversity to the Allied attack, in that it portended the day when Germany would be subjected to a round-the-clock offensive. But it was not until 27 January 1943, when the operational strength of the US Eighth Army Air Force was barely more than 100 heavy bombers – Flying Fortresses and Consolidated Liberators – that they attacked a target in Germany – Wilhelmshaven. And by then, in defence of targets in France, the Germans had discovered ways of avoiding the heavy machine-gun fire from the Fortresses in order to inflict significant losses. Of 64 bombers dispatched, three did not return, seven German fighters were shot down – and the bombing failed to attain the concentration on target demanded. Moreover, subsequent raids on Germany suffered a worsening of losses without much improvement in bombing accuracy. Inevitably the weather and Luftwaffe defensive measures, which were intensified as the attackers gradually built up their strength, prevented the Americans from making the impact their pre-war crystal-gazing had suggested. The hard realities of war denied survival of unescorted bombers in daylight and the dropping of a bomb into a barrel (as was once claimed to be so easy). And in any case, the maximum bomb load of the American heavies, at about 8,000lb, did not compare with the maximum 12,000lb carried by the British Lancaster, while the Liberator could carry only 5,000lb.

Nevertheless it was to a US air contingent of suspect effectiveness and a British force which was only then on the eve of receiving H_2S and Oboe, and whose GEE system had already been jammed (although, through countermeasures, never entirely made useless) that the formal Directive at Casablanca in January 1943 to mount a major bombing effort against Germany was given. But which ever way Harris or General Ira Eaker, his opposite number commanding US Eighth Army Air Force, chose to interpret the Directive, the fact remained that it only demanded '. . . the progressive destruction and dislocation of the German military, industrial and economic system and the undermining of the morale of the German people to a point where their capacity for armed resistance is fatally weakened'. And it further stated that the primary targets, in order of priority, were the German submarine construction yards, transportation, aircraft industry, oil plants and 'other targets in enemy war industry' — together with the caveat that other targets, as required, could be attacked, including Berlin 'when conditions are suitable'. Like Directive No 22, it was not an order to win the war single-handed. Yet Harris, to a greater extent than Eaker, treated it as a mere instruction, in so far as he paid only lip-service to the order of priority laid down, and concentrated his efforts upon attacking a wide range of German industry through area bombing of centres of population and manufacturing.

The natural by-product of this single-mindedness was a vehement rejection of what Harris inaccurately termed 'panacea targets' such as dams, power stations, transportation systems and oil plants, most of which were included specifically in the directive. He would complain that, since attempts to destroy them in the past had proved unavailing, there was no purpose in trying again, forgetting that the failures of the past had been caused by fundamental technical deficiencies which were now in the process of being rectified. For some time he went his own way as Portal concurred with his approach, partly because Portal probably did not wish to lean heavily upon Harris in the exercise of his command — and always bearing in mind that Harris was by now in regular correspondence with Churchill and a frequent visitor to the Prime Minister's official residence. And the Prime Minister not only was wholly in favour of making Germany suffer for her crimes, but ever sympathetic to colourful personalities such as Harris. Harris caught Churchill's imagination and at the same time seemed to offer an alternative, no matter how impracticable, to the heavy and bloody fighting in the amphibious operations and subsequent land battles to come.

Since the summer of 1941 Britain's prime intention had been to divert the Luftwaffe from Russia by engaging it in battle in the West. Over France and Belgium the Luftwaffe had frequently refused the challenge, preferring to conserve its strength. But the Allied bombing of Germany did contribute to this aim by remorselessly compelling the Germans to commit fighters and special technology to the defence of cities which now endured extremely heavy attacks. Berlin only occasionally was hit. At a range of 580 miles from the Allied bases in Britain it was almost the most difficult target to reach and find, besides lacking quite the concentration of vital industrial points such as were to be found close at hand in the Ruhr and in ports such as Bremen and

Hamburg. The capital city was attractive not simply because it was a communications centre, the heart of German bureaucracy (the destruction of whose cloying effects many Germans would have welcomed) and of sentimental importance, but for political reasons because, in August 1942, Josef Stalin had stressed to Churchill the desirability of bombing it – which was beyond Russian capability. Churchill had reacted favourably at that moment because he was in trouble with Stalin in the absence of the establishment of a Second Front in Europe that summer. And Stalin had sent a rare message of congratulations to Churchill when, in March 1943, the RAF had bombed Berlin.

The major operations of the spring and summer of 1943 revolved around a concentrated bombardment of the Ruhr and cities in western Germany. The Eighth Army Air Force took an as yet small part and the RAF effort fell to less than anticipated because of the new four-engine bombers only the Lancaster was proving capable of meeting the exacting operational requirements over Germany. The Short Stirling was well below its promised performance in payload, altitude and speed, besides being extremely unreliable – faults which Harris, with good reason, blamed on the manufacturers. And the Handley-Page Halifax was only slightly better although capable of improvement and use against the easier targets. In June a supplementary Bombing Instruction and a directive called 'Pointblank' was issued telling Eaker to concentrate his daylight efforts against the German aircraft factories and ball-bearing industry (the latter denigrated by Harris as 'panacea'), and Harris to continue much as before but to be 'as far as practicable' complementary to the Eighth Army Air Force. The need to attack German fighter production was seen as paramount to the continuance of US daylight operations and might even be having an effect on Bomber Command at night. But the real threat to both the Eighth and Bomber Command was Kammhuber's efficient combination of radar and radio control of his fighters, the depredations of which were all too well exposed to the Allies by SIGINT. Of 117 Flying Fortresses sent to bomb the Focke-Wulf aircraft factory at Bremen on 17 April, 16 were lost and 46 damaged; and the RAF missing rate over the Ruhr was running at 4.7 per cent with its total casualty rate 16.2 per cent – an unsustainable figure.

The unprecedented, interrelated attacks by both air forces between 24 July and 3 August on Hamburg fulfilled, however, many purposes. They not only struck at U-boat production and a variety of industrial and transport facilities, and laid waste the second city of Germany, but opened a new chapter in German air defence tactics. For the first time 'Window' was dropped by the Allies; metallic chaff to baffle the German radar and successfully throw into disarray the German air defences. It brought a commensurate reduction in RAF bomber losses from the 4.7 per cent missing rate in the previous, so-called Battle of the Ruhr (March to July) to 4.1 per cent, the total loss rate falling to 10.7 per cent for the first time. German leaders thought they were threatened by a holocaust which would smash Germany's will to continue the war. The shock and gloom which pervaded their contemporary written comments (not to be confused with post-war commentaries by Albert Speer, which tend to be biased) were summed up by Josef Goebbels when he spoke of problems 'that are almost impossible of solution', and were confirmed by Intelligence reports and SIGINT reaching London. The Germans feared similar destruction, city by city. Vastly encouraged by the evidence, Harris did all in his power to oblige, while Portal, writing on 19 August, said: 'In the present war situation attacks on Berlin on anything like the Hamburg scale must have an enormous effect on Germany as a whole.'

It did not work out that way. For one thing the Luftwaffe reacted immediately to Window with a totally new system of fighter intercep-tion, called *Wilde Sau*. It aimed at directing fighters (even single-engine types without AI radar) into the bomber stream to enable them to freelance without further ground control. And it worked. When the Hamburg formula was attempted three times against Berlin between 23 August and 3 September, by which time *Wilde Sau* was being employed on a large scale, it cost 126 aircraft of the 1,447 sent over. Raids such as the one on 23 August when 719 aircraft took off, only 625 claimed to have got there and 57 failed to return, were a serious waste of effort which might have been better employed elsewhere. Because of H_2S's inability to project a clear picture of the target on the CRT (which assuredly already was known) the bombs were scattered and only a few landed within three miles of the aiming-point. That precision bombing could be achieved by night on clearly defined small targets had been demonstrated, however, on 17 August when 596 Lancasters and Halifaxes, controlled over the target by voice radio from a circling Master Bomber, did immense damage to the

---

CRITICAL FLAWS

▶ Roosevelt's careless public announcement of the Unconditional Surrender policy.

▶ The common pre-war mis-evaluation of strategic bombing's effects and British obstinate adherence to this miscalculation until well into 1941.

▶ Harris's initial inherent resistance to scientific assistance and his distaste for attacks upon so-called panacea targets.

---

rocket experimental and testing centre at Peenemunde. At a single stroke the German rocket programme, which was intended to be the substitute for their lack of a long-range bomber force, was put back by several months, a pre-emptive blow made possible by numerous lapses of security on the German part which led to the discovery of what was in train. Nevertheless, the losses suffered by the RAF this day (despite clever deception measures which for a time deluded the German fighter controllers) were at the high missing rate of 6.37 per cent.

The missing rate figure was, of course, of greater significance than as a simple measure of performance set against bomb hits on target or enemy aircraft destroyed. It was fundamental to continuance of a sustained offensive. If, over a period of about three months, it exceeded 5 per cent with the addition of the normal casualties to crews from crashes, wounds or ill-health, the bomber force would be crippled since replacements could not keep pace and training standards would slip. It applied to the Americans quite as much as to the RAF so that when, on the same day Peenemunde was hit, they lost 60 bombers, 16 per cent of a force sent to bomb aircraft and ball-bearing factories, a halt had to be called. It would be 14 October before they ventured deep into Germany again to bomb the important ball-bearing works at Schweinfurt – and they did so in the full knowledge that the Germans could muster some 800 single-engine and 725 twin-engine fighters and that the whole concept of the unescorted bomber in daylight was as impracticable as the British had been telling them it was from the start. The Luftwaffe did not bother to tackle the bombers until their short-range fighter force turned back, but then carried out the execution of 60 bombers, with 138 damaged, out of 291 which started off. Good strikes on target and 30–40 fighters shot down (not the 186 claimed) were not enough to offset defeat. The daylight theory had collapsed and would not be tried again in deep penetration until a reliable long-range fighter was made available in numbers.

12

DECISIONS OVER BERLIN
The Bomber Offensive, 1944

The Schweinfurt massacre prompted Harris to launch what he considered to be the crucial battle of the war. On 3 November 1943, in a much quoted minute to Churchill, he proposed an all-out assault against Berlin during the longer winter nights, employing the entire resources of Bomber Command plus the Eighth Army Air Force. He was well within the terms of the Casablanca directive and 'Point-blank' in his choice of target since Berlin did also contain many factories contributing to German fighter production. However, he was being technically unrealistic in suggesting that the Americans join in at night, since neither their equipment nor their training were suited to it. And politically naïve if he thought that Arnold* was likely to permit him to dictate orders to the Eighth. For upon the success of the Eighth in strategic operations hung, to a very large extent, the aspirations of airmen in the US Army Air Force who schemed for the day when a fully independent Air Force would be conceded by President and Congress. If Arnold had even hinted at agreement with Harris when the latter went on to claim to Churchill, as often quoted, 'We can wreck Berlin from end to end if the USAAF will come in on it. It will cost between us 400 and 500 aircraft. It will cost Germany the war', it would have been a betrayal of the USAAF's most cherished ambition to attempt it by any means other than daylight operations. And though Arnold was willing to work in conjunction with the RAF, in accordance with 'Pointblank', he much preferred to win a victory which was demonstrably American in execution.

That Harris believed an attack on morale would be decisive is virtually irrefutable, although why is another matter. He had behind him the memory of the German Blitz on Britain and had witnessed the manner in which casualties had been kept within bounds by shelters

*General Henry H. ('Hap') Arnold, Commanding USAAF.

and how citizens had learnt to live with the Blitz without breaking. Only in one city in 1940 had there been the slightest hint of a crack in morale and that was the result of inferior civic leadership and example. He had before him, however, Intelligence describing the devastation of Hamburg and many other conubations. The day after he had written to Churchill, a Ministry of Economic Warfare and Air Intelligence report stated that 'The maintenance of morale is the greatest single problem confronting the (German) home front authorities . . . the increasing death roll is an important factor and coupled with military failures the general attitude is approaching one of peace at any price, and the avoidance of wholesale destruction of further cities in Germany.' Moreover, three days later, a further Air Intelligence report reinforced this view but also served a warning:

'Though forces of repression, hopes of compromise with one or other of the belligerents and the favourable climatic conditions of the past three months have so far prevented a general break in morale, it is not unreasonable to infer that no such break can occur [sic], and we do not exclude the possibility that, in conjunction with further large-scale military reverses and the advent of winter, air operations can exercise a decisive influence on conditions inside Germany.'

This was pure conjecture unsupported by the sparse, generalized and often non-committal information coming out of Germany at this time, which is revealed by Hinsley in the British History of Intelligence. Admitting the scale of destruction but noting that support for Hitler was still firm, there was consensus in the reports on only one aspect of German morale – the people's apathy in the face of severe adversity. Within the Air Staff, its Assistant Chief for Intelligence (ACAS(I)), needless to say, supported Harris; but DCAS and ACAS (Ops) were in opposition. They feared that, as with Goering's adventure against London in September 1940, the diversion of effort to Berlin would give the Luftwaffe a chance to recuperate; that even if Berlin were destroyed like Hamburg, Germany would not throw in her hand; and that if the attempt failed the Allied bomber force would be seriously weakened.

With the support of Churchill and Portal, Harris went his way and launched the Battle of Berlin on the night of 18/19 November with a force of 444 bombers of which only nine (2 per cent) failed to return. Four nights later a much stronger force of 764 was sent of which only 3.3 per cent were posted missing. But the next night, 382, 5½ per cent were lost. Every night the weather was appalling, the bombing invariably blind through thick cloud, and the results unrevealed by air photographs until a gap in the clouds in daytime on 20 December provided an impression of considerable damage, but no true indication of the success of various tactics or guidance as to the selection of future aiming points. Harris remained optimistic about the final outcome, writing to the Air Staff on 7 December that, so long as he could maintain the attack's tempo '. . . the Lancaster force alone should be sufficient, but only just sufficient, to produce in Germany by April 1st 1944, a state of devastation in which surrender is inevitable'. In the same letter, however, he uttered a warning of the possible fatal consequences of 'ever-increasing' enemy defences. And he did not mention the Americans whom he had temporarily written off as a helpmate.

The German defences were indeed becoming formidable, aided significantly by errors on the British part, particularly in the electronics field. Early warning of intentions to raid were always provided by aircrew warming-up their radios in pre-operational flights over Britain on the day of attack, transmissions which were monitored by the B.Dienst. However, the major course of electronic insecurity resided in active equipment within the aircraft upon which the German fighters were homing with comparative ease. Two years previously, Dr R. V. Jones, the Assistant Director of Intelligence (Science) (ADI(Sc)), had warned against this danger in connection with the Identification, Friend or Foe (IFF) set carried by British aircraft to indicate their nationality to British radar operators. Bomber crews thought, quite wrongly, that IFF confused enemy searchlight radar operators, and therefore kept it switched on. Moreover, Bomber Command's scientists unscientifically discounted Jones's assertions and went on to say that to discourage the use of IFF for this purpose might have 'psychological effects on the crews'. Not until 5 January 1944 was irrefutable evidence via Enigma produced to show that IFF was a source for homing, leading to an order from Harris to 'those idiots who believe in the joss-like protection of IFF' to desist. Yet some crews continued to use IFF and one was enough to betray an entire bomber stream. A comparison with Doenitz's difficulties and errors with electronics is not inappropriate.

Transmissions from H_2S and Monica (a device to give warning of a fighter approaching from astern) were also being exploited by the

German freelance fighters because they were usually left switched on even when unneeded. Against H₂S centimetric radar they used the same *Naxos* as would help the U-boats against centimetric ASV. As a result of all this the Germans were able to improve on *Wilde Sau* with *Zahme Sau* and commence intercepting the bombers far out over the North Sea. Helped by several new electronic devices and SN 2, a greatly improved AI Radar set, they shot down bombers with deadly consistency. From the night of 23/24 November onwards, with few exceptions, the missing rate exceeded 5 per cent and on 2/3 December was as high as 8.7 per cent. Stern and prompt Civil Defence measures in cities attacked by Bomber Command ensured that there would be no pronounced crack in morale or discipline. As many as 50,000 men from the Army and the SS were drafted into Berlin to give aid and clamp down hard on looters and defeatists, a number of the latter being duly arrested and taken to the nearby Sachsenhausen concentration camp for summary execution or hard labour. Casualties in Berlin were contained to less than 10,000 dead during the 'battle' terminating in March 1944, a figure kept relatively low by the use of thick concrete shelters and the previous evacuation of the population and dispersal of industry. Yet, despite the Berlin raids and many more elsewhere, German industrial production continued to rise under the inspired direction of Speer who, with Schmidt (Kammhuber's successor) and Himmler's SS, frustrated Harris with a ruthless determination even he could not match.

In war simple plans work best. By their very nature, Bomber Command's plans to maintain momentum against the weather and the diversified enemy defences, together with its crews' and machines' fallibilities, could never be simple. The assembly, briefing and launching of an air fleet, the provision of diversionary measures and distractive sorties, involved intricate planning and staff work which could never be foolproof. From take-off, accidents, mechanical failures or misjudgements could put the operation in jeopardy, threats which were always compounded by the risk of attacks from enemy intruder aircraft over the bombers' home bases. With interceptions taking place over the sea, there was scarcely a moment when the crews could feel safe, as William Anderson, a survivor wrote:

'There was no glamour in this winter Battle of Berlin . . . The trips were long, dull and dangerous. Lining the route, we would see strings of fighter flares, generally in threes, and every now and then the gunners would report an aircraft falling in flames. You just sat there and waited for your time to come.'

Neither he, nor any one else in Britain at this time, were aware that the Germans had discovered that if a fighter got underneath a Lancaster or Halifax it could fly safely undetected because no member of the bomber crew could see it. The Germans experimented with two 20mm cannon mounted in the roof of a Messerschmitt 110 cockpit to fire almost vertically upwards and slightly forwards. The idea was codenamed *schräge Musik* (literally, slanting music, though the term actually means jazz music).

On the other hand the German fighter pilots had awkward problems to solve, winning though they were. The strain of being called upon to fight by day and night in dangerous skies was about to be compounded by the appearance of long-range fighters in their midst. It might have happened earlier if their enemies, unlike themselves, had given priority to such machines pre-war. But neither the British nor the Americans, prior to 1938, had envisaged such a requirement since they expected long-range bombers to be able to take care of themselves. Now the British felt the need to give impetus to the conversion of the excellent Mosquito light bomber and Oboe carrier to the night fighter role, equipping it to home in on enemy night fighters in an effort to disrupt attacks on the vulnerable bomber streams. Here was a nice irony bearing in mind that, pre-war, the Air Staff had resisted adoption of this de Havilland private venture for a bomber which could outfly enemy fighters (partly because de Havilland did not normally specialize in military aircraft) and had built the Mosquito as a long-range fighter in 1940 as a gamble. Likewise the Americans, now desperate to give their favoured P-38 and P-47 fighters a long-range capability with drop fuel tanks to escort the Fortresses, found themselves in possession of the P-51, which had been built in the USA to an RAF specification and which, re-engined with the British Merlin, proved a superior machine, in virtually every category (not simply that of long range) to all others, friend or foe.

Despite the introduction of navigational and aiming aids, hits on target were still difficult to achieve, especially over Berlin which was beyond the range of Oboe – a handicap which might have been avoided if, in October 1943, an improved 'Oboe repeater' system had not been abandoned as 'unprofitable'. Since only a few models of the latest 3cm H_2S were as yet available, clear definition of aiming-points within the city was impossible and therefore the Pathfinders had to do their best by dropping their markers at the end of a timed run on a fixed bearing from such prominent features as a nearby suburb or a large lake. Thereafter, the Master Bomber would rely on the light of the differently coloured flares maintained by Pathfinders, or on the markers' glow through the clouds, as aiming-points for the incoming mainforce crews. The chances of error were considerable. Repeatedly even experienced H_2S operators mistook the correct aiming-point leading to complete misdirection of bombing. Quite often the markers faded and were not replaced in time, forcing bomb-aimers to drop blind. Timing was crucial and extremely difficult to maintain at the end of a long flight in which wind conditions were a critical and often misjudged factor. Sometimes control of the stream would collapse if the loitering Master Bomber were shot down and his deputy slow to take over. It was a game of chance at extremely long odds with even a minor error leading to total failure. Under these conditions the ditching of bombs in the North Sea, over Denmark and scattered around Germany were an inevitable, wasteful outcome, even when the German controllers were effectively spoofed by diversionary measures and the bombers got through unopposed.

By the end of March, Bomber Command had lost in attacks on Berlin 495 aircraft representing 4.5 per cent of the aircraft dispatched. During the same period many major attacks were made on different cities. They included, at the express orders of a disenchanted Air Staff, despite Harris's vehement protests against 'panacea-mongers', the accurate bombing of the ball-bearing works at Schweinfurt, the British being led to the target by night on 25 February by the fires started on the 24th by Eighth Army Air Force. The price to Bomber Command between November and March was 1,128 bombers missing from 28,903 sorties, with 2,034 bombers damaged, a phase in operations which included such notorious disasters as 78 lost against Leipzig on 19/20 February and the record figure of 98 out of 795 against Nuremberg on 30/31 March. Nuremberg, indeed, was the death knell of Harris's supreme ambitions, a disaster to which he had contributed by faulty diversionary tactics, rejection of adverse weather forecasts showing cloudless skies, and an under-estimation (even at this late stage) of the efficiency and morale of the German fighter force. He was also in ignorance of the menace posed by intercept of a H_2S radiations and *schräge Musik* − information of which was not hinted at until July 1944. To Bomber Command's losses against Berlin had also to be added about 140 from Eighth Army Air Force in five separate daylight attacks during March, attacks which usually involved between 600 and 800 bombers, escorted by up to 800 long-range fighters, and which despite assistance from H2X (the American version of H_2S) achieved concentrated bombing on target only on the one day when gaps were found in the clouds.

Come 1 April, Berlin had not been destroyed and German production was still rising. The price of about 640 Allied bombers lost (well above the 400–500 figure originally staked by Harris and the 300 he admitted to post war) had not cost Germany the war. She was still fighting hard on all fronts and it was Bomber Command which had been defeated. It was a defeat which coincided with a demonstration by the Americans that their daylight, precision attacks actually did hold the key to winning the battle against the Luftwaffe. The British Air Staff, at last convinced that night area bombing was outmoded, decided to bring Harris into line. Like Doenitz, Harris had persisted single-mindedly in pursuit of a doctrine and tactics which habitually tettered on the brink of frustration by technical countermeasures − and also, like Doenitz, he had done so in ignorance of the diversity, quality and nature of the enemy's technology. Like Doenitz, too, he had clung to a pre-war notion, in his case that a bomber offensive would prevail over a fighter defensive − the same misguided policy, of his own shaping, which so nearly had placed RAF Fighter Command in second place to Bomber Command in 1938 with the almost certain subsequent loss, in 1940, of the Battle of Britain. By neglecting in 1943 to contribute to the destruction of enemy fighters in battle as well as their factories and airfields, he had not merely, in cavalier fashion, ignored directives − he had abandoned a leading Principle of Air Warfare, the winning of air supremacy. Now it was the Americans who showed him the error of his thinking − and who began to force the leaders of the Luftwaffe into fresh mistakes of their own.

It was the courage of General 'Hap' Arnold, in facing up squarely to the lessons of the October Schweinfurt disaster which paved the way for the American presence with manageable losses over Berlin in March. On 17 October 1943, with complete honesty, he wrote to Portal of the need for 'immediate scrapping of some outmoded tactical concepts, closer co-ordination between all elements of our commands and more effective use of combined resources'. Arnold's aim was the winning of air supremacy through the destruction of the Luftwaffe as an essential precondition to the launching of Operation 'Overlord' in 1944, the great amphibious invasion of France. Portal's immediate response, unsupported by senior colleagues within the Air Staff, had been to give Harris his head over Berlin and thus transgress the principles of air power by relegating the struggle for air supremacy. On the face of it, this can be seen as the elevation of an unproven theory in the interest of sectional Service ambitions above Allied and national considerations at a crucial moment in the war. Be that as it may (and the dust of such controversial matters continues periodically to fly) the Americans, with all the vigour for which they are celebrated, proceeded to concentrate on the fight for air supremacy. With a ruthless disregard for formalities, they pressed ahead with the introduction of expendable drop fuel tanks for their fighters. At the same time, they reshaped their fighter escort tactics as they worked to restore the confidence of their bomber crews in daylight combat, simultaneously resisting Portal's attempts to have them adopt night bombing. Practice in local attacks on French targets and on the periphery of Germany, was gradually extended to deeper penetrations as experience was acquired and the enemy fighter force began to suffer.

German fighter tactics against escorted bombers had always been cautious. Like U-boat Command, the Luftwaffe Fighter Command, led by General-Leutnant Adolf Galland, preferred to attack only where the enemy was weak – which they had managed to do with commendable skill and success even with obsolete machines, often by standing off from bomber formations and shooting at them with mortars from long range. This 'Happy Time' was ended when superior long-range enemy fighters began, from higher altitudes, to overwhelm outmoded opponents over Germany. Faced with a problem similar to that of the British over England in 1940, Goering laid it down that his pilots should avoid American fighters in order to concentrate on the bombers – a mistake which Dowding had carefully avoided in 1940 when he insisted upon attacks against both fighters and bombers, with preference only to shooting down the latter. The result was a free hand to American fighter pilots to hunt down German fighters, the latter's morale sagging when, as one remarked, 'The safest flying that was ever possible was that of an American fighter over Germany.' Also, the bombers began to break through regularly and often without being intercepted – which was why accurate daylight attacks could be resumed effectively against aircraft factories, and against Schweinfurt in February, and against Berlin in March 1944.

As with so much else, it was the ineptitude of Goering and Udet which lay at the root of the Luftwaffe's troubles, plus the induced errors stemming from a numerical and technical inferiority. Quite apart from the fundamental weakness of the German nation's position, which was at the heart of all their troubles, their 1940 moratorium on development of electronic devices had taken its toll (and had only been partially made up by prodigious efforts since 1942), together with the failure to produce the superior fighters which, in 1940, had been within the Luftwaffe's grasp. The jet aircraft which had emerged in 1939 could have been the fighter butterfly of 1943 had sufficient priority been allocated to it and had Goering stamped firmly upon the wishes of Hitler and others that it should be developed as a fast bomber. It was not that its function as a bomber would not have been important or that the two types were incompatible in operational terms. Multi-purpose twin-engine aircraft, such as the Mosquito, were proven. Goering's error was in permitting debate to rage without reaching and imposing a firm decision, thus repeatedly delaying development of any one jet type. Thus the best jet project did not come into action until 1944.

The penalty for ambivalence was the progressive destruction of the German aircraft industry (some sources admitting to lost production of 1,000 aircraft between 20 February and 1 April alone) and the admitted loss (as opposed to American over-claimed figures) of between 300 and 400 fighters per month in air combat. Indeed, it was knowledge through SIGINT of these figures which prompted the Americans in March to suspend concentrated attacks upon aircraft factories and challenge the Luftwaffe to fighter combat over Berlin – a strategy which paid off handsomely since the Germans could not ignore the gage. Their fighter losses rose to the unacceptable level of 10–15 per cent and included highly trained and irreplaceable night fighter crew whom Goering insisted upon throwing into the daylight battle in their outclassed machines. And when Galland attempted to engage the American fighters at their altitudes, by hastening the development of a high-altitude fighter, it was Goering among other conservatives who frustrated him. But as one critic of Goering once remarked, 'His thinking never rose above that of a wing commander.'

Benefits to Bomber Command naturally accrued from this superbly conducted and victorious American offensive which put Harris's clumsy efforts in the shade. In April, as the Luftwaffe began to wil and to refuse combat even over central Germany, the night bombers began to enjoy safer access to peripheral targets. In the course of preparations for 'Overlord', they made attacks on the sites for guided weapons under construction in France, provided support for devastating operations on land, and were able to operate in daylight with significantly improved accuracy and concentration of effort. The defeat of Harris contributed to measures taken from on high to bring him under control of Supreme Allied Headquarters in the conduct of 'Overlord' and in the prosecution of a genuine combined bombing offensive. This was a blessing in disguise since it put an end to his go-it-alone activities and prevented needless waste of men's lives. For it is sometimes forgotten that on average, each four-engine bomber missing took with it to oblivion eight or nine high-grade men; that only a small percentage of these escaped death; and that among the many machines returning damaged was a quota of dead. Perhaps most important of all, the 'panacea-mongers' in Harris's vitriolic words, had won and were being proved right. Henceforward attacks upon key targets, usually as nominated by experts with Intelligence of critical enemy industries and economic systems, would be heeded so that the bomber effort could be directed against sensitive objectives to a co-ordinated plan instead of vacillating from one target to another to suit the operational requirements of Portal and Harris in their crusade for independent air power. Enemy transport systems and oil production next became the victims of a sustained programme of destruction aimed at the sinews of the German war effort. The attack on the enemy's brain and nerves, although by no means nugatory, would be incidental to the strategy.

At last Bennett's original 1937 desire for 'destruction with the least possible expenditure of effort on each type of target' was fulfilled. And as an example of what could be done it is worth quoting the effects of the mining of sea and waterways by bombers, which received far less attention in the official histories than ordinary bombing, but which sank or damaged far more shipping, and hampered transport systems to a much larger extent than did

---

CRITICAL FLAWS

▶ Harris's miscalculation of bombing's effects upon German morale and his single-minded commitment to the wrecking of Berlin, with a technically inadequate force, without sufficient evidence to justify his claims.

▶ German delay in developing jet fighters with a priority (well within her capacity) to defeat daylight bombing.

▶ Resistance by Allied air commanders to making concentrated attacks upon enemy transport systems.

---

bombing until the closing months of the war when the Allied Air Forces finally enjoyed almost unopposed access to enemy air space. As a specific example, totally omitted from the Official British History of the Bomber Offensive, was the blocking of the River Danube between April and September 1944.

Based on Foggia in Italy, Liberator and Wellington bombers crossed the Alps and, against the scantiest of opposition, began laying sea mines in the Danube. In April and May alone, 152 sorties laid 531 mines resulting in the river's immediate closure, instantly notified by SIGINT. The Danube carried almost exclusively the oil production of the Roumanian fields which, until their overrunning by the Russians in September, had to be diverted to already overloaded rail routes, effectively halving Germany's imports. The cutting off of all manner of supplies disrupted wide sections of the economy which traditionally depended upon bulk transport by water. By the middle of May alone, 10,000 tons of ammunition destined for the southern Russian front were held up. Desperate efforts to reopen the river were frustrated by a dire shortage of sweeping equipment for a task of unforeseen magnitude, and the difficulties of recuperation were hindered by attacks on port installations by American bombers. Supplied through SIGINT with a running commentary of the German countermeasures and the occasional reopening of lengths of waterway, it was simply necessary for the RAF to fill in gaps as they were created to maintain the blockage to the end.

The most interesting aspect of this prolonged operation, with its incalculable damage to logistics (let alone the sinking or damage to

170 vessels by the end of June), was its remarkably light cost. A mere eleven aircraft were posted missing, despite strenuous enemy efforts to set up anti-aircraft defences along the length of the river with a diversion of manpower and equipment which could be ill afforded. As Churchill minuted Portal: 'You are on a good thing.' The surprising thing is that it was not tried earlier along all the German inland waterways; the economy of effort might well have produced a proportionately far greater impact than certain elements of the extremely costly main bomber offensive against heavily defended focal targets – especially since, to Harris, minelaying was a cost-effective activity, useful for accustoming fledgling aircrews to operational conditions and therefore not distractive to the bomber offensive.

But the surprise discovery of Churchill's 'good thing' pointed to the fundamental error of both British and American Air Forces in their unflagging unwillingness to concentrate, on enemy communications. As Lord Zuckerman has pointed out in the RUSI Journal, 'Communications are the common denominator which affects all possible target systems.' The evidence would be there for all to see later in 1944 as the Allied armies advanced from Normandy to the frontier of Germany, and from captured documents which proved the dislocation inflicted on industrial as well as military enterprises in the communications desert created by the air forces in the run-up to and execution of 'Overlord'. This was a devastation which Harris and Eaker refused to admit almost until the end as they went on attacking targets of their own preference, creating a desolation, ironically, which was to compound the errors of the armies in the field as they strove to end the war before Christmas 1944.

13

GAMBLING AT ARNHEM

The Airborne Offensive, 1944

There is a story – apocryphal no doubt – of a paratrooper tramping back from defeat at Arnhem and coming across a tank of 4th/7th Dragoon Guards which had been among those of the relieving force struggling to reach the beleagured 1st Airborne Division. 'Where have you been?' asked the disgruntled and weary paratrooper. 'Listen, mate,' came the reply from an equally disconsolate tank commander, 'we've been here since D-Day, not just bloody Sunday.' It might be thought that the story was symbolic of mutual rancour between members of two élite fighting formations, whereas, it was an expression of acute disappointment at the failure of a desperate and seemingly worthwhile mission to shorten the war by several months – the dramatic culmination of a series of Allied victories which the Dragoons had spearheaded in Normandy on 6 June 1944.

The need for the Allies to invade France in 1944 had been caused by the series of errors made by the Anglo-French alliance during the 1940 campaign which had permitted German conquest of western Europe. Equally it could be said that the underlying reason why, four years later, the Germans themselves stood on the brink of defeat, was Hitler's unwillingness to invade Britain when the chance was offered after the fall of France. Most command errors contribute gains to the enemy in much the same manner as a combatant who learns fast and correctly from his own mistakes stands to benefit considerably. For example, the Normandy invasion (as well as almost every major Allied landing in North Africa, Europe and the Pacific) owed its overwhelming initial success to lessons learned from the costly débâcle at Dieppe in August 1942 when a large Allied raiding force was mauled by the port's defenders. Rarely again would an Allied amphibious assault be projected against such entrenched strength without adequate beach reconnaissance, close integration of air and ship bombardment of the defences and the means to land armoured vehicles among the leading troops to provide close support as the landing craft came ashore.

Uncluttered by the need to conciliate allies, the Germans never-theless contributed to Allied success through disagreements at the highest level in the prosecution of their defence. Field Marshal von Rundstedt, as C-in-C, West, saw no hope of holding an invasion at the water's edge. He therefore proposed counter-attacking enemy penetrations with a massive concentration of armour after the landing had taken place. The Commander of his Army Group B, Field Marshal Rommel, took the opposite view. He considered that an already defeated Luftwaffe would be unable to prevent the dominant Allied air forces from shattering the armoured force before its concentration was complete. Hitler arbitrated and arranged a compromise, telling Rommel to defeat the landings on the beaches with the help of some armoured forces held nearby and let von Rundstedt retain a diluted central reserve for the main punch if the enemy was not checked on the shoreline. In the event, the landing was not stopped at the beach, but, in the face of a quick and strong German reaction, the Allies could not penetrate far inland. As a result, a steady stream of German reinforcements were attracted to Normandy to withstand the strain of mounting Allied attacks in what became a battle of attrition. Severely hampered in the movement of men, equipment and stores along lines of rail and road communications devastated by air attack, the Germans rapidly became overstretched against an opponent whose movement of forces by sea to the bridgehead was restricted only by the availability of shipping and the depredations of the weather on cargo handling across open beaches.

The close co-ordination of the Anglo-American armies in Normandy was evidence of a triumph of good sense by the Supreme Commander, General Dwight Eisenhower, who insisted that everything be shared, who squashed nationalistic inclinations to 'go-it-alone' and who supported to the hilt General Montgomery, who had overall command throughout the Battle of Normandy. Set-backs there would be, but the breakout from the bridgehead at the end of July which released the pent up strength in a pursuit of the broken Germans into France and towards Germany in August, was the product of unified command and purpose. The only serious ripples to disturb the surface of Allied accord were largely those generated by certain RAF officers. Air Marshal Sir Arthur Tedder, Eisenhower's deputy, was among those who intrigued against Montgomery because he rated the commander of 21st Army Group over-cautious, blaming him for taking far too long to expand the bridgehead to make room for fighter airfields and for missing opportunities to make an early breakout. And Air Marshal Harris still resented orders to send his heavy bombers against communications targets in support of the invasion, centres of enemy resistance on land and the V-1 missile sites which threatened England, regarding these attacks as a wasteful diversion of airpower from the business of winning the war on its own. But these British inter-Service squabbles were scarcely permitted to distract Eisenhower or Montgomery from their main aim of defeating the enemy totally on land. Only after the breakout had taken place would nationalistic undertones rise to the surface, and the majority of these were the outcome of the utter completeness of the German collapse which, to some extent, was compounded by the inflexibility clamped upon the German defence by Hitler's insistence on holding grimly to almost every inch of ground.

All at once the Allied mobile forces had room to plunge far and deep into the enemy rear, rapidly outstripping their logistics and communications systems' ability to keep pace. It was not shortage of stores already dumped ashore which caused a petrol famine at the front, but, on the one hand, incompleteness of the necessary transport and signal services (whose scheduled arrival was geared to a slower rate of advance into Europe) and on the other the destruction inflicted by Allied air power plus German demolitions of the French and Belgian railway and road links – showing how critical communications were. With each mile advanced the volume of supplies reaching the spearheads became less, and the difficulty of communicating with them in a rapidly changing strategic situation became acute.

In the matter of keeping in touch with his superiors, his staff and his subordinates, Eisenhower came face to face with his greatest dilemmas. While the fighting was compressed into Normandy, with Montgomery solely responsible for conducting the battle, it was sound for the Supreme Commander to be based in London at the centre of the diplomatic and military communications network, commuting only occasionally to his small Advanced Headquarters in Normandy when the need arose. But once the 12th US Army Group and 21st British Army Group fanned out and placed nearly 400 miles between the front and Normandy, Eisenhower found himself losing touch and control. This came to a head on 17 August when Montgomery suggested to Bradley that, instead of fanning out, their

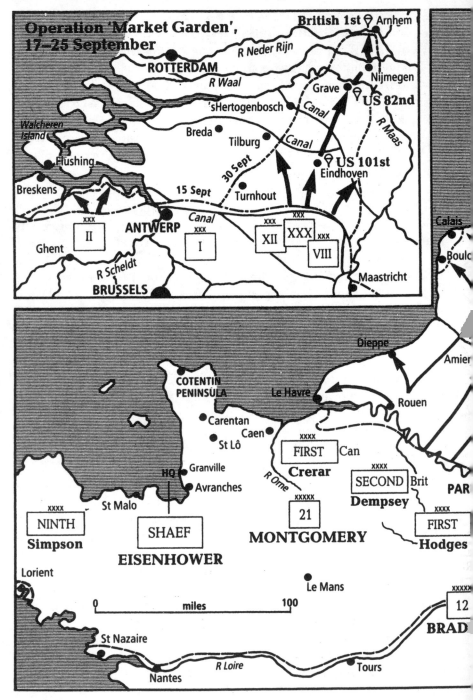

Operation 'Market Garden', 17–25 September

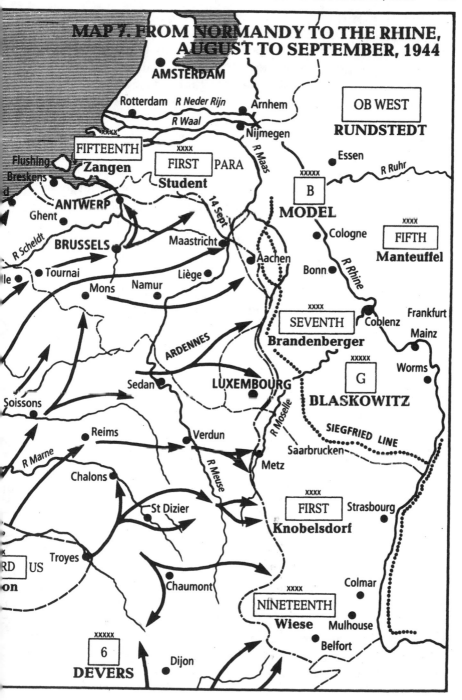

MAP 7. FROM NORMANDY TO THE RHINE, AUGUST TO SEPTEMBER, 1944

two Army Groups should remain side by side and, in a solid phalanx of forty divisions with their administrative resources pooled, they should advance northwards, with their left on the Pas de Calais (directed on the great port of Antwerp), their right on the Ardennes and their axis pointing towards the vital Ruhr industrial complex and the North German plain. It was decision by consensus when Bradley had concurred with what was to become known as 'the narrow front policy' – even if the frontage proposed was by no means very narrow! But it was not what Eisenhower had in mind.

No doubt it was this friendly collusion between his subordinates which prompted Eisenhower to decide to take personal charge on 1 September and to conduct operations from a newly located, semi-permanent residence in his Advanced Headquarters beside the seaside at Granville at the south-west corner of the Cotentin Peninsula. Granville, as Eisenhower's Chief of Telecommunications, Brigadier L. M. Harris, has pointed out, 'was a delightful seaside resort and together with Jullouville had been left practically untouched by the war. . . . But, although this was a poor place from a signal communications point of view, our objections were overruled as other considerations were more favourable' – meaning comfort, presumably. Not only was it about as far from the front as was possible, the long-distance communications to the rest of France and Belgium were in ruins. The volume of traffic passing to and from Advanced Headquarters and Main Headquarters in London, and between Advanced Headquarters and the Army Groups and Armies in the field overloaded the meagre facilities provided to the extent that long before 1 September when the front in Belgium was 400 miles distant, even the highest priority messages were taking 24 hours (and sometimes longer) to reach their destination. And naturally personal contact by air travel was by no means reliable, the Supreme Commander's aeroplane being as susceptible to delay by mechanical failure or adverse weather as any other.

If the front had been all but static such hindrances might have been bearable. But with all in flux and the pace of advance increasing they were dangerously intolerable because they created misunder-standings at a vital and tense juncture leading to hesitations and mis-calculations when an agreed plan, known to all, ought to have been in operation to make action unified and economic. Eisenhower had formulated such a plan designed to advance on a broad frontage (the broad front policy). But it was not shared at once with his army group commanders. Bradley only got to hear of it on the 19th after he had gone along with Montgomery's narrow front proposal. Eisenhower's concept, which was to send 21st Army Group northwards, but to split 12th Army Group (its First Army under Lieutenant-General Courtney Hodges moving north of the Ardennes to link up with Seventh US Army advancing from the south) had considerable merit. It was the lateness of his decision and its transmission to his subordinates which sowed the seeds of disarray. Eisenhower did not discuss it with Montgomery until 23 August, by which time Bradley had been persuaded to withdraw his support for the narrow front policy. And Montgomery was unable to persuade Eisenhower to back the narrow front approach at a meeting when it was agreed that a logistic crisis was looming.

The logistic crisis blossomed into a major issue less than a week later. On 25 August both Army Groups lunged forward with unprecedented velocity from their bridgeheads across the River Seine in an expanding torrent which, by 4 September, found the Third US Army in the vicinity of Metz, the First US Army close by Liège, General Dempsey's Second British Army in possession of Antwerp and General Crerar's First Canadian Army investing the Channel ports and approaching the mouth of the River Scheldt as a start to clearing the approaches to the port of Antwerp. A new situation had arisen, therefore, beyond the scope of prevision. The capture of Antwerp with its docks intact was of paramount importance since it offered an early improvement to the deteriorating logistics system if only the approaches up the Scheldt could be cleared. Yet not one senior army commander made this necessity clear to his subordinates. Eisenhower's directive of 4 September called for the 'securing' of Antwerp without emphasizing the need for its use. Montgomery, with his eyes fixed on the far side of the River Rhine, paid it but scant attention, difficult though his supply situation already was. As a result no specific instructions were issued through HQ Second British Army or First Canadian Army to subordinate formations to give priority to opening up the approaches – despite a demand for action on 3 September from Admiral Ramsay to Eisenhower, pointing out the urgency and the difficulty of clearing 80 miles of waterway. In consequence Montgomery did not at once exploit beyond the Antwerp docks, with the result that the bridges to the north over the Albert

Canal were not secured and the subsequent arrival of German reinforcements enabled a prolonged defence of the approaches which otherwise would have been reduced to a mere day or so. Hence the opening of the port was delayed until 28 November and only after a costly series of battles. The First Canadian Army, meanwhile, concentrated on the capture of the Channel ports, all of which were severely damaged, while Second Army began to shift its axis of advance to the right in readiness for the drive across the Rhine.

One logistic alternative was, of course, the use of transport aircraft and these, in the opinion of Bradley among others, should have been kept exclusively for that purpose. But to a significant extent they were withheld since, in the view of Supreme Headquarters, their primary task, was to deliver into battle the First Allied Airborne Army. This Army had been formed on 2 August under Lieutenant-General Lewis Brereton and consisted of XVIII US Airborne Corps (Major-General Matthew Ridgeway), with the battle experienced 82nd and 101st Airborne Divisions, and the 1st British Airborne Corps (Lieutenant-General F. A. M. Browning) with the experienced 1st Airborne Division and the 'green' 52nd (Airportable) Division. As Charles Macdonald, the American official historian, remarks, this Army was 'burning holes in SHAEF's pocket'. Between 6 June and 5 September 1st Airborne Division had planned, stood by and seen cancelled at the last moment no less than 14 different operations, the twelfth of which ('Linnet') would have included part of 1st Airborne Corps together with all the other Allied airborne divisions plus the 1st Polish Parachute Brigade; the thirteenth ('Linnet II') a plan to close the gap between Aachen and Maastricht, which was rejected by Bradley, and the fourteenth ('Infatuate') a project to seize control of the Scheldt estuary and thus hasten the clearance of the approaches to Antwerp. But 'Infatuate' was called off on 5 September partly, one suspects, because the fall of Antwerp on the 4th seemed to make it no longer necessary, but largely due to what was called the unsuitability of the landing zones (they were not easy) and to the abiding fear of all airmen of fighters and heavy anti-aircraft defences which might play havoc with slow, low-flying transport aircraft.

In a last convulsive effort to employ the airborne formations upon which so much effort and expense had been lavished, and which their sponsors so ardently backed in order to demonstrate their decisive role in the land battle, Operation 'Comet' was prepared. At first light on 10 September, the bridges over the Maas at Grave, the Waal at Nijmegen and the Neder Rijn at Arnhem would be secured by 1st Airborne Division and 1st Polish Parachute Brigade as a preliminary to a link up with Second Army's armoured formations and the establishment of a bridgehead over the Rhine, threatening the Ruhr. Its chances of success were good, for Intelligence accurately showed that the enemy were in poor shape and unprepared for such a surprise blow. A few days earlier, indeed, and it might have been 'a pushover'. But at 0200 hrs on the 10th, as the troops embarked, 'Comet' was abruptly cancelled. The deadening effect on their morale at this crucial point can be imagined.

In place of 'Comet' stood 'Market', a product of the slow, maladroit evolution of Allied plans at the hands of Eisenhower and Montgomery, the former having imposed an even greater handicap on consultations by retiring to bed for 48 hours on 2 September with a wrenched knee after a forced landing on the beach near Granville. Out of touch with the battle and sticking hard to the broad front strategy, Eisenhower had been in no psychological condition to square with the inspiration of Montgomery's signal, sent on the evening of the 4th immediately after the fall of Antwerp. Montgomery, uplifted by victory, and promotion to Field Marshal on the 1st, was calling for 'one powerful and full-blooded thrust towards Berlin', a blow that would require all the transport available and which, therefore, would mean shutting down Patton's thrust in the south in order to concentrate in the north. Montgomery was of the opinion that an immediate thrust on the northern front might be decisive, but he insisted that time was vital and that a compromise would only prolong the war. To guarantee disagreements the two important signals initiated between Eisenhower and Montgomery on the 4th, took four days in transmission and were further confused because the second half of Eisenhower's signal reached its destination one day ahead of the first part.

If it had been anybody else other than Montgomery making this proposal the American commanders might have willingly acceded. As it was, Eisenhower, Bradley and Patton resented the incisive British Field Marshal who had several times tactlessly ruffled their feathers, whose autocratic ways were anathema to them and whose grasping for glory competed with their own ambitions. With Eisenhower's blessing, Bradley told Patton on the 5th to continue his drive to the

Rhine, consuming precious supplies in abundance as he went. Instead of a quick resolution of the controversy over the broad and narrow front strategies, a round of negotiations took place while Montgomery instructed Dempsey to persevere with 'Comet' in the full knowledge, through Intelligence, that the way to the Ruhr was almost undefended.

A single, relatively low-calibre fortress division alone covered the 50-mile front from Antwerp to Hasselt along the Albert Canal, and a disorganized German rabble was pouring through it to be slowly incorporated in the thin defences to Germany's northern gateway. Among these were the remnants of 9th and 10th SS Panzer Divisions who occupied the terrain selected for 'Comet', there to reorganize and re-equip with a view to attacking the flank of Allied troops approaching Aachen. With each day that passed, these forces, under the command of General Student's First Parachute Army, were strengthened by the arrival of various Parachute Regiment units which were instantly thrown into abortive counter-attacks against a British bridgehead over the Albert Canal at Beeringen – and considerably reduced in strength by 10 September as a result. Nevertheless the success of this German defence certainly had an impact on 'Comet' since there was no guarantee now that the British forces available at Beeringen on the 9th could link-up with 1st Airborne Division if dropped in Holland.

Indeed, on the 9th, Dempsey had reached the conclusion, based on Intelligence reports of the enemy build-up and the resistance at Beeringen, that it was advisable to call off the northward movement along with 'Comet'. Instead he wanted to conform to the eastward movement of First US Army and advance, with airborne assistance, in the direction of Roermond and Wesel where the northern arm of the pre-war Siegfried Line was weakest and as yet thinly garrisoned. But already the decision to shift the axis of Second Army's advance had, to some extent, been taken out of Montgomery's hands. A signal had arrived from London announcing the fall on the 8th of a large V-2 rocket missile, stating that it had probably been launched from the vicinity of The Hague, in west Holland, and indicating that a northward move by Montgomery to cut the supply lines to the launching pads would be welcome. Behind that signal stood Churchill who, previously mislead by false Intelligence which credited the V-2s with a vastly greater destructive power than they actually possessed, had on 18 July reacted violently when told by R. V. Jones that some thousand or more might be ready for use. A deluge of these missiles upon England in the aftermath of victory in France and the quelling of the V-1s, could, he feared, have a disproportionate effect on public morale. Simultaneously, the Air Force commanders warned Montgomery that while the Dutch bridges were extremely well protected by anti-aircraft batteries, those along the Rhine (including Wesel) were doubly secure since they lay within the belt of guns covering Germany's principal industrial areas. So a northward thrust it would have to be, but only if Eisenhower agreed and allocated sufficient logistic support.

Eisenhower, with his knee in plaster, flew to meet Montgomery at Brussels on the 10th, a confrontation at which, according to the usually reliable reporter and historian, Chester Wilmot, Montgomery was particularly undiplomatic in his exposition of what he thought was wrong with Eisenhower's strategy, causing Eisenhower to utter a clear and effective reproof. In the absence of written minutes but in the light of a letter to Portal by Tedder (who was present) and various subsequent messages between the participants it is fairly clear that, in receiving Eisenhower's permission to employ the entire First Airborne Army to spearhead 'Market', and an indication of increased logistic support, Montgomery believed he had obtained priority for the northern thrust and that Patton would be stopped in the south. Whereas, in fact, Eisenhower had no intention of abandoning the broad front strategy which, like Montgomery's Chief of Staff, Major-General de Guingand, he was convinced was right. He was simply giving Montgomery temporary extra support in furtherance of a project which he believed to be very important (and within the context of the main effort in the north), even if it were unlikely to achieve the war-stopping result Montgomery claimed for it.

It was not the merits, or otherwise, of broad and narrow front strategies which failed the Allies that September, for the arguments in favour and against were finely balanced with much on the side of broad front. The fundamental error concerning the adoption and launching of 'Comet'/'Market' lay in the time wasted on their gestation, delays which must be laid firmly at Eisenhower's door for endeavouring to command by remote control, at such long range and through an inadequate communication system. The time wasted not only presented the enemy with the chance to reinforce his defences, it also denied First Airborne Army time to study the situation and develop its plans. The delay also imposed a need to more than redouble the size of force required to overcome enemy opposition which, to the certain knowledge of the commanders, was accumulating to protect the bridges and the Siegfried Line's open flank. Where for 'Comet' a single brigade had been deemed sufficient at each of the three bridges, where but little opposition was expected to bar the way of Second Army's link-up drive, a division for each bridge was now demanded for 'Market' together with an air landed division to exploit success northwards of Arnhem along with a specially mounted operation called 'Garden' to effect the link up with XXX Corps. And while ample air transport had been available to carry 'Comet' to its landing zones in one lift, there was now a shortfall with the need to bring in reinforcements in three lifts spread over three days – weather permitting.

The weather's inclemency must always pose a higher degree of risk for airborne than for ground operations. By comparison, enemy resistance can be calculated quite accurately and for 'Market' the fears of the air force commanders regarding the anti-aircraft defences of the bridges were predominant. Both Army and Air Force agreed that a daylight landing was essential if the dispersal and confusion of all previous night landings were to be avoided and if enemy night fighters were to be evaded. But whereas for 'Comet' the airmen had been content to attempt a dawn descent, close by the bridges, allowing glider *coup de main* parties to prevent demolition taking place, for 'Market' they insisted upon a wholly daylight effort with landings at a distance of up to several miles from the bridges but within full fighter cover. At the same time, they also resisted requests that each air crew should fly two sorties from England on D-Day (17 September) in order to be sure of achieving maximum concentration and supply in one day, not only for fear of the weather breaking but also to deal overwhelmingly with the enemy in case he was found in greater strength than expected. The decision to go by day and land away from the bridges was that of commander First Allied Airborne Army, General Brereton, who, as an airman, sympathized only too well with the airmen's problems. He was probably right in insisting upon mainly daylight movement. But his acquiescence with the soldiers' abandonment of the night-time glider *coup de main* attempts against the bridges' ends is less commendable, since their presence on the ground at first light would have upset local anti-aircraft gunners and very likely prevented the bridges being blown. This was crucial. If the main bridges were destroyed the entire operation stood in jeopardy, cutting off the forces at Nijmegen and Arnhem from 'Garden'. Unfortunately, Brereton was not the man to brook protest from subordinates, as General Browning, his deputy and commander of British Airborne Corps, had discovered when he had argued against certain aspects of 'Linnet II' and had been threatened with instant dismissal as deputy.

To dispose of the German side of things, it has to be said that, despite the presentation of several highly imaginative scenarios from German officers who, with prescience, foresaw a threat something like 'Market Garden'; and despite a completely unsubstantiated post-war assertion that the plan had been divulged by a Dutch traitor, the Germans were taken by total surprise. At that moment their attention centred upon the American approach to the Saar and Aachen. Perhaps, too, they had lapsed into what was, by this time, a common view on both sides of the line that Montgomery was an excessively cautious commander who lacked the vital spark of daring in his execution of offensive operations. 'Market Garden' was the antithesis of that and even stunned the Americans, as well as some of the Field Marshal's colleagues, as something of a gamble.

In terms of risk to the airborne divisions, those for US 101st looked the least because it landed closest to the start-line of the British relief, Operation 'Garden'. Its drop zones, like those of the other two airborne formations, were flat land but intersected by drainage systems and waterways and profusely vegetated. Its flanks extended alongside the only main road which linked the British bridgehead over the Meuse Escaut Canal with Eindhoven, and northwards across the big bridges at Grave and Nijmegen (the objectives of 82nd US Airborne) and Arnhem. Because this route into Holland was so difficult to defend and easy to attack from the flanks, a pre-war Dutch staff study had rejected it as impractical – as the Allied planners were aware. 101st Airborne's task was to secure the main road, including its smaller bridges, and keep it open for the passage of British 1st Guards Armoured Division as it spearheaded 'Garden'.

Like most other elements of the Airborne Army delivered on 17 September, the 101st Division dropped accurately and well concentrated on to its intended zones, although compared with the other two divisions, its aircraft sustained the highest losses, mainly from ground fire. Nevertheless it was able rapidly to take possession of the road and would have seized all the bridges intact had not two of the parachute battalions wasted two hours moving to a bridge at Zon, only to see it blown up in their faces. It was a familiar kind of error, the product of lassitude after an initial success's over-confidence. Yet on a day in which only 75 aircraft were lost out of 4,676 committed (a mere 2.8 per cent compared with a gloomy estimate of 30 per cent) this was a trivial set back and would soon be rectified. The only really serious loss on the Allied part during the air delivery was the shooting down of an American glider containing a copy of the complete Operation Order and which, placed in front of General Student two hours later, told him all he needed to know when preparing the defence of the bridges. Some written information has to be carried into battle but this item seems to have gone beyond the bounds of security prudence.

Meanwhile 82nd Airborne had also made an exceptionally good arrival, one of its platoons landing within a mere 700 yards of the Grave bridge and managing to prevent the bridge garrison from setting off the demolition charges. Orders to do so had, in any case, not been forthcoming since General Hans Reinhard, the German Corps Commander, was neither present nor in touch with a totally unexpected situation. Similar breakdowns in the German chain of command due to the surprise factor also saved several more smaller bridges from destruction. The great bridge over the River Waal at Nijmegen, however, remained intact and in German hands, the failure to make for it at once being the shortage of air transport which allowed only two of 82nd's three regiments to be lifted that day. As a result, not only was a *coup de main* denied, but a major effort to seize the bridge was at once prevented because Major-General James Gavin, the 82nd's commander (with the full concurrence of Lieu-tenant-General Browning) considered it of greater importance to seize and hold the high ground to the south-east of Nijmegen. For, to lose that to an enemy force attacking out of the Reichswald from the east, would, they both appreciated, make command of the Grave and Nijmegen bridges untenable. The likelihood of having the bridge blown in their faces, when finally an assault on it was mounted, simply had to be accepted as a risk of war, a contingency which could be solved, but with further delay, by bridging the river once a lodge-ment had been made on the opposite bank.

Yet, Lieutenant-Colonel Shields Warren's battalion from Colonel Roy Lindquist's 508th Parachute Regiment was given a forlorn hope *coup de main* task by Gavin to seize the bridge immediately after landing (which was feasible). A mere eighteen poor-quality troops guarded the bridge. Resistance was patchy, resulting in the blowing of one or two minor bridges but not the big one since the Germans wanted it for themselves and reckoned to hold it. No sooner was he aware, by early evening, of what the Allied objectives were, than the German C-in-C of Army Group B, Field Marshal Walter Model, ordered 9th SS Panzer Division to secure the Nijmegen bridge, and a little later 10th SS Panzer also was instructed to take part. But the Germans were impeded by the landing at Arnhem and only a few troops from 9th SS Panzer managed to cross the bridge there before its northern end was seized by British paratroopers.

For some unaccountable reason the immediate post-combat reports from 508th Parachute Regiment are missing from the US Army's files. The post-war reconstruction by Charles Macdonald, an official historian of high merit, shows, however, that there were mis-understandings between General Gavin and Colonel Lindquist about the priority attached to the *coup de main* by Warren's battalion. Gavin said the battalion was to move 'without delay after landing'. Lindquist thought that 'no battalion was to go for the bridge until the regiment had secured its other objectives', which were several and important. As a result Warren was instructed by Lindquist to take some inter-mediary objectives and only be prepared to go into Nijmegen later. Therefore it was not until 1830 hrs, five hours after landing, that Warren ordered a patrol towards the bridge. But that patrol's radio failed and it was not heard of again until next day.

A few minutes later, Gavin took a firm grip of the situation and, through Lindquist, ordered Warren's battalion forward. Without delay Warren complied, sending ahead A and B Companys with a Dutch guide. But only Captain Jonathan Adams's A Company reached the rendezvous south of the bridge since B Company 'got lost en route'. A charitable view suggests this was all too easy to do in a strange, hostile environment as darkness was falling. A Company, however, got to within a very short distance of the bridge's southern end before a single burst of machine-gun fire made them deploy. In the dark, the paratroopers were about to attack when, with a clatter, the leading elements of 9th SS Panzer belatedly arrived to be instantly embroiled in a furious fire-fight. A Company was stopped by a superior force and called for reinforcements, but by the time they arrived it was too late, without armoured support, to overcome a consolidated defence.

Imprecise orders among the higher echelons of the division, allied to Gavin's and Lindquist's justifiable concern to secure their airhead as an essential preliminary to subsequent moves, had led to a failure in personal communications which unnecessarily delayed the *coup de main* party in accomplishing a vital and dramatic task, one which was well within the Americans' grasp. But at the root of the uncertainty leading to this failure lay the overriding unwillingness of Brereton, who took council of his fears and declined to plunge with all the stakes at his disposal into what was recognized as a gamble. One prize of immense value which Adams believed he had won, nevertheless, gave rise to hope that the bridge might yet be saved for the Allies. Acting on information from a Dutchman, he had been led to the post office where, it was said, the bridge demolition controls were located. Fighting his way in, Adams and his men destroyed some promising-looking equipment, but they then had to depart as enemy activity began to build up all around them, pressure which forced Lindquist, eventually, to pull Warren's battalion back.

For similar reasons, the British 1st Airborne Division found itself at once in far worse plight than its American colleagues to the southward. Precluded from an admittedly difficult glider *coup de main* attempt against the south end of the big road bridge or the railway bridge over the Neder Rijn at Arnhem, Major-General Robert Urquart, in his first experience in command of an airborne operation, was also denied the drop of the 4th Parachute Brigade north of the river until the 18th, and of 1st Polish Parachute Brigade south of the river until the 19th. Moreover, in order to comply with Brereton's insistence that landing near the bridges must be avoided, the dropping zones had to be sited at least six miles from the road bridge. This posed an impossible task to a *coup de main* party, consisting of the division's 1st Reconnaissance Squadron in armoured jeeps, and the 1st Parachute Brigade with long and hazardous journeys through built-up areas to their objective upon which their survival, let alone the ultimate success of 'Market', depended. They were being directed into the heart of a defensive system known to include armoured forces against which infantry were invariably at a severe disadvantage with only light artillery and anti-tank guns for protection.

Generals Browning and Urquart both thought they might hold out at Arnhem unrelieved for four days, but they knew too that if the armour and artillery of Lieutenant-General Brian Horrock's XXX Corps were not within reach in two days, the chances of 'Market Garden's success would be poor. As a measure of how unduly pessimistic Brereton had been over the danger from anti-aircraft fire, not a single transport aircraft was lost by enemy fire at Arnhem. And as a measure of how easily a *coup de main* party might have found it to capture the bridge if they had landed at its southern end, it has merely to be mentioned that the garrison of 25 men bolted when the air drop began six miles away and that, until about 1945 hrs, the bridge's principal custodian was a lone Dutchman, Constable von Kuijk. But the 1st Reconnaissance Squadron had been ambushed and prevented from getting to the bridge in the afternoon. And before the vanguard of Brigadier Gerald Lathbury's 1st Parachute Brigade – its 2nd Battalion under the extremely experienced Lieutenant-Colonel J. D. Frost, put in an appearance on its feet at 2030 hrs, after the Germans had arrived at the northern end, the latter had already blown up the railway bridge downstream in the face of a *coup de main* company from 2nd Battalion.

It is not inappropriate to reflect in this case upon the 'what might have beens' if the air drop at Arnhem had been made just a little closer to the bridge and thus saved time. If a Company had arrived one hour earlier at the northern end of the bridge, the platoon which Frost sent across to seize the southern end might well have reached its objective. Two hours earlier and it is very unlikely that the Company from 9th SS Panzer which, by only a few minutes, frustrated Adams in his attempt to seize Nijmegen bridge, would have been unable to cross the river from Arnhem on its mission. In that event the narrow carpet from the Meuse Escaut canal would have been laid almost in one piece, broken here and there only by minor demolitions and a gap of six miles separating the southern bastion of 82nd Division from the vanguard of Guards Armoured Division.

But already Guards Armoured Division and its flanking infantry division supports had run into precisely the kind of trouble envisaged by the pre-war Dutch study. It was simplicity itself for handfuls of German troops to block defiles and delay the advance, despite the preponderant firepower brought to bear by waves of rocket-firing fighter bombers and intense artillery fire. By nightfall the Guards were only six miles on (the resistance of high-grade paratroops and SS troops proving extremely hard to overcome) with the town of Eindhoven, Horrock's objective for the first day, still five miles distant. And there they stopped for the night in close harbour as was the usual procedure except in the most special circumstances.

In the aftermath of Arnhem, opinions were passed around that if the 11th Armoured Division had been employed instead of the Guards there would have been no halt, that Eindhoven would have fallen that night and that the charge to Nijmegen and Arnhem would have been that much swifter and perhaps crowned with a full link-up and success. This opinion seems largely to have been based upon the remarkable 40-mile advance in darkness which had been made by 11th Armoured to Amiens on 30/31 August. But the situation to the south of Eindhoven was a lot different from the previous one in Belgium. The enemy were fighting better, the terrain was enclosed, not open; and there was only one good road. So utter confusion might have been caused in a night action, perhaps by a disastrous collision with the Americans, whose positions were not known, if not from enemy ambush. Yet, although the Guards Armoured waited until dawn, one is left wondering why its infantry did not attempt to push forward patrols on foot, especially since the distance was short and there was nothing to indicate a monstrously strong enemy presence to the front. But nobody, not even General Horrocks, who was renowned for calling for special efforts to maintain momentum, applied dynamic pressure. Instead routine procedures of replenishment and rest were permitted, leaving the enemy to re-establish his defences in the woods ahead. Maybe the infantry would have been held up. Probably they would have shaken the enemy and made it easier for the armour to break through on the 18th. Also let it be noted that a complete squadron of armoured cars from the Household Cavalry did manage initially to break through on its own to join the Americans, the enemy having abandoned their guns and fled.

XXX Corps's wasted 24 hours, plus the inclement weather, determined the failure of 'Market Garden', sealed the fate of 1st Airborne Division and lost Montgomery's praiseworthy gamble to shorten the war by several months. It would be 0820 hrs on the 19th before the Guards made contact with 82nd Division at Grave and another 36 hours before brilliant and gallant charges by paratroops and guardsmen at last seized crossings over the Waal, the big road bridge falling intact into Allied hands because of Model's insistence that it be preserved for German use. For it was not the destruction of the alleged demolition mechanism which preserved the bridge, but the vague directions given by Model and his Chief of Staff, allowing discretion to the bridge garrison commander, which permitted the bridge to be blown only when under threat of imminent enemy capture. Not until four hours after the bridge had been stormed, crossed and its demolition charges actually made safe, did Model give the order to blow, by which time all contact had been lost with the garrison for at least two hours.

As for the weather, in England it had turned unkind before dawn on the 18th, thick mist delaying the departure of the second wave of airborne reinforcements and supplies to First Airborne Army. When they did arrive, five hours later, having this time suffered heavier casualties en route, the momentum of the offensive had diminished as German pressure against the flanks of the corridor and the by now tightly encircled 1st Airborne Division at Arnhem increased. Command and communications problems grew more acute and eroded the initiative. The intended link-up between 101st Division and XXX Corps was impaired because a glider containing the British signals detachment failed to arrive, thus also forfeiting what might have proved a useful relay link with 1st Airborne Division, which was completely out of touch with the outside world. When Gavin suggested to Browning on the 18th that he should at once attack the bridge at Nijmegen, the Corps Commander demurred because XXX Corps was nowhere in sight and it seemed prudent instead to concentrate on strengthening the division's perimeter against attack. He might have done better to adopt the motto of Sergeant Paddy McCory, a tank commander in Guards Armoured Division: 'When in doubt, lash out.' As it was, he seems mentally to have written off the entire operation's chances by timidity and adherence to the pre-operation appreciation of ground and enemy threat.

Enemy pressure, communications black-outs and command breakdown inevitably plagued 1st Airborne Division in a situation of wilting initiatives. They piled one upon another in favour of the Germans who had only to maintain their strong defensive positions. When it proved impossible for the remainder of 1st Parachute Brigade to fight its way through to Frost at the bridge, a purely defensive perimeter had eventually to be occupied in Oosterbeek, a suburb far distant from the drop zones, thus making re-supply extremely difficult and haphazard by aircraft flying in the face of intense ground fire. In the absence of Urquhart, the divisional commander, who was cut off among the enemy and with his radio destroyed, Brigadier P. H. W. Hicks, commander of 1st Air Landing Brigade, had taken over and attempted to push through to the bridge. With the unavoidably late arrival of Brigadier J. W. Hackett with his 4th Parachute Brigade on the afternoon of the 18th, tension arose between him and Hicks due to anomalies in their age and seniority. Such things matter to ambitious leaders! Hicks was older than Hackett but junior in seniority. Lewis Golden, who was present at the meeting between the two men, at which a revised plan was imposed by Hicks, recalls his embarrassment 'to hear two senior officers expressing strong differences over the best way to use the newly arrived brigade'. This did not prevent them resolving their difficulties sensibly and having the division in as good shape as possible in the circumstances before Urquhart escaped to his own side next morning.

1st Airborne's main internal difficulties were to a large extent caused by radio communications failures. Long ago it had been realized that none of the sets in use were sufficiently reliable or robust enough to withstand the shock of air dropping. Furthermore, only the No 19 Set, which was issued to armoured and infantry units, had a range greater than 5 miles in daylight working conditions, and this was frequently reduced through static interference at night. These technical weaknesses, compounded by a maladroit signals plan, loss of sets in action, persistent interference from nearby enemy and friendly sets working on overcrowded frequencies, constrained signallers to desperate improvizations to make contact attempts which rarely worked. The end product inevitably was a debased command and control network together with impaired co-ordination leading to still greater waste of severely diminished combat and administrative resources.

The unreliability of airborne radio sets has frequently been criticized, but it merely reflected the long-standing inadequacy of all British infantry communications. Unlike the armoured and artillery arms which, pre-war, had struggled hard to obtain suitable sets, the infantry's inertia and lack of interest in the subject had worked to their considerable disadvantage. Starting with the premise that the subject was 'too difficult', infantry leaders proved this to their own

---

CRITICAL FLAWS

▶ The bad compromise of German strategic deployment and subsequent mis-employment of mobile forces in the defence of France.

▶ The existence of an inadequate SHAEF command and control network in the aftermath of the breakout from Normandy.

▶ The failure of Montgomery to give priority to the clearance of the sea approaches to the port of Antwerp.

▶ The approach of Eisenhower and Brereton to the employment of First Airborne Army.

▶ The failure of the Army and Corps commanders to impose Montgomery's aim and the sense of urgency needed to capture the vital bridges at all costs without a moment's delay.

▶ The existence of inadequate field radio communications for Allied airborne forces due to misdirected development in the past of the necessary radio sets.

---

satisfaction by understating their requirements, allowing themselves to be lumbered with useless equipment and not insisting upon higher standards of radio usage by their commanders. Instinctively they clung to the cumbersome methods of the First World War without understanding what a boon to tactical control good, manpack sets might be.

Better communications at Arnhem might just have turned the scales. For example, the stream of demands from Urquhart and his staff, giving precise tactical Intelligence and underlining the urgency of immediate relief, might have stirred Browning and Horrocks to greater offensive activity and Brereton to intensifying the air effort before it was too late. It was, indeed, far too late when, due to continuing bad weather, the Polish Brigade was dropped two days after it should have been, south of the bridge on 21 September in the face of intense enemy fire and just two hours too late to make firm contact with the British on the north bank at Heveadorp. And although XXX Corps's armour and infantry was at last advancing from Nijmegen, it was across difficult ground in the face of stiff enemy resistance and sapped by an administrative tail which was being threatened and cut every now and then by German attacks against the single main supply route.

By the 22nd any chance there had been of sustaining 1st Airborne to make 'Market Garden' prevail had vanished. The best that could be hoped for was an operation to save as many men as possible from the trap in which they were held with ever-dwindling supplies, above all, ammunition. Yet time and again, because of inadequate radio communications, the weary paratroopers had watched brave pilots flying through a hail of fire to discharge those cargoes into enemy hands, since, it had proved impossible to notify the airmen of the correct dropping zones. Likewise, frequent opportunities to direct air attacks and artillery fire against the enemy pressing in from all sides were forfeited because it was impossible to speak to the airmen or to the gunners. It was a major reason for 'Market's failure that a long-range airborne penetration was attempted without compatible long-range radio communication facilities.

Without doubt both the paratrooper and the tank commander whose cross words preface this chapter had something to complain about. The fault was not theirs. They and their junior commanders had given all they had, staking everything on Montgomery's justifiable gamble. Unfortunately not all the senior players at the table were convinced of the game's feasibility or psychologically adjusted to so risky a venture. Virtually all the errors had been shared by all the senior commanders, the buck starting at the top with a future President of the United States. Chiefly, however, the blame, in my opinion, has to be borne by the two Corps commanders for not over-riding their divisional commander's natural concern for security at Nijmegen (instead of driving all-out for the bridge at once) and for permitting ordered procedures to prevail south of Eindhoven. This is supported by the memory of a remark in my hearing by one of those involved, General Horrocks, who said that the main – perhaps the sole – function of a corps commander in battle is ruthlessly to ensure that the aim of the operation is maintained. Neither he nor Browning effectively did this at the crucial moments of 'Market Garden'.

14

ILLUSIONS OF INVINCIBILITY

The Pacific Campaign, 1942

Five months after the half-successful gamble at Pearl Harbor, Admiral Yamamoto was still planning for the complete naval victory which would ensure his nation's survival in the war to save its honour. The sinking by aircraft of two British battleships off Malaya in December 1941 (the outcome of operating them without fighter cover); the overrunning of the Philippines, The Dutch East Indies and Burma; the crushing of Allied naval power in the Java Sea and the Indian Ocean and the establishment of the complete outer perimeter of defence covering the new Japanese empire (as envisaged by the original War Plan) offered no guarantee of security in the eyes of the Naval C-in-C. In the spring of 1942, with the American carrier force still at large and the war in the West and in Russia by no means settled in Germany's favour, the US Pacific Fleet had yet to be brought to the ultimate confrontation. At the same time the Japanese Army deemed it essential to strengthen by expansion its outer perimeter of defence.

The fact that two major operations were being planned to take place within a short period of each other was an indication of high Japanese morale verging on an overconfidence such as had prompted the Germans to invade Russia after the conquest of Western Europe. Unlike the situation of 1941 in the West, however, that in the East was less in the predator's favour. Capture of oil fields had not yet been turned to good account in having them deliver significant quantities. Possession of so large an empire now demanded excessive expenditure of fuel against an undefeated opponent who, on 18 April, had the audacity to bomb Tokyo, rather ineffectually, with carrier-borne aircraft, resulting in the fateful Plan MO to expand the southern defensive perimeter. Unbeknown to the Japanese, almost every operational plan they hatched and sent via radio messages encoded by their sophisticated Type 97 machine (the equivalent of, but not the same as, Germany's Enigma) was being read by the American Magic and Ultra organization (with the assistance of Bombe computers). This was largely due to a serious security lapse on the Japanese part when they persisted in compromising the Type 97 by transmitting simultaneously the similar Type 91A, whose cyphers had already been broken by the Americans. Furthermore, although Japanese warships, aircraft and their excellent Long Lance torpedoes gave their extremely well-trained officers and men a distinct and quite unexpected initial superiority over the Americans and British (both of whom out of traditional disrespect for Orientals, had been far too prejudiced and, therefore, inclined, pre-war, to ignore or underrate Japanese technology and talent), they lacked one vital instrument of modern battle – radar. Only scanty information about it had filtered through veils of secrecy from Europe and America, with no help at all from their ally Germany. Such research as Japan's own scientists and technologists had attempted, had little bearing upon the essential areas of detection and ranging. By modern standards the Japanese were half-blind, depending on the aid of old-fashioned optical instruments and, by night, flares and searchlights.

Plan MO, aimed at the seizure of Port Moresby in New Guinea, demanded a serious diversion of carrier strength from Plan AL, an attack upon the Aleutian Islands, and Plan MI, an advance into the central Pacific via the island of Midway, to which Yamamoto attached the greatest importance designed as it was to bring the US Pacific Fleet to battle, which MO did not pretend to do. The planning errors committed by Yamamoto for MO were the products of overconfidence and inadequate Intelligence. In the belief that the American carrier force was somewhere to the northward, returning from the strike on Tokyo, and with nothing to indicate that a part of it might be in the South-West Pacific, he committed only two heavy and one light carrier to the support of the Port Moresby invasion squadron and proceeded to divide his forces into no less than seven groups. This he would not have done if he had known that Admiral Chester Nimitz, C-in-C, Pacific Fleet, at Hawaii, had before him, on 24 April, clear evidence of MO along with indications that the landing would take place on 10 May. It was thus possible for Nimitz to prepare a welcome for the Japanese by having Task Force 17 (Admiral Frank Fletcher) concentrate to the east of the Coral Sea in sufficient time to make a surprise blow against the three Japanese carriers, a manoeuvre which might have had bountiful results if only Fletcher had kept secret his forces' presence. But the fruits of Intelligence are the measure of its users' belief in its credibility, and at Coral Sea (as elsewhere noted in this book) American users were prone to distraction by reports of what were subsidiary or diversionary operations.

A summary of the battle is a catalogue of tactical mistakes. Of, initially, the absence of Admiral William Halsey's two carriers since they were unable to return from the Tokyo raid, replenish at Hawaii and reach the Coral Sea in time to take part. Of the premature disclosure of the American carriers to the Japanese under Admiral Inouye at Rabaul, by the employment of *Yorktown*'s aircraft against a minor Japanese landing on the island of Tulagi, and the subsequent gropings by both sides to locate each other and get in the first blow. That Admiral Takagi preferred, for some obscure reason, to use only the limited number of floatplanes carried by his battleships and cruisers instead of the larger number of aircraft in his two heavy carriers; and that Nimitz was handicapped by the strict rule that forbade him sending reconnaissance aircraft into the operational zone of General Douglas MacArthur (who lacked sufficient aircraft to cover his sector of the battle zone) are just two reasons why contact, when it happened, was memorable for a series of surprises and hasty, inaccurate judgements. Errors by individuals in the heat of combat far from the scan (visual or radar) of their commanders generated dire repercussions. A Japanese pilot who, on 7 May, reported an American oil tanker and its escorting destroyer as, respectively, a carrier and a cruiser, lead to a series of attacks which were not only fatal to the targets concerned, but thoroughly misleading to Inouye and Takagi who momentarily concluded that they had found the main enemy force and were therefore able to continue MO without fear. Likewise, the report by an American pilot of two enemy cruisers and two destroyers, which was wrongly decoded as two carriers and four heavy cruisers, led to the light Japanese carrier *Shoho* receiving the full and fatal attention of Fletcher's combined carrier strike forces in clear weather. While hesitation on Takagi's part again to commit his strike force against the two American carriers (which at last had been properly located), led to his weary pilots being dispatched into thick weather, late in the day, and without locating their targets; a disastrous encounter with fighters compounded by further losses from landings in the sea due to shortage of fuel at dusk. In this débâcle chance played its part, but Takagi's ineptitude cannot be overlooked.

When the two opposing heavy carrier forces did at last come to blows on the 8th, the outcome simply underlined the superiority of the

Japanese airmen's training, command and control procedures. The American airmen, although they managed to inflict serious damage with bombs on the carrier *Shokaku*, wasted time co-ordinating their attacks (thus enabling the Japanese to launch fighters) and failed to score torpedo hits because they attacked out of range. But the Japanese worked as a superbly practised team, scoring torpedo and bomb strikes which eventually sank the carrier *Lexington* and badly damaged *Yorktown*. Thus in terms of carriers sunk, the advantage accrued marginally to the Japanese and should also have been their complete victory if Inouye at Rabaul had not, even in the incorrect belief that both enemy carriers were sunk, postponed MO and if Takagi had, despite his heavy loss in aircraft, once more sent out his few remaining machines from the carrier *Zuikaku* to finish off *Yorktown*. Yamamoto's order to Inouye and Takagi to continue the action and destroy all enemy forces arrived too late for implementation. A half-hearted spirit, similar to Nagumo's at Pearl Harbor, took precedence over Admiral Togo's single-minded example at Tsushima. So Yamamoto's Plan MI was deprived of *Shokaku*, in need of extensive repairs, and *Zuikaku*, rendered ineffectual for five weeks due to losses of aircraft and crews.

Many of the errors committed during MO came from inexperience in the tactics and techniques of a totally unique form of naval combat in which the main combatants were scores, if not hundreds, of miles apart. Practice alone would teach the Admirals and their squadron commanders how to make better use of their equipment, although the chances of the Japanese benefiting in full were reduced by the fundamental errors of their airmen in claiming two American carriers sunk in the Coral Sea. That being the case, to launch MI against Midway with four (instead of six) heavy and two light carriers to spearhead the Fleet's seven battleships seemed to achieve safety in numbers set against the 'certain' knowledge that the Americans were without battleships and had only two carriers available, both of which were assumed (without good reason) to be in the South Pacific. It never occurred to the Japanese that Halsey had returned to Hawaii or that the damaged *Yorktown* had also escaped there; she, by the prodigious efforts of 1,400 men, would be patched up for battle in three days. For neither their patrolling submarines nor their agents in Hawaii spotted or reported these developments to the Japanese commanders.

The Combined Japanese Fleet which set forth in four main groups at the end of May to execute Operations MI and AL had lost that fine cutting edge which had distinguished the one which had struck in December 1941. After six months of virtually ceaseless operations, men were in need of rest and re-training, ships and machines required overhaul. At the top of the command tree there brooded unhealthy divisions of opinion and loyalties amidst a dangerous over-confidence amounting to swollen-headedness. Yamamoto had failed completely to convince even his closest colleagues of the soundness or practicality of MI–AL. There were those who said that even if the American carrier force was brought to its doom, the capture of Midway must eventually lead to over-extension of Japanese resources in its defence and thus be counter-productive. And Admiral Nagumo, who rated American fighting spirit poor, it is said declined to criticize the plan's defects to the C-in-C's face because he knew Yamamoto blamed him for witholding the third strike at Pearl Harbor. 'If I opposed Midway this time, I'd almost certainly be labelled a coward, so I'd rather go and get killed at Midway just to show him.'

Several of the key men in the air strike force were sick and unable to pull their full weight or to fly. At crucial moments Yamamoto would suffer from stomach troubles which eventually were diagnosed as worms. Physical weaknesses brought on by strain impaired mental clarity and conviction. Elaborate plans were laid without access to credible Intelligence about the enemy. The submarines, which might have discovered the true whereabouts of the American carriers, were 24 hours late getting into position and thus missed sighting Nimitz's only trump cards, his three carriers as they sailed from Hawaii for a precise rendezvous with an enemy whose plans were fully laid bare by SIGINT. Yamamoto was indeed gambling without security, yet not without a certain logic if it is accepted that a thoroughly decisive victory over the American carrier force, which had escaped in December, was to offset the otherwise inevitable wrecking of his nation due to its initial cupidity. For if the American carriers were destroyed the dividends from this coup would be boundless. Every Allied naval installation from Australasia through Hawaii to the West Coast of America would be exposed to raiding forces.

Sloppy planning, poor staff work and an unusually high percent-age of mistakes perpetrated by the lower echelons of command plagued the Japanese throughout. Whereas the American high com-

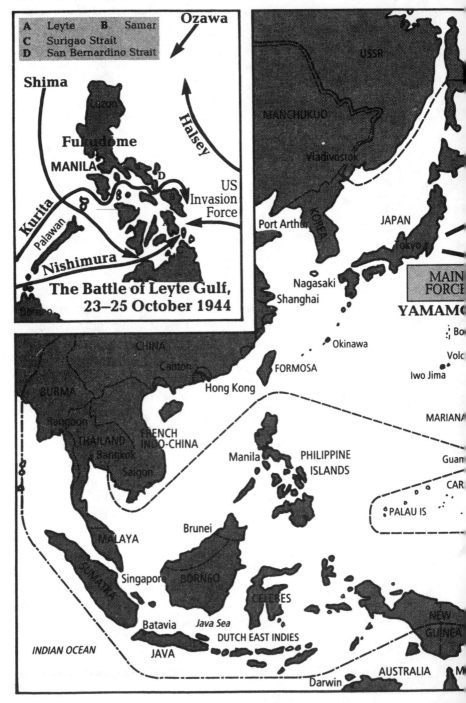

A   Leyte   B   Samar
C   Surigao Strait
D   San Bernardino Strait

Ozawa

Shima

Luzon

Fukudome

MANILA

Halsey

D

Kurita

Palawan

US
Invasion
Force

Nishimura

**The Battle of Leyte Gulf,
23–25 October 1944**

USSR

MANCHUKUO

Vladivostok

KOREA

Port Arthur

JAPAN

Tokyo

MAIN
FORCE

YAMAMO

Nagasaki
Shanghai

Bo

Volc

Okinawa

Iwo Jima

CHINA

Canton

FORMOSA

BURMA

Hong Kong

MARIANA

Rangoon

FRENCH
INDO-CHINA

THAILAND
Bangkok

Saigon

Manila

PHILIPPINE
ISLANDS

Guam

CAR

PALAU IS

MALAYA

Brunei

SUMATRA

Singapore   BORNEO

CELEBES

NEW
GUINEA

Batavia   Java Sea

DUTCH EAST INDIES

INDIAN OCEAN   JAVA

AUSTRALIA   M

Darwin

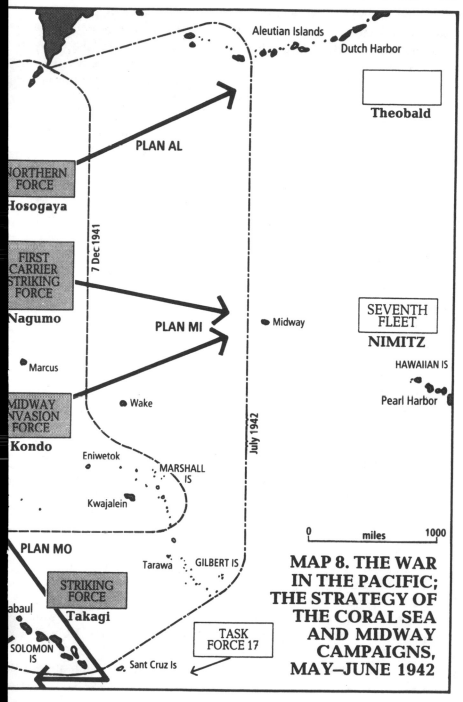

Aleutian Islands

Dutch Harbor

Theobald

PLAN AL

NORTHERN FORCE

Hosogaya

7 Dec 1941

FIRST CARRIER STRIKING FORCE

Nagumo

PLAN MI

Midway

SEVENTH FLEET

NIMITZ

HAWAIIAN IS

Marcus

Wake

MIDWAY INVASION FORCE

Kondo

Pearl Harbor

July 1942

Eniwetok

MARSHALL IS

Kwajalein

0   miles   1000

PLAN MO

Tarawa   GILBERT IS

STRIKING FORCE

Takagi

abaul

SOLOMON IS

TASK FORCE 17

Sant Cruz Is

MAP 8. THE WAR IN THE PACIFIC; THE STRATEGY OF THE CORAL SEA AND MIDWAY CAMPAIGNS, MAY–JUNE 1942

mand, well provided as it was with excellent Intelligence, made few mistakes of fundamental importance. Nagumo was not told that reconnaissance of Pearl Harbor by a long-range sea-plane had been called off. He therefore operated in a fool's paradise of over-security to the last, a security impaired by Yamamoto's faulty plan. For fundamentally the C-in-C, by his deployment and allocation of forces, pushed Nagumo's strike force out on a limb. At the distance of about 350 miles, which separated the Combined Fleet from Nagumo, no immediate support whatsoever could be given to the carriers, the two battleships and their three cruiser escorts. Furthermore, when committing Nagumo to the vanguard role with the task of pounding Midway on 4 June, Yamamoto denied him the maximum air support possible by diverting two light carriers to AL and keeping a third with the MI Support Force.

But it was the basic and totally unjustified assumption of the absence of an American carrier force upon which all foundered. To begin with there was the strange loose end of a contradiction. If the enemy carriers were far off elsewhere, when and how would the much-desired 'decisive battle' take place? Be that as it may, because of false assumptions, Nagumo carelessly ordered only a perfunctory search reconnaissance ahead by a minimal number of float planes from three cruisers as he concentrated upon the blow against Midway. At that moment he was aware only that his force had been discovered by Midway-based aircraft and submarines. Soon, he assumed, his bombers and fighters would overwhelm the defenders of Midway, creating immense damage while his carriers' defences would make short work of Midway's bombers. Nevertheless, at 0700 hrs, Lieutenant Tomonaga Joichi, the bombing force commander, over-impressed by the anti-aircraft fire, radioed that a second strike would be needed.

Within the space of the next 30 minutes the fate of Nagumo's carriers, the war in the Pacific and the Japanese nation was decided by a bizarre mixture of chance and Japanese incompetence. As Nagumo was mulling over the pros and cons of a second strike with Commander Genda Minoru, his very experienced but fever-ridden Air Staff Officer, Admirals Fletcher and Spruance were supervising the launch of a strike force of fighters, dive-bombers and torpedo aircraft against Nagumo's carriers, whose location had now been accurately plotted by reconnaissance. If the experienced Commander

Fuchida Mitsuo had been well enough to command the Japanese bombers over Midway, instead of the less experienced Tomonaga, he might have rested content with a first strike. But, with the air attack from Midway actually in progress at 0710 hrs, Genda and Nagumo, haunted by irresolution at Pearl Harbor, felt unable to refuse a second blow. This meant striking below the aircraft ranged on deck in order to remove their torpedoes and fit general-purpose bombs – a time consuming and laborious process which started at 0715 hrs. But a safe enough decision by Nagumo in the absence still of reports by his reconnaissance aircraft of enemy surface forces. Yet had he delayed but fifteen minutes history might have been changed. The maxim, 'order, counter-order brings disorder' prevailed, with worse to come.

The minimal reconnaissance by the float planes had been reduced further by bad weather and one plane's engine trouble. Of rather far-reaching importance, the cruiser *Tone*'s machines had been delayed for 30 minutes by a catapult fault, and it was these whose zones of search pointed at the American carriers. As it happens, if Amari Hiroshi, the pilot of *Tone* 4, had correctly calculated his course, he would have missed seeing the enemy ships, leaving Nagumo to continue in blithe ignorance of what was in store and perhaps saving him from his next fatal error. For when Amari came through on the radio at 1728 to report '10 ships, probably enemy . . . distance 240 miles . . .', and at 1745 confirmed it but still without mentioning carriers, Nagumo correctly guessed that there would be carriers present and changed his mind again. 'Remove the bombs and put back the torpedoes' was the order which threw the by now weary aircraft and armament handlers into turmoil, littering the hangers with bombs with no time to send them below to the safety of the magazines. But at 0820 it all looked worthwhile when *Tone* 4 came through to report, at last, what looked like a carrier. Why he had taken nearly an hour to verify this is unknown.

The Midway first strike force was due home in 20 minutes, was short of fuel, damaged and needing to land. Faced with the sudden dilemma about whether to risk the returning aircraft and give priority to launching the anti-carrier strike, Nagumo decided to have the Midway strike land in order to prepare it as soon as possible for a second blow at Midway. This meant delaying the anti-carrier torpedo force by about an hour, but to him the risk seemed acceptable even if that meant abandoning the principle of making the first strike against enemy carriers. Chaos above and below decks reached fresh heights as the second strike force was struck below prior to the torpedo bombers being sent above deck. Yet they were so close, a mere ten minutes short of launching, when the American torpedo bombers arrived. For the Americans, the ideal tactics, a fighter escort covering dive-bombers attacking simultaneously with torpedo bombers, had gone disastrously astray. The fighters and dive-bombers failed to make their rendezvous and, because of failures in communication and initiative by squadron leaders, the fighters orbitted at 20,000 feet while the torpedo bombers made their attack in glorious isolation – and were shot to pieces without scoring a single hit. All they seemed to achieve was further delay to the Japanese launching their own anti-carrier strike force, because of the need for the carriers to take evasive action. They did at least dislocate the Japanese defence formation and divert the air defence controller's attention, thus encouraging the fighters and the carrier's anti-aircraft gunners to neglect high-altitude search while combat went on at sea level. Yet it was enough. At this moment of general disorientation and confusion, American dive-bombers by luck found their targets and were plunging to the attack almost unopposed.

It required but nine bomb hits to alter the naval balance in the Pacific and lose Japan the war. It was the timing of their explosions amid a jumble of aircraft, loose bombs and torpedoes and open fuel lines above and below unarmoured flight decks on all four Japanese carriers which produced the fatal infernos. The only consolation for Yamamoto came with the report that aircraft from the carrier *Hiryu* had, on the 4th, damaged *Yorktown*, before she was herself put down by repeated American air attacks on the 5th; and that the submarine *I 168* had finished off *Yorktown* on the 7th. Apart from that he had merely to be firm with members of his staff who, anxious to save honour, counselled persisting with the attack on Midway with the battleships. 'That of all naval tactics, firing one's guns at an island, is considered the most stupid,' he said in dismissal, in the realization that his ships, lacking air cover, would be overwhelmed by enemy air attack. Mistakes quite often appear absurd and this one by Yamamoto was no exception. Bombardment by battleships and smaller warships had already repeatedly been demonstrated as a far more potent, accurate means of *sustained* fire support of landings than bombing. The crux of the débâcle lay in Yamamoto's initial basic error of

---

CRITICAL FLAWS

▶ The unwieldy complexity of Japanese plans.

▶ Inadequate Japanese staff work, reconnaissance and Intelligence.

▶ Yamamoto's failure to concentrate his forces and Nagumo's inflexibility when using them in crisis.

---

dispersing his forces. If he had kept the Combined Fleet united there would have been no need for Nagumo to writhe on the horns of a dilemma, torn between the conflicting desire to hit Midway, attack the enemy carriers and protect his own. Warships, shielded by carrier aircraft, could have concentrated upon supporting the landing while bombers sought out the enemy carriers. It was not simply, as has been suggested, that Yamamoto's gamblers' luck was running out. He had got his basic doctrine wrong and allowed it to dictate a faulty plan.

Victory for Yamamoto and Nagumo at Midway would have ensured their ability to make life hell for the Allies for at least another year. Destruction of the carriers, compounded by the losses of Coral Sea, robbed them of the initiative and snapped the linchpin of their nation's security. Denied the strong carrier force with its incomparable and virtually irreplaceable air crews, defence of the empire's new outer perimeter by the intervention of an invincible central reserve was undermined. Worse still, the enemy took fresh heart. The Allies were vastly encouraged to attack and, in August, to launch a tentative – so tentative in its risks that some on the Allied side nicknamed it Operation 'Shoestring' – counter-offensive designed to seize the island of Guadalcanal as the first step in the way back to the Philippines and along the road to Tokyo.

Beyond any doubt, even after making full allowance for the random workings of chance and luck, it was Nagumo and Genda who, between them, lost the Battle of Midway for Japan. It was their counter-orders which, for dubious advantages, prevented the Japanese anti-carrier strike force being launched on the mission which, at all times, demanded priority over all else. Nagumo, by inflexibility of mind in sticking rigidly to the original plan had apportioned too great an importance to an unsinkable island instead of to the much more vulnerable and powerful enemy aircraft carriers. It was as if his natural reservations about carriers had dictated his advice. For it was hardly likely that, as commander of a line of battleships, he would have similarly denied them the use of their main armament in battle. Be that as it may, Midway could have waited and still been ripe for the picking; the enemy carriers simply had to be knocked out even if, in the meantime, one or two of Nagumo's carriers were sunk or damaged. Only by delaying the strike could he risk annihilation. He therefore chose the only wrong course possible.

15

SUICIDAL IMPULSES
The Battle of Leyte Gulf

A mistake which the Japanese made, almost to the bitter end, was their under-estimate of American combat prowess. Even so imaginative a commander as Yamamoto, with his firsthand knowledge of and contacts with westerners, was prone to fall into that trap – and pay the penalty. Like the Germans who, on first contact with the American Army in November 1942, chose to denigrate their latest opponent, the Japanese Army's contempt for the Americans in the Philippines in 1941 and after was not in the least bit diminished by evidence of the brave resolve with which their enemy had shattered the Japanese Navy. When American marines and soldiers landed at Tulagi and Guadalcanal on 7 August, the Army command not only knew very little about their enemy's élite Marine amphibious force (which for more than 20 years had prepared for the sort of battle in which they now were engaged), but they also chose to despise it and, in the months to come, repeatedly sent inadequate forces to rout out the intruders. The outcome was a prolonged battle of attrition without hope of victory for the Japanese when they condemned their limited naval, air and land forces to a slugging match with an opponent whose resources were almost inexhaustible.

Repeatedly as would the Japanese inflict heavy losses on American warships and aircraft in the battle for supply to the Japanese Army on Guadalcanal, they were defeated eventually in their aim by sheer weight of numbers and technology. At one point neither side had an aircraft carrier remaining serviceable and it was battleships, cruisers, destroyers and land-based aircraft which held the stage. Here, again, the more experienced Japanese repeatedly outfought the Americans – especially at night – yet finally they were checked by two decisive developments, neither of which they had foreseen. First, the almost impenetrable barrage of anti-aircraft gunfire being produced by batteries of automatic weapons filling every spare space on the American ships. This not only acted as a sure shield against conventional low-level attacks, it rapidly annihilated the crack members of both the Navy and Army Air Arms and led to the moment at which it was recognized that, even if an aircraft did manage to complete its attack, it was most unlikely to escape. This led to the adoption of suicide missions in which experienced pilots flew their aircraft into the targets simply as a guarantee that their almost inevitable death would not be wasted. Second, the demonstration of radar's value as a detection and ranging device when the US battle-ship *Washington* picked off the battleship *Kirishima* in the dark at 8,400 yards and wrecked her with nine hits out of 75 shots in eight minutes. This to the Japanese, who still were years behind in radar development, was a disaster.

The withdrawal imposed upon the Japanese at Guadalcanal, because they were no longer able to supply the garrison, was the inevitable outcome of their failure to face up from the outset to an inherent imbalance of power. With the strategic initiative snatched away and an increasingly preponderant and, more importantly, far better led and trained opponent hustling them, the Japanese commanders generated errors to a disproportionately larger extent than the Americans. Naturally both sides made mistakes and both, as was to be expected in a war taking place across an immense expanse of the globe's principal ocean, suffered from communications break-downs, misunderstandings and disagreements. In addition, common-or-garden outbreaks of ineptitude at all levels of command were inevitable among forces the vast majority of whose personnel had so recently been civilians without a morsel of military upbringing or background. But in the higher direction of the war it was the Japanese who suffered most because of two basic failings – chronic under-estimation of the enemy and errors induced by ignorance of certain key aspects of technology.

In basic terms, the credo of superiority ingrained in the Japanese élite, which had encouraged them to make war by astute surprise with a technically superior force, also conspired to shut their minds (even sometimes their eyes) to the concept or evidence that the enemy might be capable of overtaking them. The use of radar to sink ships at night was one early and shocking example of this looming imbalance. Far more unsettling was the abrupt breaching of their island-based, linear defences by long-range, self-contained amphibious forces which concentrated upon seizing key locations in a concerted drive towards the heart of the Empire, bypassing and neutralizing strong points as they advanced. Commonplace as bypassing tactics are in land warfare, this was a naval technique unforeseen in its depth and scope by the Japanese because they had been industrially incapable of it themselves and therefore excluded it from their forecasts of future enemy intentions. They could never have built so many sophisticated landing craft or logistic support equipment such as American dockyards and factories turned out in a deluge. And even if they had foreseen the advent of deep amphibious penetration and island-hopping, they would have been hard pressed to counter it once their vital carrier force had been dissipated, as dissipated it must have been even without Midway. Japanese lapses in intellectual performance could only occasionally be laid at the doors of individuals. Their roots lay in a social and military system which educated and conditioned an entire caste to take up arms as the better and more evocatively honourable way of satisfying the demands of ambition and expansion. But, as they were learning the hard way, the pursuit of honour has a nasty habit of leaving even the bravest in the lurch.

The exaltation of the Japanese honour code was not only costly, it included anomalies and inconsistencies. For example, whereas aircrew were provided with parachutes to preserve their undeniably valuable expertise (and their lives) in the event of being shot down, there prevailed an idea that a ship's captain should go down with his ship, copied from an old British tradition of the captain being the last to leave a stricken vessel – a practical tradition linked, in part, to the ramifications of salvage law and, the need to do everything possible to the last to save the crew and command. As a result of this tradition, warped by bushido, a very high proportion of top naval commanders – figures up to 90 per cent are quoted – were lost, thus depriving the navy of men whose 20 years service or more was invaluable. Indeed the entire concept of dishonour in surrender, which had its roots in the *samurai* tradition of a past age, was entirely inappropriate and utterly wasteful in a modern setting where no industrial nation could afford to waste its best brains and technologists. That was simply a short cut to the nation's suicide at the hands of an outmoded system. Moreover, the Japanese ban on surrender, stiffened only in part by the Allies' proclamation of the Unconditional Surrender policy, doomed to extermination in hopeless situations thousands of Japanese who might otherwise have been saved for their country's service in the future.

Nothing like these errors were ever made by the Americans and their allies who, though prepared to sacrifice lives for a worthwhile project, would always be bound by political, economic and humanitarian Western philosophies to economize in their expenditure of lives. Whenever serious losses or problems occurred, whether errors of omission or commission, the tendency to press on regardless with faulty methods was usually suppressed. Take, for example, the multiple set-backs and casualties of the landings by Rear-Admiral Kelly Turner's amphibious forces at Makin and Tarawa in November 1943. At Makin the landing craft grounded at an unacceptable distance from the shore because the hydrographic hazards had not been thoroughly explored by close personal reconnaissance beforehand. Turner described the landing as 'My poorest appraisal of beach areas for a landing during the whole war . . . That's why I pushed the development of Underwater Demolition Teams (UDT) so hard.' It was just fortunate that the enemy at Makin did not put up as tough a fight as they later did at Tarawa, at the price of 980 Marines killed out of 5,000 put ashore. At Tarawa, of course, there were many other causes for the slaughter besides minimal beach reconnaissance by air reconnaissance also – such errors as inadequate anticipation of known adverse currents, insufficient allowance for the restrictive performance of landing craft and miscalculations of H-Hour in relation to speed of approach – all of which lead to confusion and loss. These upsets, plus an over-optimistic reliance on naval gunfire, to neutralize the defences, and poor planning and execution of air support for the landing, all contributed to the excessive casualty bill. Yet so much which went wrong could have been averted if lessons of a similar nature learnt at Dieppe, fourteen months before, had been studied and applied in the Pacific – for the Dieppe Report had been circulated widely in plenty of time and acted upon in many other aspects. So far as embryo UDTs were concerned, if only Turner had been kept informed of work going on in connection with what would become known in Britain as COPPS (Combined Operations Pilotage Parties) and in the USA as Beach Jumpers, his problems would have been fewer. But space and time do tend to take their toll of communications, and staff are not infallible in picking out what is essential amid a plethora of information. And even the best of commanders, due to the load placed upon him, cannot be all-seeing and understanding – and Turner was a very good, foresighted commander indeed.

In the ten months following the capture of Makin and Tarawa, the Allied pincers began closing in on the Philippines via the Marshall Islands and Marianas (whence long-range heavy bomber attacks could be mounted against the Japanese homeland) and from the Solomon Islands via New Guinea. In this same period, too, the blockade of Japan was tightened to such good effect by American submarines that the oil famine, which Japan's rulers had gone to war to prevent, became acute. To some considerable extent this was their own fault for failing to promote modern anti-submarine measures. Intent upon main fleet operations on the grand scale, it was not until mid-1943 that they at last instituted a convoy system and began to replace minelaying and minesweeping gear on destroyers with a sufficient number of the latest depth-charge throwers. Yet their detection devices and techniques fell far below those practised by the Allies in the Atlantic and elsewhere. Nor did the Japanese at first realize that American submarines, choosing largely to work on the surface, were plotting their favoured night attacks with the help of radar. Short-comings caused by so serious an oversight in technique and technology went far to cripple the Japanese economy. Some 57 per cent of the 8.5 million tons of merchant shipping she lost during the war went down to Allied submarines, along with 201 out of 686 warships. As a result her logistic distribution of vital stocks became unbalanced. In September 1944, for example, there was ample oil but a shortage of ammunition in Singapore, whereas it was the other way about in Japan – with the result that instead of, as was strategically desirable, stationing the Combined Fleet in Japan, it had to be based on Singapore.

Perhaps the most serious of all Japan's failures continued to be her ignorance of enemy penetration of her codes and cyphers which revealed all her plans and operations and, incidentally, divulged the schedule of Yamamoto's last flight when he was shot down by American fighters precisely positioned for the task. Close to a state of collapse, the Japanese should have sought the war's end at the best terms possible. But this the code of military honour resolutely forbade. As the American carrier aircraft roamed the Philippine Sea and began landings in the Marianas in June 1944, Admiral Toyoda Soemu, the C-in-C, began preparations for major action by the Combined Fleet, the final, so-called decisive, defensive battles under the name 'SHO' (meaning Victory) which, because Japanese Intelligence was totally unaware of where the Allies might strike, had to be planned to cope with any one of three contingencies – a potent recipe for last-minute haste and numerous forced errors.

The fate of 'SHO' depended absolutely upon air power which, since 1942, had slipped from Japan's grasp not only through being outnumbered but also due to her failure to introduce into service a fresh generation of aircraft to replace those which were increasingly outclassed by the latest enemy planes. The Japanese aircraft industry was beset by a mishmash of problems, exacerbated after 1941 by the onset of material shortages which delayed into production large numbers of the latest types under development. The fighter types alone, whose difficulties overlapped and were similar to those of the bombers, suffered from a policy and procurement organization which permitted research and development into many types without ensuring that improvements to power plant and armament matched advances in airframe design. Thus machines which were outclassed continued in service. In the air battles of 1943, Japanese fighters, whose pilots were mere tyros compared to the paragons of 1941, were cannon-fodder, though continuing to give a better account of themselves than is sometimes implied.

It was not only when being outflown and outfought that the Japanese pilots' inexperience told against their cause. They also marvellously exaggerated their successes with claims which, if they had been utilized only for propaganda purposes, might have been justifiable for uplifting morale (as they did), but which were wholly pernicious when accepted at face value by the staffs and taken up by commanders as data for planning. Announcements that Admiral William Halsey's Third Fleet had lost 11 carriers, 2 battleships, 3 cruisers and a destroyer, with 8 more carriers and 2 battleships damaged between 10 and 16 October 1944 off Formosa (when, in fact, only one carrier was damaged and two cruisers put out of action), led the Japanese to regard the forthcoming Operation 'SHO' with far greater optimism than it deserved.

The American landings which began on the island of Leyte in the central Philippines on 20 October, supported by the 6 old battleships, 18 light carriers and 8 cruisers of Vice-Admiral Thomas Kinkaid's Seventh Fleet, and protected to the eastwards by Halsey's 12 battleships, 9 heavy and 8 light carriers of the Third Fleet, was the trigger which set Operation 'SHO' in motion. Apart from earlier contingency planning, there was little more Admiral Toyoda could do, once he issued the alert on the 18th, to help the converging five separate groups of ships. Some came from Japan, but the majority from Singapore and Brunei while reinforcements of land-based aircraft were ferried south to provide virtually the only air cover possible in the Philippines. Loose ends remained to be tied up and it was this process, in company with previous orders issued by radio, which, of course, provided Nimitz with ample notice of what was in train. Almost as fast as the Japanese admirals received their instructions, Nimitz, by courtesy of SIGINT, was reading them too and learning that Vice-Admiral Kurita Takeo's Forces A and B (reinforced from Singapore) would sail from Brunei on 22 October, bound for the San Bernardino Strait to hit the landing area from the north, while Vice-Admiral Nishimora Shoji's Force C, reinforced by elements under Vice-Admiral Shima Kiyohide from Japan (!), was to cross Force A's course to pass through the Surigao Strait to complete a pincer movement on Kinkaid. Meanwhile, to distract attention from these diffuse manoeuvres, Vice-Admiral Ozawa Jisaburo's Mobile Strike Force would sail from Japan, taking with it one heavy and three light carriers (all that remained in service of the mighty Japanese carrier fleet, and this time embarking only 108 aircraft). This group was to act as bait for Halsey in the hope that he would be drawn away from Kurita and Nishimura in accordance with Halsey's overriding ambition to destroy what he took to be the principal enemy striking force. Meanwhile the combined Navy and Army Air Arms in the Philippines, under Vice Admiral Fukudome Shigeru, were told to give absolute priority to protecting Kurita and Nishimura in their dash for the invasion beaches, and try also to avoid getting heavily involved with Halsey.

The approach of the Japanese Admirals to the battle can only be described as fatalistic. This was a 'decisive battle' in name only, implemented in a dramatic atmosphere created by Toyoda when he referred to their 'divine mission'. The stated aim was prosaic and materialistic, with scant genuine belief in doing much more than save the Navy's honour by fighting in support of the Army to defend territory which could not, without the unacceptable moral and military consequences, be relinquished undefended. 'Hit the American transports, break up the invasion and sink as many ships as you can,' was the essence of Kurita's and Nishimura's instructions from Toyoda – without for one moment minding what happened to the virtually impotent Ozawa in the north, or what would happen if and when Halsey decided to defend the two key straits. Apart from being a complicated plan, in which only a miracle could bring about a neat junction of the southern forces, and in which the chances of Halsey's falling for the deception were remote indeed (entirely unlikely when it is realized that, through SIGINT, he knew perfectly well that Ozawa's force was a decoy), this was just about the worst project ever devised by the Japanese. Even at the time, this seems to have been realized by all those in the know (on both sides). The Americans approached the confrontation in a mood of sublime confidence, amazed that the Japanese were coming out to fight. While the Japanese, ignorant of what the enemy was doing to stop them, bore themselves into battle like *samurai* on the eve of ritual suicide, the doubters among them rallied by Kurita's pre-sailing address: 'I know that many of you are strongly opposed to this task. But the war situation is more critical than any of you can possibly know. Would it not be a shame to have the fleet remain intact while our nation perishes? . . . I am willing to accept even this ultimate assignment to storm into Leyte Gulf.'

In addition to divine inspiration, the Japanese also required good luck, and ironically, at once received it in an undesirable way. On the evening of 18 October, three days after Shima's group had departed from Japan and two days prior to Ozawa's departure, Commander T. L. Wogan, commander of a US submarine pack watching the exits from the Inland Sea, reported to Vice-Admiral C. A. Lockwood, Commander Submarines (Pacific), that since only fast vessels were entering the Inland Sea, there was no prospect of battle. Could he now return to the far more lucrative task of sinking merchant shipping? Which Lockwood permitted. This was a strange lapse on the Americans' part. Since SIGINT had warned Nimitz of Ozawa's impending movements, how was it he permitted this premature with-drawal of cover? Or, bearing in mind that virtually only Nimitz and a very select few (none of whom were allowed to be placed in a position where they might fall into enemy hands) were informed about the workings of Magic and Ultra, how was it that the Special Branch officers, tasked to feed their vital information to selected officers such as Lockwood, failed to do so? Or, if they did, how could Lockwood put hunting before vital reconnaissance as ordered by Nimitz? Whatever the cause, the fact that Ozawa sailed unobserved on the 20th was contrary to his wishes. As the essential decoy, he desired, in due course, actually to *be seen* and reported. But this was by no means the only occasion over the next few days when anomalies in the handling and exploitation of decrypts on the American part had a crucial effect on the development of the Battle of Leyte Gulf.

Less fortunate in concealing his approach was Kurita who, at 0116 hrs on the 23rd, a mere seventeen hours after sailing from Brunei, was picked up by the radar of US submarine *Darter* (in company with *Dace*) off the southern approach to Palawan Island. This provided Nimitz, Kinkaid and Halsey with their first positive Intelligence of the enemy approach, along with verification of the forecasts so confidently made by 'I'. But to the commanders of *Darter* and *Dace* the most satisfactory aspect of their encounter lay in the extraordinarily vulnerable formation adopted by the Japanese, one which was all the more incomprehensible in the laxity of its anti-submarine measures since, from the outset, Japanese ships' companies had demonstrated exaggerated fears about the submarine threat. On a frontage of 9,000 yards the Americans beheld two columns of battleships (including, in the starboard column, the mighty 64,000-ton *Yamato* and *Musashi*) headed by cruisers and flanked by destroyers, but without a single escort hunting for submarines ahead. As a result, at crack of dawn *Darter* was able, at a range of 900 yards to torpedo two cruisers in the port column, the first of which was *Atago*, Kurita's flagship. She sank eighteen minutes later, depositing Kurita and his staff in the water. A few minutes later *Dace* also managed to bag a cruiser in the starboard column.

Kurita was in advanced middle age and suffering from dengue fever. Jumping overboard from a ship engulfed in flames, swimming in the sea, being picked up by a destroyer and rapidly transferred to *Yamato*, where he had hardly been dried out before fresh problems engulfed him, was, to say the least, highly disturbing of his composure. Without doubt his subsequent performance must be judged in relation to that tragic overture with its loss of 25 per cent of his cruiser force. Such equanimity as remained to him was further eroded when, throughout the morning of the 24th in the Sibuyan Sea, great air battles raged and *Yamato* received two bomb hits, one of which caused her to list temporarily after 2,000 tons of water were let in. Yet Kurita's most shattering disappointment that morning was the absence of Fukudome's fighters to disrupt, if not prevent, the waves of bombers roaring in from Halsey's carriers.

Fukudome, an élite naval airman who, as Yamamoto's Chief of Staff in 1941, had keenly supported Pearl Harbor, had ever since retained his conviction that the best method of air defence at sea was to attack enemy carriers. Every major engagement since then had proved it to his satisfaction. Discount by half, as he might, his airmen's recently exaggerated claims to have sunk more ships off Formosa than Halsey possessed, he adhered to the opinion that land-based aircraft were superior to the carrier-borne type. It was, therefore, contrary to his experience and instincts when Toyoda ordered priority for defensive air cover of Kurita's centre Force A and B before direct attacks upon Halsey's carriers. With only 200 aircraft available he put his faith in killing the enemy at source rather than wearing down his smaller force to extinction through the process of attrition in air combat. So he ignored Toyoda's orders and Kurita's pleas for fighter cover, and unwisely went after the American carriers. For it is a fairly safe bet that aircraft which attack a radar forewarned enemy, whose fighters are positioned aloft and whose guns throw up a deadly hail of fire, will suffer far heavier losses than forewarned fighter aircraft operating defensively under land-based control and in conjunction with a fleet's anti-aircraft fire curtain. But obduracy allied to ritual suicide again obtruded into the Japanese choice of options. Fukudome sank but one enemy light carrier and for his pains lost nearly his entire force within a few hours.

Free from interception by Japanese fighters, and therefore barely impeded, the hundreds of American attackers had nothing except intense anti-aircraft fire to face over their target, and lost only 18 shot down. But they sank the great *Musashi* (designed as unsinkable), damaged two other battleships (including *Yamato*) together with two cruisers and two destroyers, and had compelled Kurita to turn away before, 1¼ hours later on the approach of nightfall and in the absence of further air attacks, he resumed course for the San Bernardino Strait. But the reason he resumed course also had something to do with the pilots whose attacks had hurt him so, since they, like their Japanese opposite numbers, were prone to exaggerate their successes. Almost coincident with a sighting report at 1540 hrs of Ozawa steaming down from the north, Halsey had been presented with his airmen's claims and concluded, according to his report next day, that Kurita's force 'had been so heavily damaged in the Sibuyan Sea that it could no longer be considered a serious menace to Seventh Fleet [covering the Leyte beachhead and Surigao Strait]. Also, he was aware that Nishimura's Force C, in the south, had been detected early on the 24th and attacked with indeterminate results, and concluded, with some justification, that this was a menace which could be contained by Seventh Fleet. He was not to know, however, that Nishimura, while resolutely forging ahead towards the Surigao Strait, had already radioed to Kurita his concern at the mounting opposition and that Kurita, faithful to his orders and not by any means as crippled as Halsey was led to suppose, was about to turn eastward again for the San Bernardino Strait.

Halsey was far better informed than his enemies who were groping throughout. When he made his crucial decision at about 2000 hrs on the 24th to lead the entire Third Fleet against Ozawa in the north, he was beyond doubt aware, through Special Branch which processed Ultra, that Ozawa's Force was a decoy with the task of tempting him away from the San Bernardino Strait so as to leave it completely unguarded.* And he made his decision despite an ensuing report that the coastal navigation lights in the straits had been switched on, quite obviously for Kurita's benefit. Halsey could not ignore Ozawa of course. But nor, with the immense strength at his disposal and in full knowledge of the 'SHO' plan, need he have feared splitting his force, leaving a strong element to guard the straits while he chased Ozawa's one heavy and three light carriers, and their accompanying pair of hybrid carrier/battleships. Indeed, Vice-Admiral Willis Lee, the designated commander of the Third Fleet's Battle Line should Halsey decide to detach the six battleships included within his four Carrier Groups (and which as he had already intimated at 1512 hrs, he might do), offered to cruise in the straits, if necessary without air cover. For Lee, a very shrewd and cool commander, had already sensed that Fukudome was spent and, without Halsey's benefit of Special SIGINT, had actually deduced that Ozawa's force was a decoy — and had passed his conclusions to Halsey, whose staff acknowledged the message without comment or subsequent change of plan.

* When writing the official history Morison, for security reasons, was forbidden from mentioning the assured SIGINT factor, with the result that his criticism of Halsey was a lot less trenchant than many thought it should have been.

Despite the smoke-screen of excuses thrown out by Halsey after the event, one is left with the indelible impression that he was hellbent on annihilating Ozawa by a stupendous show of force regardless of what happened elsewhere. The behaviour of his staff supports this view, even though they, like Lee, were not officially conversant with Special SIGINT. When Rear-Admiral Gerald Bogan, commanding Task Force 38.2, asked by speech radio if the information about the straits navigation lights had been received, he was brushed off with an impatient 'Yes, yes, we have that information.' Which deterred the formal protest he had contemplated. Nor did Lee get anywhere when, also by speech radio, he repeated his earlier suggestion that Kurita remained in fighting trim and was on his way eastwards. It is abundantly clear that Halsey, whose previous triumphs had won him renown within the Fleet and fame with the public, was grimly intent upon crushing dramatically an enemy force which he *knew* was there for the picking, rather than on hanging about for a similar opportunity against a battered target which he had been deluded by his airmen into thinking might not put in an appearance. To this impression, to some extent, his staff also contributed. But Halsey was an extremely strong character who, once his mind was made up, did not brook further dispute – characteristics of most great commanders, of course. The irony of it is that, by detaching, say, one quarter of his carriers along with the Battle Line to watch the San Bernardino Strait, while leading the rest northwards to tackle Ozawa, he might have accomplished both missions safely and without imperilling the invasion. But Halsey was not really the sort carelessly to share glory with others and it was to be the irony of the day that, eventually, the vice of selfishness, allied with impetuosity, would deny him not only the fruits of his endeavour, but also the clash between a line of battleships, as well as carriers, which would emboss the hallmark of his career.

If Halsey's selfishness had been confined to imperilling his own command, the obloquy he subsequently earned might have been mitigated. The enormity of his sin, however, is compounded by the manner in which he put at risk the entire Allied operation against Leyte, with possible severe loss of lives and perhaps the shifting back by months of a campaign then on the verge of total victory. For he did not take care precisely to inform Nimitz or Kinkaid of his action – and for that he must accept full responsibility and blame. Halsey's radio signals ordering his Task Force commanders northwards were addressed 'for information' to Nimitz, but not to Kinkaid who, in fact, only heard of them by monitoring Third Fleet's communications. Kinkaid always and naturally assumed that Halsey would cover the San Bernardino Strait to his northward but, as insurance, sent out his own air reconnaissance of it as a normal precaution. So, when he monitored Halsey's signal of 1512 hrs and read of the Battle Plan (which mentioned the formation of a new Task Force 34 composed of battleships and other heavy units under Vice-Admiral Lee, extracted from the Carrier Task Forces) he assumed that Task Force 34 had actually been formed and that, as Halsey actually did intend at that moment, it would be used against Kurita in the San Bernardino Strait. Under that impression, Kinkaid not unreasonably assumed (without at once checking) that Halsey's executive signal of 2012 hrs telling his Carrier Task Forces to head north, excluded Task Force 34, meaning that Lee and the battleships had been left behind to guard the straits. Whereas, in fact, Task Force 34 had not been formed. Its designated units remained as parts of the Carrier Task Forces and therefore was also heading north. It is worth noting that Nimitz drew precisely the same conclusions as Kinkaid from these messages – and Nimitz, let it be noted, was not also heavily distracted, as was Kinkaid, in planning in detail the reception of Nishimura's Force C as it headed for the Surigao Strait.

Maybe Kinkaid was naïve in not being as sceptical as some among his staff who, at once, smelt a rat or, maybe, a misunderstanding. Probably he should have asked Halsey at once, and certainly long before 0412 on the 25th, whether or not Task Force 34 existed and if it was guarding the San Bernardino Strait. But he could hardly be blamed for thinking that Halsey would have had the courtesy, let alone the duty, of informing him directly of his intentions in leaving the vital straits totally unguarded. Both he and Nimitz had every justification for disgust that Halsey did not leave even a picket boat to watch the strait and report anything coming through. Perhaps Halsey did not mean to delude the C-in-C and his brother Admirals, but certainly he exposed his integrity, as well as his professional competence to doubt. Perhaps he should have supervised his staff's performance. Beyond much doubt, sloppy staff work contributed to a series of false assumptions and vague orders which led to the brink of disaster – with Third Fleet a common source or centre of error – and for which Halsey's Chief of Staff, Rear-Admiral R. B. Carney, must be held responsible. This is, perhaps, the point at which to repeat Arthur Marder's quote, used in the context of comment on admirals' errors at the Battle of Jutland in 1916, but applicable to so many command situations: '. . . in the stresses of a great war the Fates are often stronger than man, even man at his best: that an enterprise may fail, and fail disastrously, without the officer responsible for it necessarily deserving castigation'.

So, as Third and Seventh Fleets diverged, Kurita's and Nishimura's forces converged on Leyte Gulf which was strongly protected by Kinkaid to the south but quite abandoned by Halsey to the north, exposing the defenceless invasion transports to a formidable threat. Nishimura's chances of joining in the feast were pretty remote from the start, however. Spotted as he was by Kinkaid's reconnaissance during the morning of the 24th, there was ample time for Kinkaid to set a trap under the command of Rear-Admiral Jesse Oldendorf, whose force consisted of six battleships, four heavy cruisers (including one Australian) and four light cruisers, plus 28 destroyers (one Australian) and a swarm of PT boats. The plan which delivered Nishimura into such narrow waters, never permitted him the slightest chance of outmanoeuvring Oldendorf. His fate was sealed once Kurita fell behind schedule, to the extent of being completely incapable of acting as a diversionary factor in Kinkaid's defence. Accepting his fate in compliance with Toyoda's *samurai*-like order of 1900 hrs on the 24th − 'All forces dash to the attack' − he charged headlong without waiting for Shima, trusting in luck and the self-presumed Japanese superior combat prowess in darkness to see him through. There is no need here to render a detailed account of Nishimura's destruction by successive rows of enemy PT boats, destroyers, cruisers and battleships. They picked off his ships one by one as they advanced until, eventually, only one light cruiser out of a total force of seven major ships survived. Or how Shima's smaller cruiser force, 40 miles astern, suffering a rather lower percentage of losses, was turned back when the evidence of Nishimura's anninilation was known. The fatalism of karma lay heavily upon Nishimura as he went to his doom amidst shoals of torpedoes and a relentless battering from battleships firing by radar at long range − a spirit which may well have induced his tactical misjudgements. For example, when, after sighting a destroyer attack, he maintained course without attempting a classic evasive 'turn towards'. And how, a little later, he actually manoeuvred so as to place his destroyers in the path of oncoming torpedoes. Truly there was exhibited here a neutralizing clash between an implacable martial spirit and an erosion of morale through being outnumbered and outclassed.

Nevertheless, Nishimura's sacrifice did win for Kurita a totally unopposed and unobserved passage of the San Bernardino Strait. By chance, the flying-boat sent by Kinkaid to search along Kurita's course at night on the 24th/25th, missed contact on the outward flight by the narrowest of margins and failed to see him again on the way back. Three hours before Nishimura went to the bottom in the Surigao Strait at 0319 hrs in the inferno of the battleship *Yamashiro*, Kurita in *Yamato* stood clear in open waters to the east of the San Bernardino Strait bearing down upon the virtually defenceless invasion transport areas 300 miles away. Barring his way, quite fortuitously, as it happened, were eighteen unsuspecting light carriers with their escorts under Rear-Admiral Thomas Sprague, whose designated task was general escort duties and whose characteristics hardly fitted them to stop a battle fleet which included the most powerful battleship in the world. For one thing they had no dive-bombers.

Halsey did not receive Kinkaid's signal of 0412 hrs querying the whereabouts of Third Fleet's dispositions at the mouth of the San Bernardino Strait until 0648 hrs, and the reply did not reach Kinkaid until after a number of extremely dramatic events off the island of Samar had rendered it superflous. For at 0646 hrs an escort carrier of Rear-Admiral Clifton Sprague's so-called Taffy 3 group, had detected a totally unexpected contact to the north-west. And a minute later Ensign Hans Jensen, on an anti-submarine patrol, confirmed the presence of hostile ships – to which Sprague's immediate reaction was one of disbelief, assuming that it was part of Halsey's fleet.

At almost the same moment a Japanese look-out reported masts at 28,000 yards and soon Kurita was aware that he had an enemy force at his mercy. But what sort and whose? To begin with his Chief of Staff, Rear-Admiral Koyonagi, thought they were battleships. But fairly quickly Kurita was satisfied that there were only five to seven carriers with destroyers when, in fact it was six carriers and three destroyers. Hardly believing his luck he gave chase.

Sprague also was quickly supplied with accurate information about the enemy strength. The odds against Taffy 3, with its few 5in guns versus many 14in, 16in and 18in pieces from four battleships, were terrible. All he could do was launch aircraft and run, calling desperately to Kinkaid for help and mouthing explosively about Halsey. Within the hour the entire force of 500 aircraft (none of them dive-bombers) from the eighteen carriers were beginning to make their presence felt with torpedo attacks amplified by the dropping of anything to hand, from light bombs to depth-charges, in gallant endeavours to hamper the enemy. But calls for help from Halsey were wasted since he had Ozawa's Northern Force just over the horizon 300 miles away. While requests for help from Oldendorf's battleships, in the immediate aftermath of their victory over Nishimura, were treated with reservation. Captain R. W. Bates, Oldendorf's Chief of Staff, recommended holding back in order to strike at the moment of his Admiral's choosing. In any case he was more than 60 miles away and conscious of a slight (and exaggerated) shortage of big gun ammunition which might impose restrictions if a major engagement developed. Meanwhile Kinkaid had to take into account the remaining presence of Shima inside the Surigao Strait, and so he declined until 0850 hrs to send Oldendorf northwards to protect Leyte Gulf and support the fast-retreating Taffies.

Kurita, amazed at the absence of Halsey and at having so juicy a prey at his mercy; still shaken by his sinking, ducking, bombing and fever – and not at all sure that Halsey actually was missing – found himself almost alone among his officers in thinking cautiously. He was beset by doubts, pessimism and indecision. Yesterday enemy aircraft had done as they pleased against his ships; might it not be the same today? Indeed, the sighting report came at the very moment when he was ordering the adoption of a change of formation and course to cater for the air threat, a re-deployment which was incomplete when, at 0652 hrs, he gave the first of a series of conflicting orders culminating at 0703 hrs in 'General attack'. These were the reactions of surprise upon a man ill at ease. In the words of Koyanagi, 'No heed was taken of order or co-ordination'. Each ship's captain did much as he pleased. The orderly lines of battle began to disintegrate. Fire control became haphazard. The pursuit developed pell-mell, but in the face of mounting enemy air attacks and, throughout, a most skilfully conducted American retreat. Frequently screened by smoke and disobliging rain squalls, the Japanese fell into a disorder which Kurita's mental state seemed incapable of controlling. Hardly ever were the Japanese captains permitted to concentrate upon the task of sinking carriers. Again and again they were compelled to take evasive action. Japanese gunnery without radar was poor in smoke and mist, finally managing to put down only one enemy light carrier and three destroyers (plus damage to others) in a mêlée which was to end with the loss of their own three heavy cruisers and severe damage to another and to a battleship.

At 0911, after two hours' frustrating inability to deliver the *coup de grace* to the Taffies, Kurita called for a temporary respite to restore some sort of order to his scattered formations. He turned north to take stock before steering once more for his prime objective, Leyte Gulf, where the richest pickings were to be found, and still unguarded by Oldendorf's battleships which were a good two hours sailing away. For two hours more he would vacillate and wander indecisively. Depressed by news of Nishimura's immolation and Shima's retreat; deprived of the vital information from his cruisers that they were closing the range with the Taffies at the very moment when he had erroneously estimated the latter force was making 30 knots – twelve knots above its top speed; he was further confused by conflicting and unconfirmed Intelligence reports about the enemy. One quite spurious report suggested that Halsey was a mere 113 miles off when, in fact, he was engaging Ozawa a good 300 miles away. Still more persuasive were reports, some corrupt, of intercepted, uncoded radio calls from Kinkaid ordering the movement of units into the Leyte Gulf. At this moment Kurita's *samurai* spirit, with its abiding loyalty to the Emperor, came into conflict with Toyoda's order, with professional competence and with the demands of bushido. It was traditional and worthy to sacrifice one's life for the code of honour and ultimate spiritual victory, but incompetent in modern times to lose an entire fleet (all that Japan had left), without achieving anything for the Emperor. And as things appeared to him at about 1100 hrs, while circling off Samar endeavouring to make up his mind, there seemed every chance that the vulnerable transports in Leyte Gulf must have escaped under the protection of a line of battleships brought up from Surigao. At 1236 hrs he gave up, turning for San Bernardino Strait and on his way to safety, in the impossible hope of finding and damaging the falsely reported American force to the northward.

As for Halsey, he had first found Ozawa's force through air reconnaissance on the afternoon of the 24th and, as previously described, had gone off in search of battle that evening. Contact between the opposing forces was intermittent, but at 0430 hrs on the 25th Halsey felt sufficiently certain of his enemy's position to, at last, form the battleship Task Force 34. Under Lee he intended it to lead the carriers into an action which he envisaged as a classic carrier-versus-carrier engagement followed by a battleship confrontation to finish off anything left over. It was bound to be a one-sided encounter since most of Ozawa's air crew were tyros and the majority of those that had been embarked in Japan had already been diverted to join Fukudome in the Philippines. The first American air strike went in at 0800; more followed over the next ten hours, with the sinking of all four Japanese carriers – a massacre which need not be described here. But Halsey's joy at having pinned down his quarry was spoiled, even as his attack was starting, when the news of Kurita's appearance off Samar (delayed by up to 90 minutes in transmission) was received in company with a steady flow of messages from Kinkaid asking for immediate help. It took 28 minutes for Halsey to decide to detach one carrier task force to attack Kurita, in the knowledge, however, that it was fuelling several hundred miles to the eastward and therefore could not reach Kurita until 1200 hrs. Lee's battleships he retained, knowing that within but a few hours they should catch up with Ozawa, thus satisfying the desire of all good gunnery officers to fire main armament at enemy capital ships.

At 1000 hrs he received from the C-in-C, Admiral Nimitz, a message which seemed to do rather more than inquire the where-abouts of Lee's Task Force 34, and was read by Halsey (interestingly enough!) as an insulting reflection upon his performance. Nimitz did not actually order the detachment of Lee, but taken in conjunction with all the other messages of alarm pouring in from Seventh Fleet, his intervention fell little short of the imperative. Against the certainty of annihilating Ozawa with a climactic shoot by Lee's six battleships overwhelming two battleship/carriers (*Ise* and *Hyuga*), Halsey had to counter-balance the odium he would acquire if harm befell Seventh Fleet and the Army ashore because he had witheld even a gesture of battleship assistance. Yet it took him an hour to relent at last and, at 1055 hrs, order Lee to turn back. By then, though, it was little more than a gesture, since Lee only steamed at 20 knots, instead of a maximum 28 knots, and spent two hours at twelve knots refuelling his destroyer escort. After the war Halsey told Morison that the decision to detach Lee was the only one in the Battle of Leyte Gulf that he regretted. Both *Ise* and *Hyuga* escaped. It almost broke his heart. He seemed to forget (or perhaps conceal) even then that he was aware of Ozawa's decoy role and that, if Task Force 34 had been retained near the San Bernardino Strait, the battleship engagement he so earnestly desired would have been his – or, rather, Lee's. Moreover, as Morison points out, if Lee had been detached by Halsey immediately Kurita's presence was reported to him, and Task Force 34 had proceeded at full speed without pausing to refuel destroyers, six modern battleships would have caught the retreating Kurita at night on the 25th/26th, and might have completed the destruction of an already weakened Japanese force. It was an irony that, in the final count, Halsey's reputation was degraded by his adherence to a misconceived aim. And worthy of note that Nimitz never condoned Halsey's pigheadedness.

American losses at Leyte Gulf were miraculously small, a mercy achieved as the result of sound employment of superior numbers and technology. Even if Kurita had maintained his aim and run riot in the Gulf, he would assuredly have been brought to book a few hours later by the combined Third and Seventh Fleets. But a nation mourning lives unnecessarily lost would not have forgiven Halsey for that. Nor, for that matter, need the Japanese nation feel any too content with the performance of Toyoda and, among his subordinates picked out for special criticism, Fukudome, for their misconceived plans which led to immense waste of life and material for only petty gain. Setting aside the emotive and political pressures upon him, Toyoda's concept and plan were incompetent from the start, doomed to failure because, fundamentally, they ignored the enemy's strength and dispositions. Fukudome's failure, however, was of another kind, encased in a typically Japanese blend of conflicting beliefs, loyalties and technical incomprehension. For, rather like Doenitz when faced with a situation of adverse technology which was wrecking his previously held concepts, he was fatally slow to come to terms with a changed situation and to embrace new weapons and methods.

When Fukudome sent his airmen in a death ride against Halsey's carriers on the 24th and by so doing denied Kurita the local protection he warranted, he should have realized that he was compelling his flyers to commit suicide without the compensation of inflicting worthwhile harm on the enemy. Yet he had at hand another suicide weapon which past experience had shown was capable of sinking or, at the least, putting carriers out of action for prolonged periods. And he turned away from it.

As early as 1931 the RAF had foreseen the possibility of Japanese airmen adopting suicide tactics and there had been several random instances since 1941 of this practice. An aircraft flown into its target had one positive advantage over normal bombing and torpedo dropping: it eliminated error from aiming. After the massacre of Japanese aircraft over the Marianas and the Philippine Sea in June 1944, Captain Jyo Eiichio proposed the formation of special attack units to carry out crash dives on enemy carriers, an idea which was taken up reluctantly by Vice-Admiral Onishi Takijiro when given the task by Fukudome of supporting Kurita in the Sibuyan Sea – but which was received with immense enthusiasm by his pilots when they were consulted. The spirit of bushido was enhanced by the sheer commonsense realization that if one assuredly was going to die it might as well be for the attainment of concrete results with a deadly blow against the foe. Preparation and training could be completed within a few hours, ready for 'SHO'. But Onishi, who concurred with Fukudome that attacks on enemy carriers were a better defence than local air cover, was unable to overcome Fukudome's initial practical and moral inhibitions to the formation and use of Kamikaze units (named after the Heavenly Wind, a typhoon which, in 1570, wrecked a Chinese invasion fleet). As a result they were denied the opportunity to make their début against Halsey's carriers, Fukudome insisting upon conventional tactics with the disastrous consequences already described.

By 21 October, therefore, only a small force of kamikaze was deployed, committed to minor operations and repeatedly frustrated either by destruction of their machines by enemy ground straffing of their airfield, inclement weather or inability to find a target. They were, therefore, just 24 hours too late when they found and struck the Taffy carriers on the morning of the 25th, their blows coinciding with the Americans' continuing embarrassment at Kurita's charge. Within four hours a few of them did more damage to Seventh Fleet than the entire effort by Kurita, sinking one carrier and seriously damaging four more. Presented next day with this evidence, Fukudome changed his mind and authorized the large-scale kamikaze operations which became easily the most effective anti-shipping weapon in the

CRITICAL FLAWS

▶ Japanese failure to develop radar.

▶ The wasteful sacrifice of good Japanese thinkers and leaders as the result of bushido's insistence on self-destruction in the event of failure.

▶ The priority given by Fukudome to air attacks against enemy carriers instead of local defence of the battle fleet.

▶ Halsey's hunt for glory in his rejection of available Intelligence, and the consequent exposure of the amphibious forces to Kurita's attack.

▶ Kurita's dithering which lost him the opportunity to benefit from Halsey's indiscretion.

Japanese armoury. At far lower cost in machines and men, they had, by 12 December, hit and damaged seven heavy carriers and sunk seven and damaged 23 other ships – with more to come. Just suppose a surprise effort had been made with, say, 100 of Fukudome's aircraft in the kamikaze mode on 24 October, leaving the other half to protect Kurita? What then might have been the outcome? It is not unlikely that a majority of Halsey's carriers, with their unarmoured wooden decks, would have been put out of action – as several were in the months to come. In that event Kurita might have emerged on time from the San Bernardino Strait in far better condition than he did; Nishimura might have had a sporting chance against a distracted Kinkaid in the Surigao Strait; and Halsey probably would have left Ozawa to his own decoy devices and been forced to fight a mainly battleship action off Samar – with imponderable results if both *Musashi* and *Yamato* had been present and fighting fit.

Fukudome had aided and abetted the loss of a fleet and thousands of Japanese lives by committing a common enough command error. Not only had he blenched at the thought of asking dedicated *samurai* types to do what was quite natural and logical to them, he had balked, in the absence of conclusive proof of feasibility, at adopting a new and revolutionary concept. Arguable, as always it is, that a new and very expensive weapon system warrants exhaustive examination prior to adoption, for fear of wasting men and material in short supply, in the context of Japan's desperate situation in the Philippines, there was but little justification in economizing on the expenditure of obsolete machines flown by men to whom both experience and statistics made clear that they were doomed. But Fukudome's inhibitions were merely another example of schism between ancient and modern, of an utter despondency and confusion in a mind which was being driven painfully towards a radical re-examination of a centuries-old philosophy, founded simply upon warrior status and invincibility.

16

THE SUM OF THEIR ERRORS

Historians and commentators, alike, sometimes lay claim to have influenced the introduction of improvements in military organizations and methods as a result of their examination of the errors and ommissions of commanders in the past. Indeed, the study of history has always been rated of prime importance to the military art. Beyond much doubt, too, those who assumed higher commands in the Second World War were mindful of what had taken place in the First World War (a mere twenty years before) and of all that had been written since. Which is not to say that they were necessarily perceptive of the revolution in warfare that had taken place. Quite frequently, in fact, their resistance to change stood rooted in loyalty and objection to jaundiced assertions by the critics which did more than imply gross incompetence – even negligence – on the part of the admirals and generals of 1914–1918. Yet it is undeniable that those who went to war in 1939 were seriously perturbed by what had gone before and for the most part extremely anxious to avoid the mistakes of the past. Despite the assertions of pundits who complained that there was a wholesale shutting of minds by sailors and soldiers to the lessons of 1918 (those who wanted only to get back to 'real soldiering', etc.) there is ample evidence of serious official attempts to make changes in order to avert pointless slaughter. At the same time, the deluge of accusations levelled at commanders, who were adjudged to have been 'donkeys leading lions to the slaughter', did create an image in the public mind that the entire military profession was a caste of ill-educated, unimaginative and insensitive nincompoops who were beyond salvation – except, of course, by inspired civilians who, it was implied, could hardly do worse than the so-called experts. Inevitably the fighting men of 1939 went into battle with a queasy feeling that they would be misused – and that had an impact both harmful and at the same time beneficial to their performance throughout the war.

The pre-1939 myth of military incompetence was, of course, as much the product of politicians seeking scapegoats for their own short-comings, or military critics and seers (such as J. F. C. Fuller and B. H. Liddell Hart) in their attempts to instigate reform (as they saw it) and earn their living in journalism, as it was the fruit of angry poets and authors working off their disgust at the horror and wastage of warfare and an attempt by pacifists to outlaw war forever. Frequently the publicists were heavily biased by self-interest and passion; rarely, due to denial of access to official archives, were they anything like fully informed. All too often the sins of commanders were vehemently presented without due regard to accuracy or objectivity. With considerable justification, scorn was heaped upon leaders who, for example, had isolated themselves at the end of a telephone from the scene of action, but without making it equally plain that detachment from the telephone hindered the exercise of command because there was, as yet, no adequate substitute for this inflexible method of communication. Reasonably enough, commanders who, post-war, clung emotionally and irrationally to the horse as the indispensible vehicle of mobility, were castigated in this hypocritical insistence upon sending an ineffectual, terrified beast they professed to adore into a charnel-house. But the political, technical and economic problems involved in mechanization were not only underrated by commentators who were technically weak or unaware (as was Liddell Hart, for example), but actually were played down in order to strengthen the slur upon those held culpable for delaying moderniza-tion. The efforts of many who did make progress with modernization in the 1920s are still, in select instances, underrated as the result of this prejudiced writing of contemporary history.

Contemporary military commentaries concerning the 1920s and 1930s frequently transmitted impressions that an influential body of senior officers and politicians persuaded themselves that the events and catastrophies of the recent war were a totally new order of magnitude in military incompetence which could have been avoided. They seemed to lack a sense of proportion and ignore the fact that the propensity to err was, as it always has been in history, in inverse pro-portion to the commander's capacity to deal with the current situation – and that, very likely, he was merely coping with the by-products of impressions and decisions handed down by predecessors over which he had had no control. Commentators who paid lip-service to new technology and techniques inevitably misunderstood the meaning themselves. It was sometimes conveniently overlooked that virtually nobody in 1914 had managed to envisage the impact upon battle of the accumulated effects of rapid technical developments despite practical illustrations of the trends in numerous wars, particularly the lessons of the major encounter between Russia and Japan in 1904. Yet the failure systematically to study and draw reasonably perceptive conclusions from current developments was not so much a criticism of the military caste as an exposure of the weakness of educational systems in schools and colleges, as condoned by governments and societies. Progress as initiated by very small, often self-educated, minorities of inventors and industrialists had out-stripped the comprehension of the intellectual majority who ruled.

We have seen how the older officers who inherited command shortly before 1939 were the graduates of a narrow educational system and how, for example, they miscalculated the increased pace induced by mechanization and radio communications and the effects of the armoured protection of special vehicles – the tank. It was not so much the case that Gamelin or von Rundstedt, both of whom failed fully to take advantage of their opportunities, were tyros or lacked the qualities of generalship. They had reached the peaks of their careers through intense application, innate talent and after prolonged and fierce competition with their rivals. They were a match for each other. But each was a prisoner of the system which had produced them. Both, respectively, were destroyed or set back by the outstanding talents of technically orientated commanders of the calibre of Guderian who possessed that spark of genius which is granted only to a handful in any profession. Guderian, in tennis parlance, forced his opponents into error by seizing the initiative. Negative qualities tend to permit the imposition of errors upon one's own side while positive qualities merely accelerate the process of an opponent's collapse – a trend in success or failure which is often associated with the manifestations of good or bad luck.

Luck to a general, as Livy remarked, is important; although Helmuth von Moltke the Elder thought that in the long run, it was granted only to the efficient. But efficiency cannot even yet, for example, forecast the weather over anything more than a few hours – and, as we have seen, the weather repeatedly governed campaigns and battles, above all those at sea and in the air. Undeniably, chance lies at the heart of war and can only be mitigated by commanders who recognize that fact and take what measures are possible to control and exploit it by granting subordinates the maximum freedom to exploit their chances intelligently. It was at the root of several errors remarked upon in this book that commanders who over-centralized control – Doenitz, Auchinleck and, of course, Stalin and Hitler being notorious – were extremely prone to make personal errors of the greatest magnitude. And they were the ones whose subordinates, all too frequently as a consequence, acted irrationally – particularly if time for consideration were denied, as it tended to be the closer to the forward edge of battle that subordinate happened to be standing.

In the heat of battle there is rarely sufficient time for the mass of junior leaders and commanders to give dispassionate consideration to swiftly evolving problems. In a life and death struggle, reactions tend to be instinctive, although a modicum of foresight in visualizing and making provision for certain instantaneous contingencies prior to close combat may be possible. Usually it is only commanders at a greater distance from the imbroglio who are granted the luxury of meditation and profound deliberation. And, as has been made plain, even the most calm and detached of commanders at the highest levels – like Gamelin, von Rundstedt, Wavell, Montgomery, Harris, King and Yamamoto – got it wrong because they were sometimes taken by surprise through being misinformed, due to misinterpretation or simply out of sheer obstinacy in sticking to a false, preconceived notion. Shortage of time for consideration may be a prolific creator of error, yet ample time is no guarantee of perfection. And a prime reason for error often can be attributed to the thinker becoming confused by exposure to a mass of poorly digested and presented information which overloads his brain. This does not necessarily imply incompetence, although every commander has a responsibility to ensure that he is well served. There is a limit to the capacity of every brain, be it human or mechanical. It is all too obvious that, while in many of the cases described in this book, commanders met defeat because of inadequate information, there were many more who plunged into difficulties because they were deluged with contra-dictory quantities of it presented in superfluity by biased individuals or inefficient systems. It is equally fair to assert that many a defeat was caused by deliberately feeding the enemy with such a plethora of conflicting, and yet credible alternative threats, that he became mesmerized into inaction. The paralysis of the Axis command prior to Operation 'Torch' is one supreme example of this condition.

Greater efficiency and better management are, in the long run, as Moltke implied, antidotes to error through chance. Superior training of all ranks in uniform control procedures, actuated by long-established staff teams whose task it is to serve their commander anonoymously and unobtrusively, is essential. Yet all warlike activities are at the mercy of personality anomalies and clashes, fear, sudden and undetected psychological or physiological breakdowns, or ungovernable changes in environment which throw men and machines out of gear. Mistakes are of the essence in human activity and all the more likely to be created or exacerbated under the stress and uncertainty of war. Even the dedicated Japanese, with their creed of bushido, discovered that. But nearly everybody is vulnerable to the imbalance of collapse when brought suddenly face to face with an inhuman, technological threat to which there appears no immediate or lasting counter. Throughout the history of the Second World War, to a greater extent even than in the First, one has to gauge the debilitating effect of advancing technology upon the thoughts and reactions of commanders, whether or not they were among the small band with minds highly receptive of technical matters. We have to bear witness to Doenitz and Harris, both of them technically aware, balking at technical innovations or allowing themselves to be fobbed off with defective and inadequate panaceas: with them, it appears, the sheer volume of new ideas saturated their mental intake at that certain age when their minds had begun to atrophy and at a moment of stress when the main stream of their mental effort had to be concentrated upon the associated functions of operational command, leadership, diplomacy and politics. Indeed, it has to be said that Doenitz and Harris, who dominated their staffs to an extraordinary degree, were no better at coping with technology than men like Gamelin, von Rundstedt, Auchinleck and Montgomery to whom it tended to be a subsidiary subject to be handled by experts. We should not turn a blind eye to the Allied commanders of 1940, to Rommel, to Nagumo and to Kurita, for example, who bent under the pressures of heavy responsibility and the collapse of ambitions which had propelled them to the upper reaches of command. Nor can we ignore the urgings of inordinate ambition such as led Halsey to commit his dangerous and impulsive indiscretion at Leyte Gulf.

If there is a common denominator for the errors mentioned in this book (and the myriad left unmentioned), it could well be the abiding inability of high commanders to come to terms with scientific and technical innovation in the requisite time while performing their day-to-day duties and higher functions in collaboration with their political masters. How fateful was Churchill's initial mistake in picking Auchinleck and then leaning upon him in moments of crisis, which led to the unfortunate selection of Ritchie as an Army commander which then led to the erosion of confidence through corps, divisional and brigade levels to the meanest fighting men. And how corrosive was Churchill's influence in persuading Montgomery to gamble via Arnhem (in order to subdue the German rocket threat) who in turn failed to convince Brereton, Browning, Gavin and Horrocks of the vital necessity to take extraordinary risks to achieve the aim of 'Market Garden'. Yet all of these commanders were affected also by difficulties in the resolution of combined technical and tactical dilemmas.

At this point I again turn unashamedly to the thoughts of Sir Hugh Dowding who, at a critical moment in history and despite misleading Intelligence and an inferiority in resources, managed to win the Battle of Britain. That was a truly technical battle, as well as one of morale, decided by the judicious integration of strategic sense, tactical expediency and technical insight – and, as he believed, an Act of God. He once asked why, in the Services, some of the best brains in Britain (although his ideas are applicable equally elsewhere) seemed to lose their critical faculty. He concluded that the process might start at school where the individualist was suppressed and the 'good citizen' mass-produced. Furthermore, 'If a junior officer puts forward a suggestion the implication is that a senior officer might have thought of it, ought to have thought of it, and didn't think of it . . . After being squashed a sufficient number of times, according to his tenacity, the junior offices ceases to put forward unwelcome suggestions . . .' In that stimulating chapter of his entitled 'Why are senior officers so stupid', he quoted instances, with examples that included his own stupidities, when senior officers had resisted, misdirected, misunderstood or had rejected valid scientific experiment. He went on to plead for the invitation of distinguished scientists and statisticians to co-operate with the Service hierarchies – well knowing the sort of obstruction R. V. Jones and his ilk had endured; how Bomber Command (unlike his own Fighter Command) had resisted scientific investigations; and how both the Navy and the Army had resisted innovations by lending more credence to inspired guesswork than practical, controlled experiments and operational research. He would not have been surprised to have found similar traits among the Services of both Britain's allies and enemies and he would have been right.

But Dowding would have been mightily indignant – as more than once he was, in his resistance to unsound proposals by Churchill and to some among his subordinates – if his young pilots had been launched into situations which seemed to him unsound in the pursuit of victory. For he possessed that inner strength of conscience which enabled him, like Auchinleck and Guderian, for example, to stand firm in his resolve even at risk of forfeiture of office.

Which leads to consideration of the impact on military commanders or heads of state who combine their political role with that of commander-in-chief. Grouse as they will, few reasonable soldiers, sailors and airmen will deny that the ultimate sanction should be vested in political government. Yet their grousing becomes justified if their professional opinions are overruled, with disastrous consequences, by politicians who are totally ignorant of the art of war or who choose to ignore serious warnings of the consequences of their politically biased military decisions. At the same time, political masters are entitled to receive fearlessly frank advice from commanders of undoubted loyalty who, even if their advice is declined, will obey unwelcome orders. It is all a matter of balance, one which hangs upon the competence of the individuals concerned and upon mutual common sense and the give and take of debate.

The Allies may be considered fortunate that President Roosevelt, as Commander-in-Chief of the US Armed Forces, was sufficiently well served by Admiral King and superlatively well served by General Marshall in achieving a reasonable balance of strategic enlightenment. And that, with Churchill, they benefited from the strategic wisdom of the British Chief of Staff, General Brooke. Likewise, despite his bullying and his pernicious dismissal of senior officers before the war, Premier Stalin and the Russian people were extremely fortunate that they had at the Army's helm a general of the calibre of Zhukov who could curb Stalin's worst excesses and steer the nation to victory without losing his own head.

The Axis powers, on the other hand, were not so fortunate in that they had over them dictators who, by the very nature of their methods, gave insufficient consideration to balanced strategies which were founded upon rational debate and decision making. Although there can be little sympathy for German admirals and generals who conspired to help Hitler to power in the 1930s, there has to be due understanding that the military errors he committed them to make were the ultimate result of his bullying methods which, in the final analysis, deprived him of sound advice from professionals who were compelled either to bow the knee or forfeit their appointments and, sometimes, their lives. Similarly, the Japanese people suffered appallingly by having over them a feudal military dictatorship which took them to war for reasons which might have looked sound for idealistic reasons but which were hopelessly miscalculated in military terms.

Cynics claim, with some justification, that we do not learn from history. The trouble is that even men at the top of their careers, who have studied history most diligently, too often forget the lessons within the turmoil of an unexpected situation, or find themselves in the grip of circumstances for which history does not offer a precedent. It is possible that, within the more liberal post-war environments to be found in some democratic nations, the inhibitions on rational command and control commented upon by Dowding and mentioned in this book have withered. Certainly there is a plethora of information available. On the other hand, there are too many dictators at large who survive in secrecy, and far too extensive an expansion of science and technology to guarantee freedom from error in the making of military decisions in the future. Yet woe betide the nation which, through emasculation of thought, permits its political and military leaders to get out of touch with the latest developments, organizations and methods. That way leads to error being piled upon miscalculation with horrendous results of unimaginable consequence which will overshadow the worst excesses even of the Second World War.

BIBLIOGRAPHY

I have drawn upon a number of official histories from various nations during the writing of this book, and include below only those that I feel were vital to its compilation.

AGAWA, H. *The reluctant admiral: Yamamoto and the Imperial Navy.* Kodansha and New York, 1979.

AIR MINISTRY. *The rise and fall of the German Air Force.* HMSO, 1947; Arms and Armour Press, London, and Fleet Publishers, Ontario, 1983.

ANON. *Naval staff history: defeat of the enemy attack on shipping, 1939–1945.* Admiralty, London, 1957.

ANON. *U-boat warfare in the Atlantic* (3 volumes). Admiralty, London.

BARKER, A. J. *Midway.* Ballantine, New York, and Macdonald, London, 1971.

BEKKER, C. *The Luftwaffe war diaries.* Macdonald, London, 1966.

CONNELL, J. *Auchinleck.* Cassell, London, 1959.

DOWDING, H. *Twelve legions of angels.* Jarrolds, London, 1946.

DULL, P. A. *A battle history of the Imperial Japanese Navy, 1941–1945.* Naval Institute Press, Annapolis, and PSL, London, 1978.

FREEMAN, R. A. *The Mighty Eighth.* Macdonald, London, 1970.

GOLDEN, L. *Echoes from Arnhem.* William Kimber, London, 1984.

GOUTARD, H. *The battle of France.* Frederick Muller, London, 1958.

GUDERIAN, H. *Panzer leader.* Michael Joseph, London, 1952.

HARRIS, A. *Bomber offensive.* Collins, London, 1947.

HARRISON, T. *Living through the Blitz.* Collins, London, 1976.

HINSLEY, F. H., and others. *British intelligence in the Second World War* (4 volumes). HMSO, London and New York, 1979–.

HORNE, A. *To lose a battle.* Macmillan, London, 1969.

HOWARTH, D. *Morning glory: the story of the Imperial Japanese Navy.* Hamish Hamilton, London, 1983.

JONES, R. V. *Most secret war.* Hamish Hamilton, London, 1978.

LEWIN, R. *Ultra goes to war: the secret story.* Hutchinson, London, and New York, 1978.

—— *The Chief.* Hutchinson, London, 1980.

—— *The other Ultra.* Hutchinson, London, 1982.

MACKSEY, K. *Tank warfare.* Hart Davis, London, 1972.

—— *Guderian: Panzer general.* Macdonald, London, 1975.

—— *Kesselring.* Batsford, London, 1978.

—— *Rommel: battles and campaigns.* Arms and Armour Press, London, and New York, 1979.

—— *Invasion: the German invasion of England, July 1940.* Arms and Armour Press, London, and New York, 1980.

—— *Technology in War.* Arms and Armour Press, London, and New York, 1986.

MELLENTHIN, F. W. VON. *Panzer battles, 1939–1945.* Cassell, London, 1955.

MESSENGER, C. *Bomber Harris.* Arms and Armour Press, London, 1984.

PITT, B. (ed.). *Purnell's history of the Second World War* (8 volumes). BPPC, London, and New York, 1966.

SAWARD, W. *Bomber Harris.* Century, London, 1984.

SEATON, A. *The Russo-German war, 1941–45.* Barker, London, 1971.

PADFIELD, P. *Dönitz: the last Führer.* Gollancz, London, 1984.

ROHWER, J. *The critical convoy battles of March 1943.* Ian Allan, Shepperton, 1977.

ROSSLER, E. *The U-boat: the evolution and technical history of German submarines.* Arms and Armour Press, London, and Naval Institute Press, Annapolis, 1981.

WARLIMONT, W. *Inside Hitler's headquarters.* Weidenfeld & Nicholson, London, 1964.

WEBSTER, R. *The RAF in the bomber offensive against Germany.* PRO Air 41.

WILMOT, C. *The struggle for Europe.* Collins, London, 1952.

INDEX

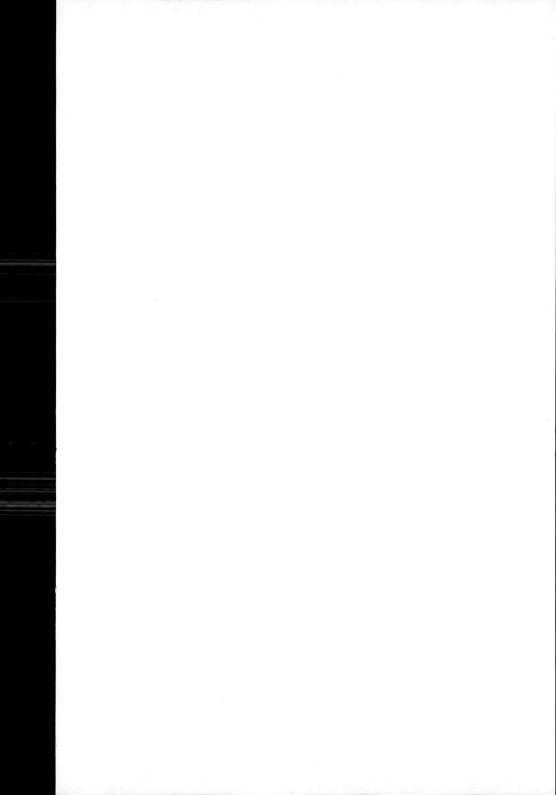